MOBILE SUIT GUNDAM THUNDERBOLT

In the Universal Century year 0079, the space colony known as Side 3 proclaims independence as the Principality of Zeon and declares war on the Earth Federation. One year later, they are locked in a fierce battle for the Thunderbolt Sector, an area of space scarred by the wreckage of destroyed colonies. Into this maelstrom of destruction go two veteran Mobile Suit pilots: the deadly Zeon sniper Daryl Lorenz, and Federation ace Io Fleming. It's the beginning of a rivalry that can end only when one of them is destroyed.

STORY AND ART
YASUO OHTAGAKI
ORIGINAL CONCEPT BY
HAJIME YATATE
AND YOSHIYUKI TOMINO

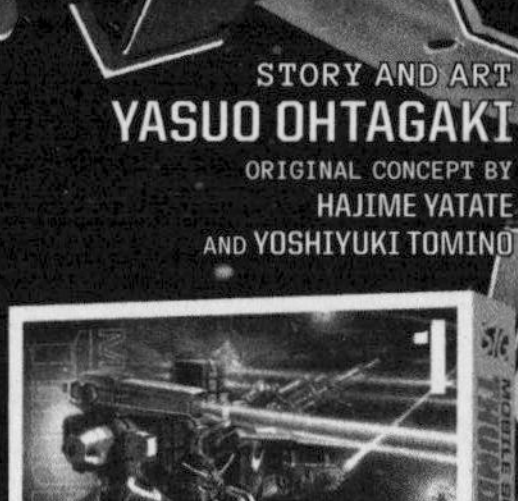
1
MOBILE SUIT GUNDAM
THUNDERBOLT

RATED T+ FOR OLDER TEEN

viz media
viz.com

RUBY ROSE

WEISS SCHNEE

BLAKE BELLADONNA

YANG XIAO LONG

RWBY

OFFICIAL MANGA ANTHOLOGIES

Original Concept by Monty Oum & Rooster Teeth Productions, Story and Art by Various Artists

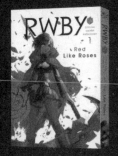

All-new stories featuring Ruby, Weiss, Blake and Yang from Rooster Teeth's hit animation series!

CHILDREN OF THE WHALES

In this postapocalyptic fantasy, a sea of sand swallows everything but the past.

In an endless sea of sand drifts the Mud Whale, a floating island city of clay and magic. In its chambers a small community clings to survival, cut off from its own history by the shadows of the past.

A deluxe bind-up edition of Naoki Urasawa's award-winning epic of doomsday cults, giant robots and a group of friends trying to save the world from destruction!

20th Century Boys

THE PERFECT EDITION

NAOKI URASAWA

Humanity, having faced extinction at the end of the 20th century, would not have entered the new millennium if it weren't for them. In 1969, during their youth, they created a symbol. In 1997, as the coming disaster slowly starts to unfold, that symbol returns. This is the story of a group of boys who try to save the world.

Sweet Blue Flowers

Story and Art by **Takako Shimura**

Akira Okudaira is starting high school and is ready for exciting new experiences. And on the first day of school, she runs into her best friend from kindergarten at the train station! Now Akira and Fumi have the chance to rekindle their friendship, but life has gotten a lot more complicated since they were kids…

Collect the series!

BEASTARS

Story & Art by Paru Itagaki

At this high school, instead of jocks and nerds, the students are divided into carnivores and herbivores.

At a high school where the students are literally divided into predators and prey, friendships maintain the fragile peace. Who among them will become a Beastar—a hero destined to lead in a society naturally rife with mistrust?

The Way of the House Husband

VOLUME 2

VIZ SIGNATURE EDITION

STORY AND ART BY
KOUSUKE OONO

TRANSLATION: Sheldon Drzka
ENGLISH ADAPTATION: Jennifer LeBlanc
TOUCH-UP ART & LETTERING: Bianca Pistillo
DESIGN: Alice Lewis
EDITOR: Jennifer LeBlanc

GOKUSHUFUDO volume 2
© Kousuke Oono 2018
All Rights Reserved
English translation rights arranged
with SHINCHOSHA PUBLISHING CO.
through Tuttle-Mori Agency, Inc, Tokyo

Printed in the U.S.A.

Published by VIZ Media, LLC
P.O. Box 77010
San Francisco, CA 94107

10 9 8 7 6 5 4 3 2 1
First printing, January 2020

VIZ MEDIA   *VIZ SIGNATURE*
viz.com   vizsignature.com

The Way of the House Husband

KOUSUKE OONO

2

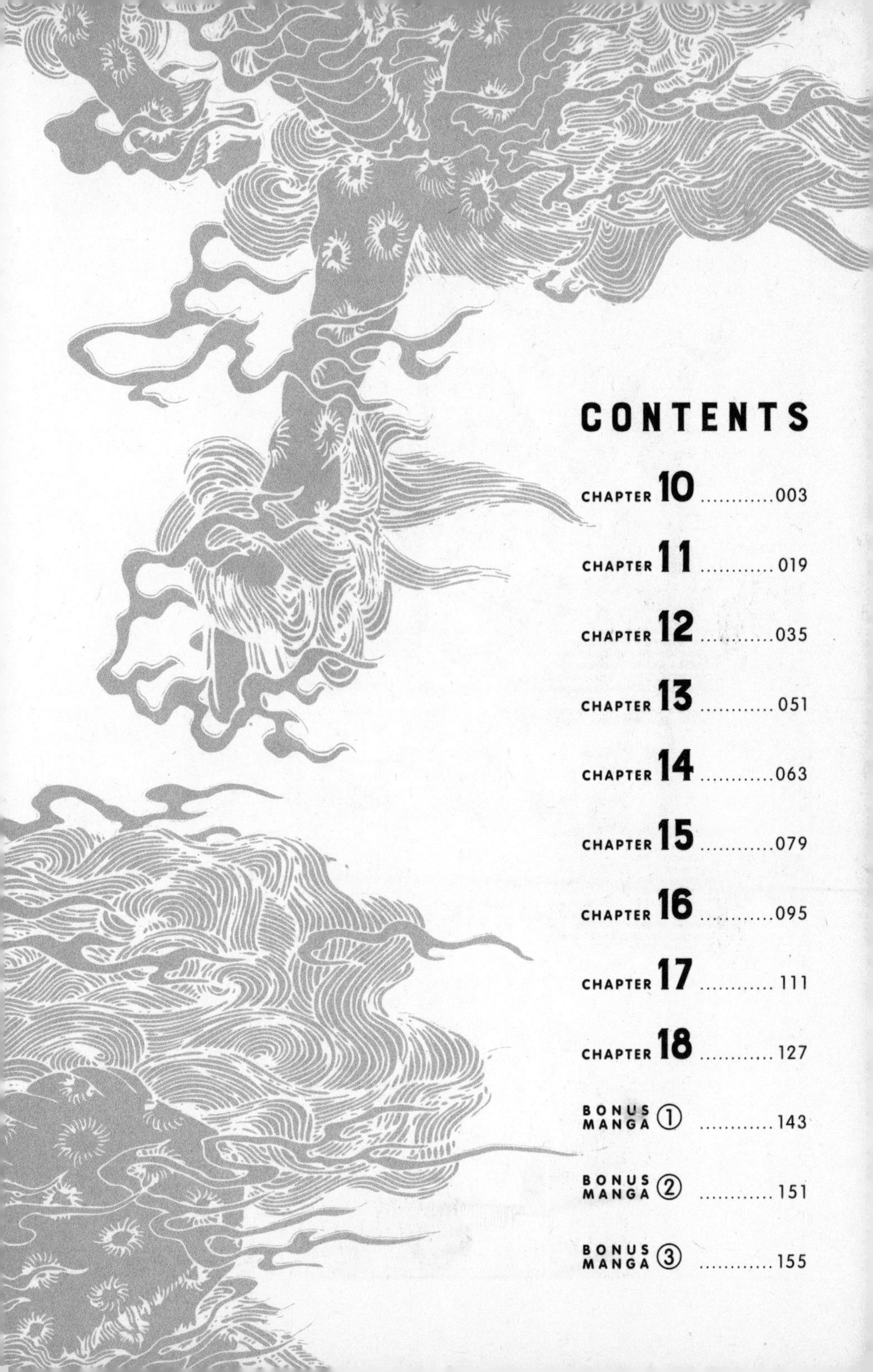

CONTENTS

CHAPTER 10

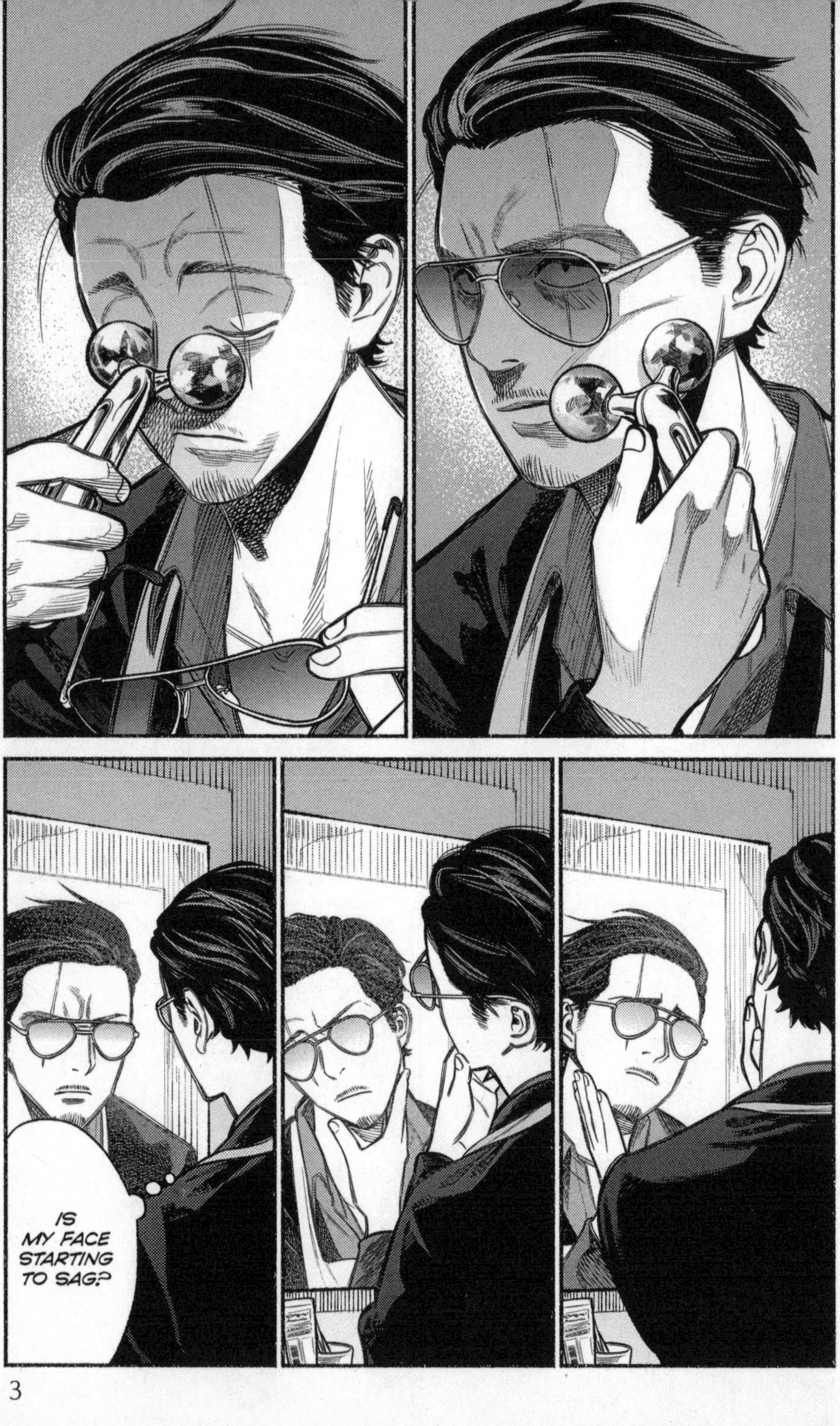
IS MY FACE STARTING TO SAG?

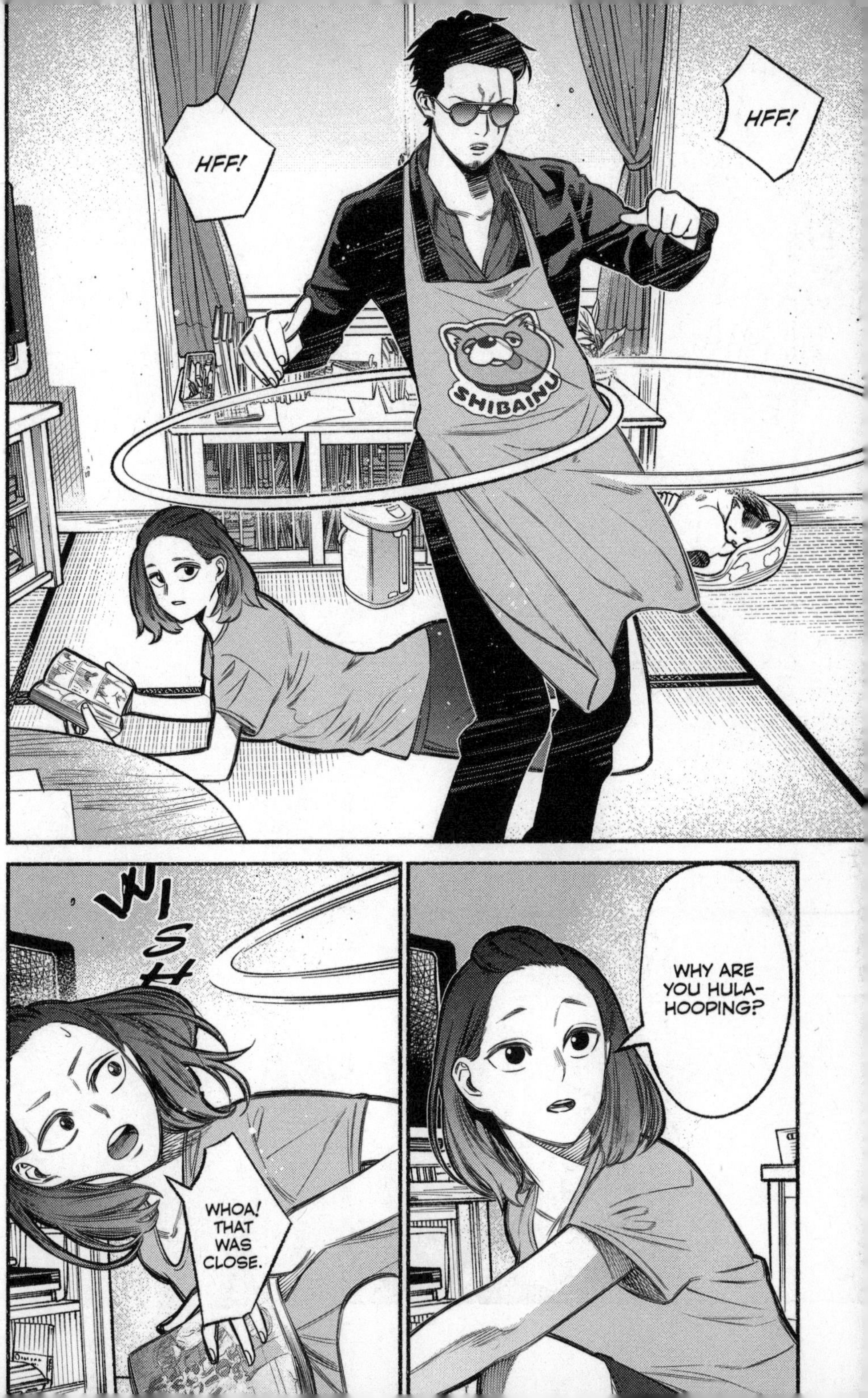
HFF!
HFF!
WHY ARE YOU HULA-HOOPING?
WHISH
WHOA! THAT WAS CLOSE.

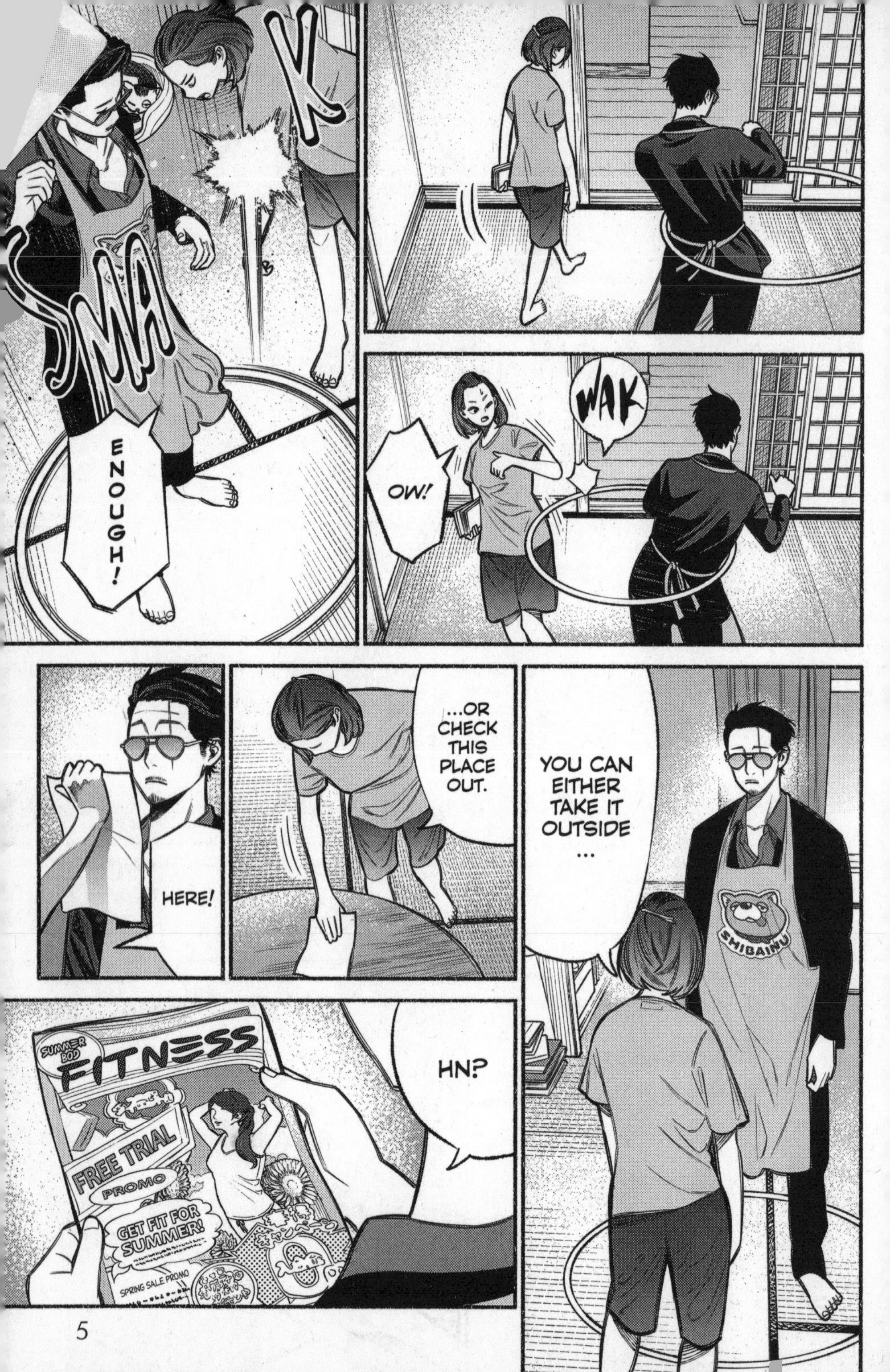
WAK
OW!
SMAK
ENOUGH!
YOU CAN EITHER TAKE IT OUTSIDE ...
...OR CHECK THIS PLACE OUT.
HERE!
HN?
SUMMER BOD
FITNESS
FREE TRIAL
PROMO
GET FIT FOR SUMMER!
SPRING SALE PROMO

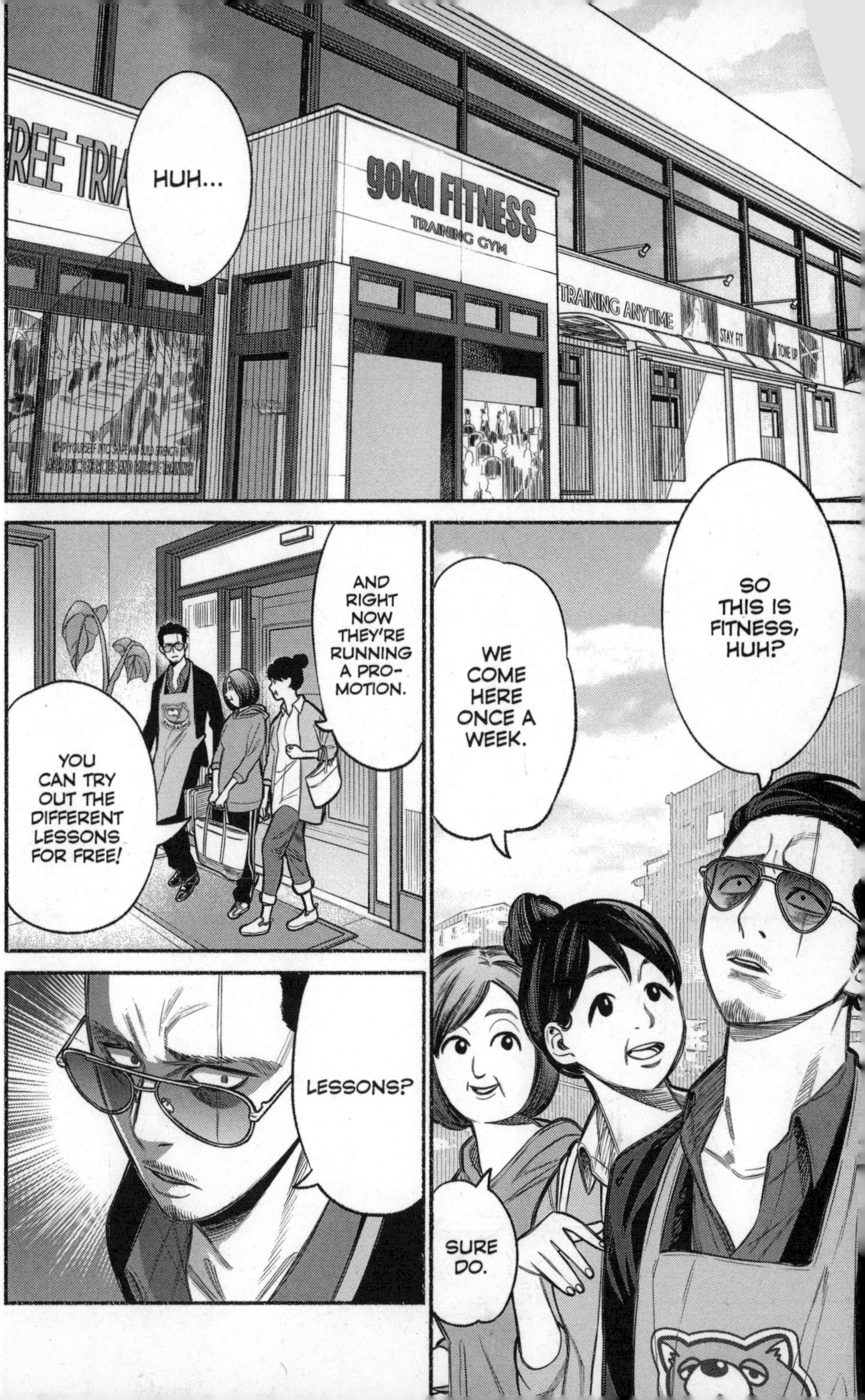
REE TRIA
HUH...
goku FITNESS
TRAINING GYM
TRAINING ANYTIME
STAY FIT
TONE UP
SO THIS IS FITNESS, HUH?
WE COME HERE ONCE A WEEK.
SURE DO.
AND RIGHT NOW THEY'RE RUNNING A PRO-MOTION.
YOU CAN TRY OUT THE DIFFERENT LESSONS FOR FREE!
LESSONS?

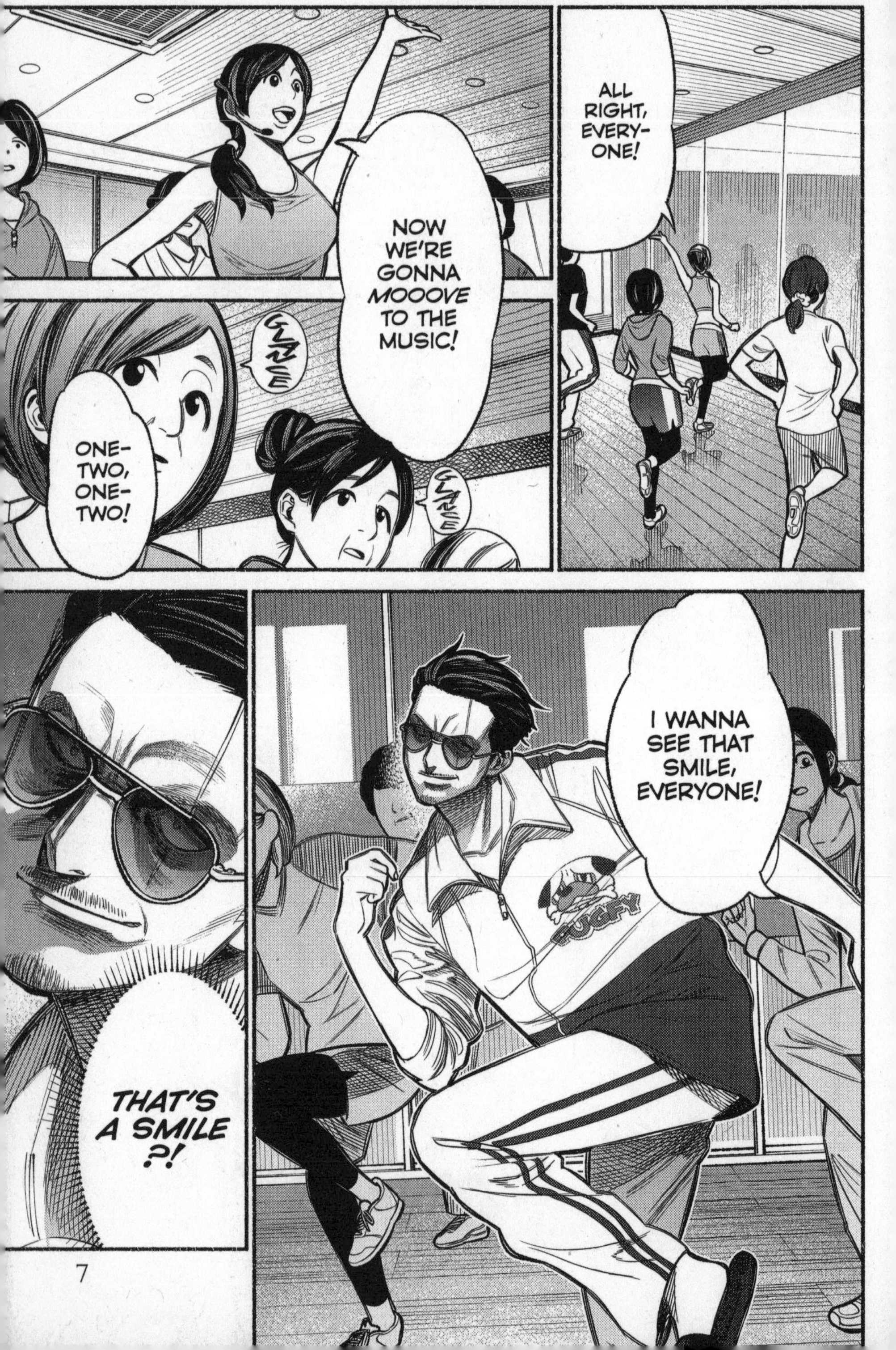
ALL RIGHT, EVERY-ONE!
NOW WE'RE GONNA *MOOOVE* TO THE MUSIC!
GLANCE
ONE-TWO, ONE-TWO!
GLANCE
I WANNA SEE THAT SMILE, EVERYONE!
THAT'S A SMILE ?!

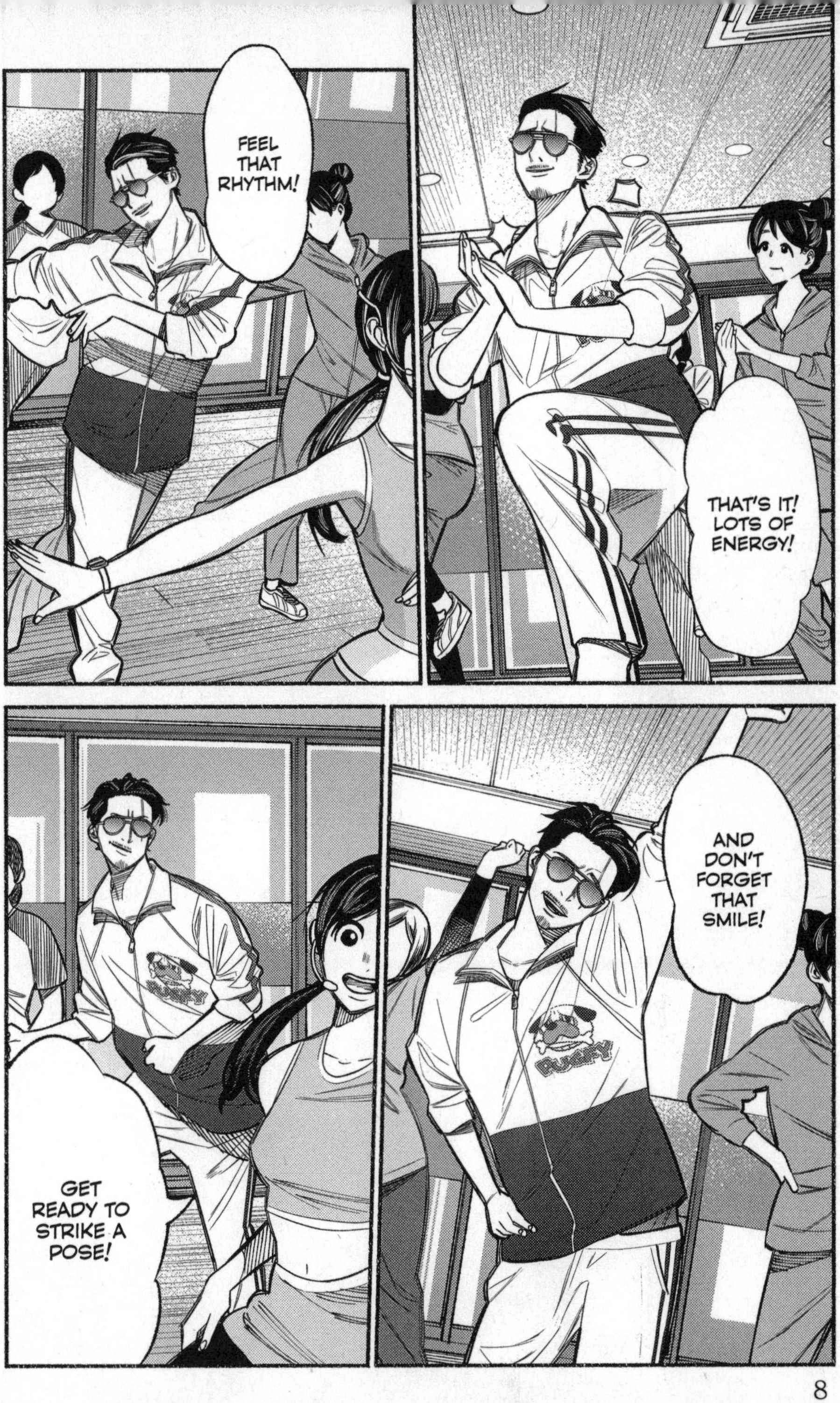
THAT'S IT! LOTS OF ENERGY!
FEEL THAT RHYTHM!
AND DON'T FORGET THAT SMILE!
GET READY TO STRIKE A POSE!

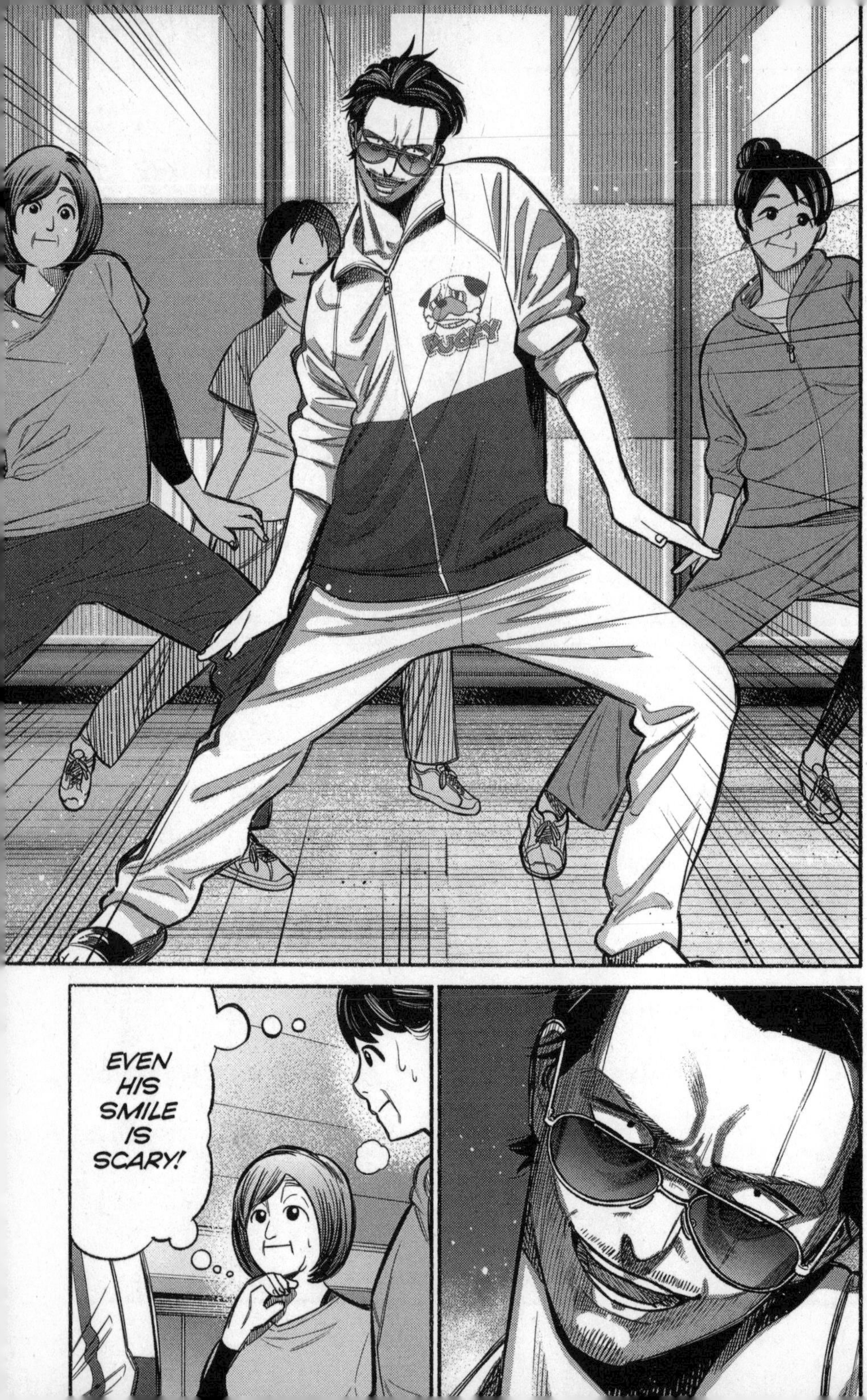
EVEN HIS SMILE IS SCARY!

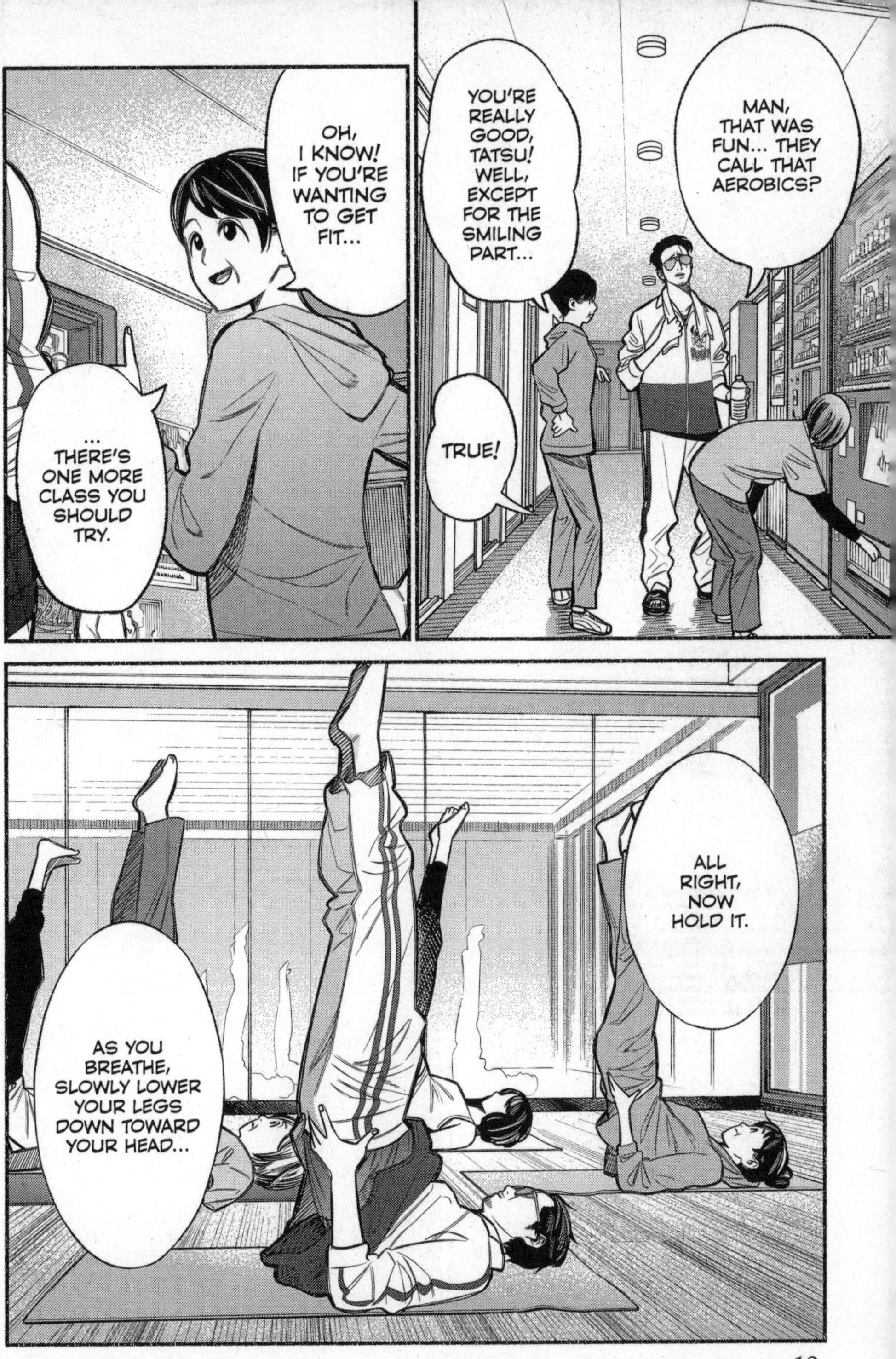
MAN, THAT WAS FUN... THEY CALL THAT AEROBICS?
YOU'RE REALLY GOOD, TATSU! WELL, EXCEPT FOR THE SMILING PART...
TRUE!
OH, I KNOW! IF YOU'RE WANTING TO GET FIT...
... THERE'S ONE MORE CLASS YOU SHOULD TRY.
ALL RIGHT, NOW HOLD IT.
AS YOU BREATHE, SLOWLY LOWER YOUR LEGS DOWN TOWARD YOUR HEAD...

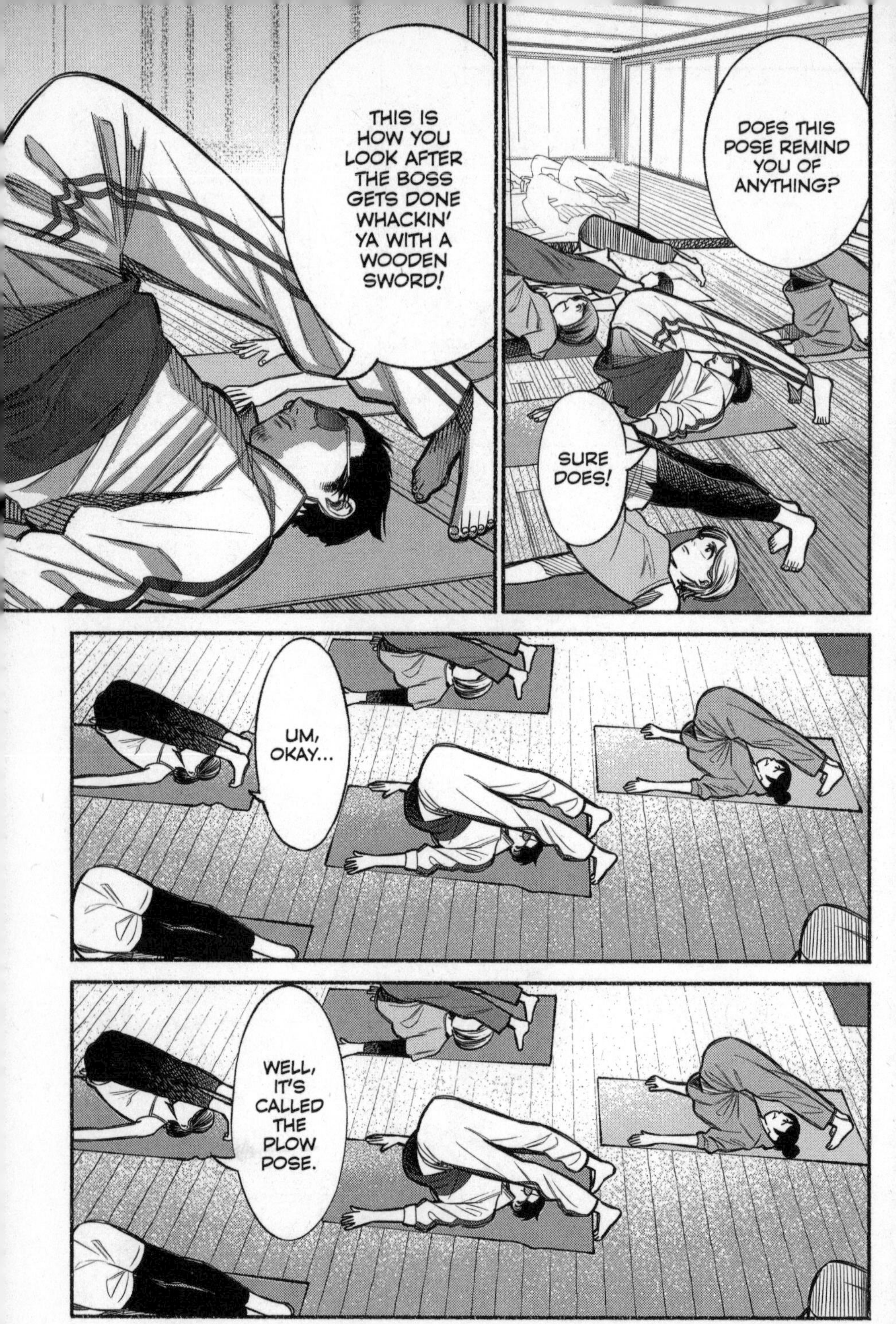
DOES THIS POSE REMIND YOU OF ANYTHING?
SURE DOES!
THIS IS HOW YOU LOOK AFTER THE BOSS GETS DONE WHACKIN' YA WITH A WOODEN SWORD!
UM, OKAY...
WELL, IT'S CALLED THE PLOW POSE.

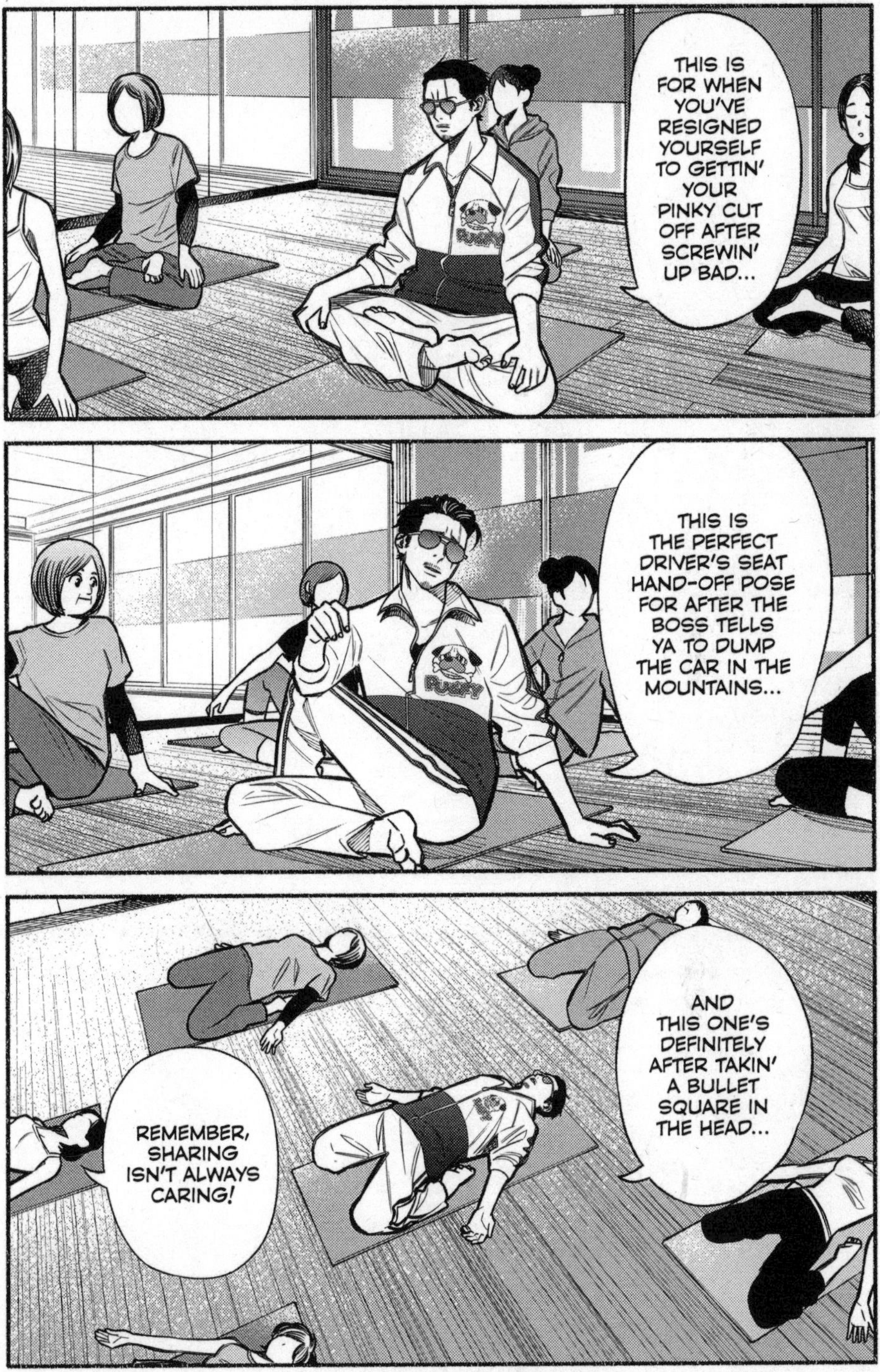
THIS IS FOR WHEN YOU'VE RESIGNED YOURSELF TO GETTIN' YOUR PINKY CUT OFF AFTER SCREWIN' UP BAD...
THIS IS THE PERFECT DRIVER'S SEAT HAND-OFF POSE FOR AFTER THE BOSS TELLS YA TO DUMP THE CAR IN THE MOUNTAINS...
AND THIS ONE'S DEFINITELY AFTER TAKIN' A BULLET SQUARE IN THE HEAD...
REMEMBER, SHARING ISN'T ALWAYS CARING!

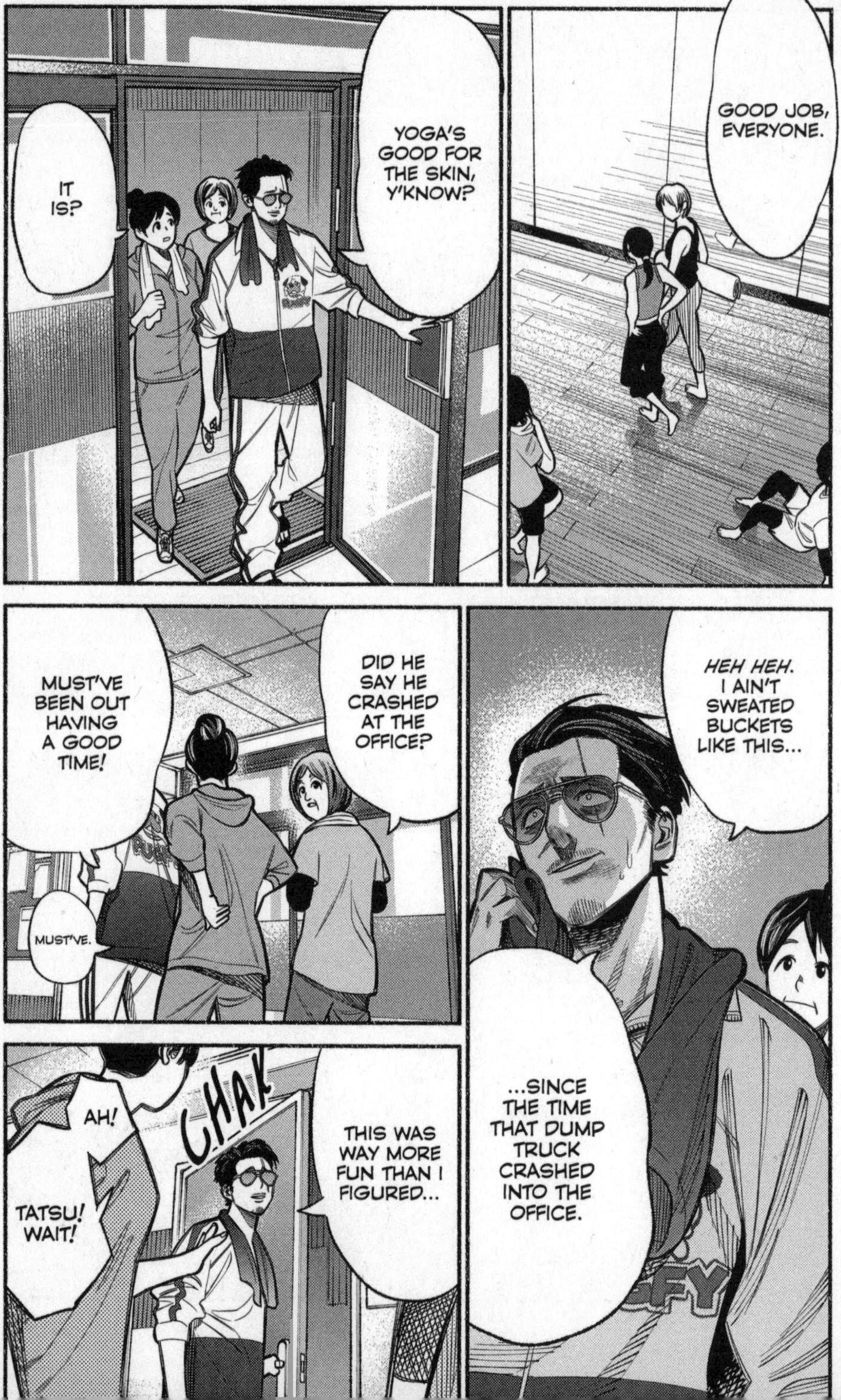
GOOD JOB, EVERYONE.
YOGA'S GOOD FOR THE SKIN, Y'KNOW?
IT IS?
HEH HEH. I AIN'T SWEATED BUCKETS LIKE THIS...
...SINCE THE TIME THAT DUMP TRUCK CRASHED INTO THE OFFICE.
DID HE SAY HE CRASHED AT THE OFFICE?
MUST'VE BEEN OUT HAVING A GOOD TIME!
MUST'VE.
THIS WAS WAY MORE FUN THAN I FIGURED...
CHAK
AH!
TATSU! WAIT!

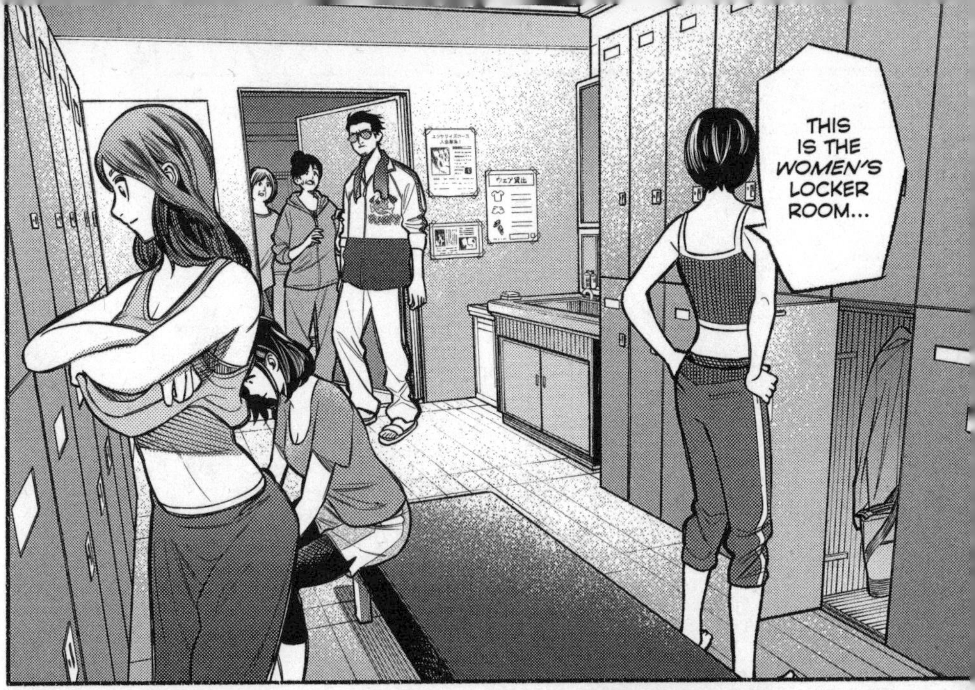
THIS IS THE *WOMEN'S* LOCKER ROOM...

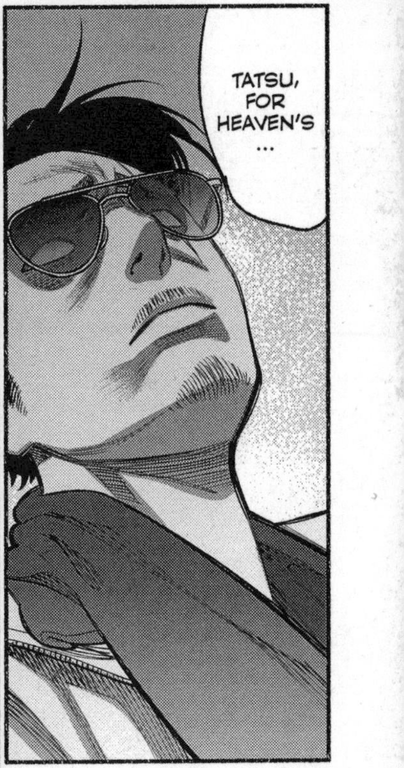
TATSU, FOR HEAVEN'S ...

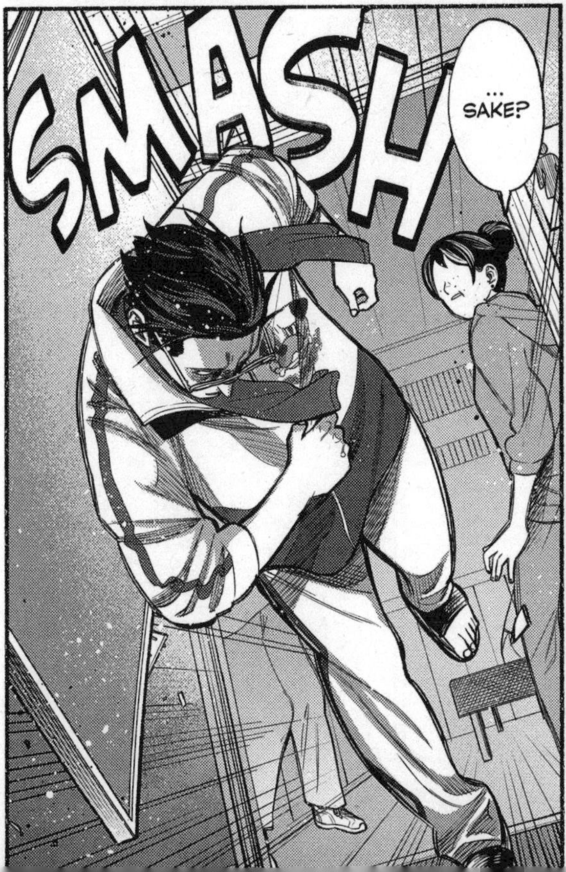
SMASH
... SAKE?

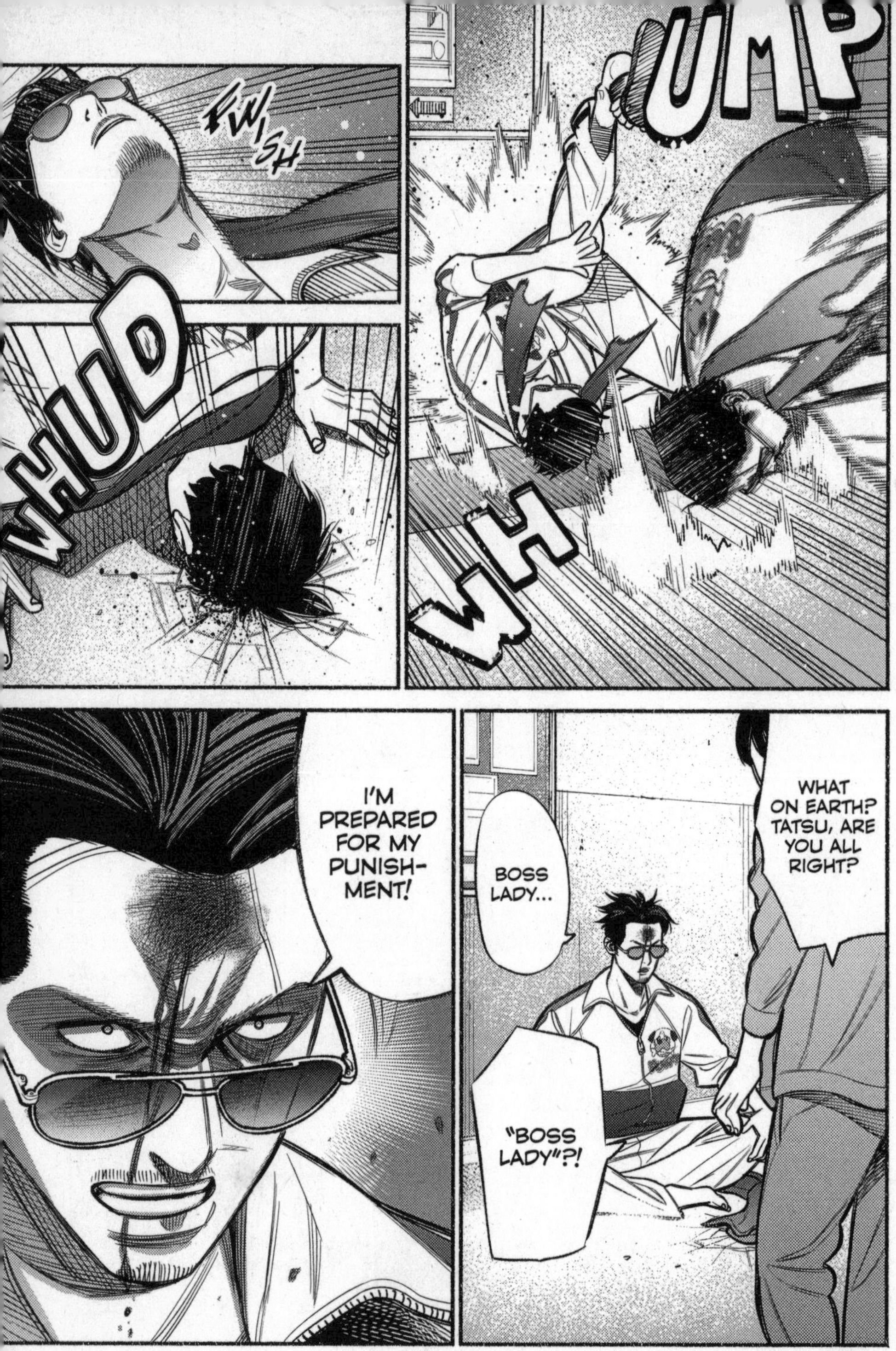
UMP
WH
FWISH
WHUD
WHAT ON EARTH? TATSU, ARE YOU ALL RIGHT?
BOSS LADY...
"BOSS LADY"?!
I'M PREPARED FOR MY PUNISHMENT!

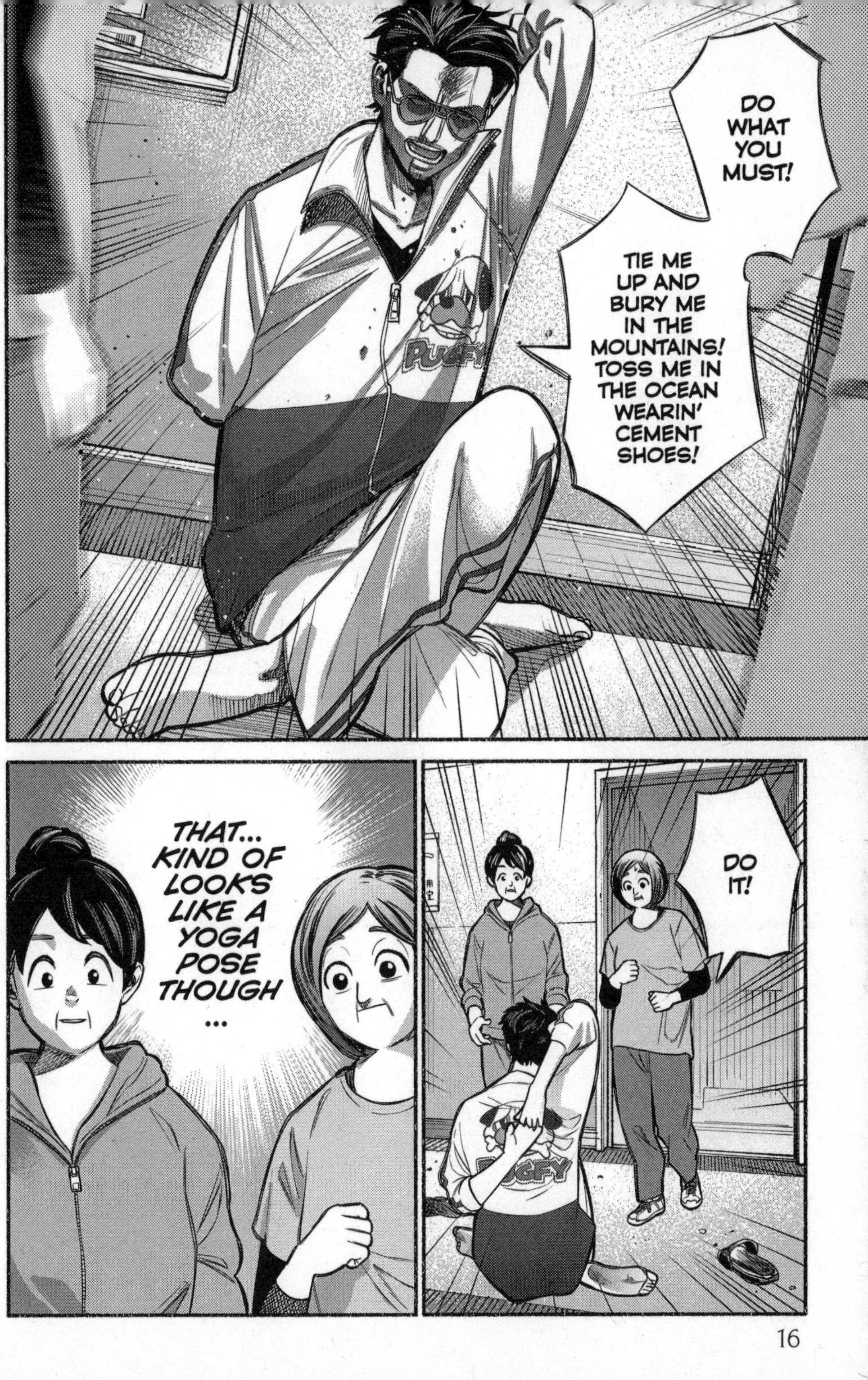
DO WHAT YOU MUST!
TIE ME UP AND BURY ME IN THE MOUNTAINS! TOSS ME IN THE OCEAN WEARIN' CEMENT SHOES!
DO IT!
THAT... KIND OF LOOKS LIKE A YOGA POSE THOUGH ...

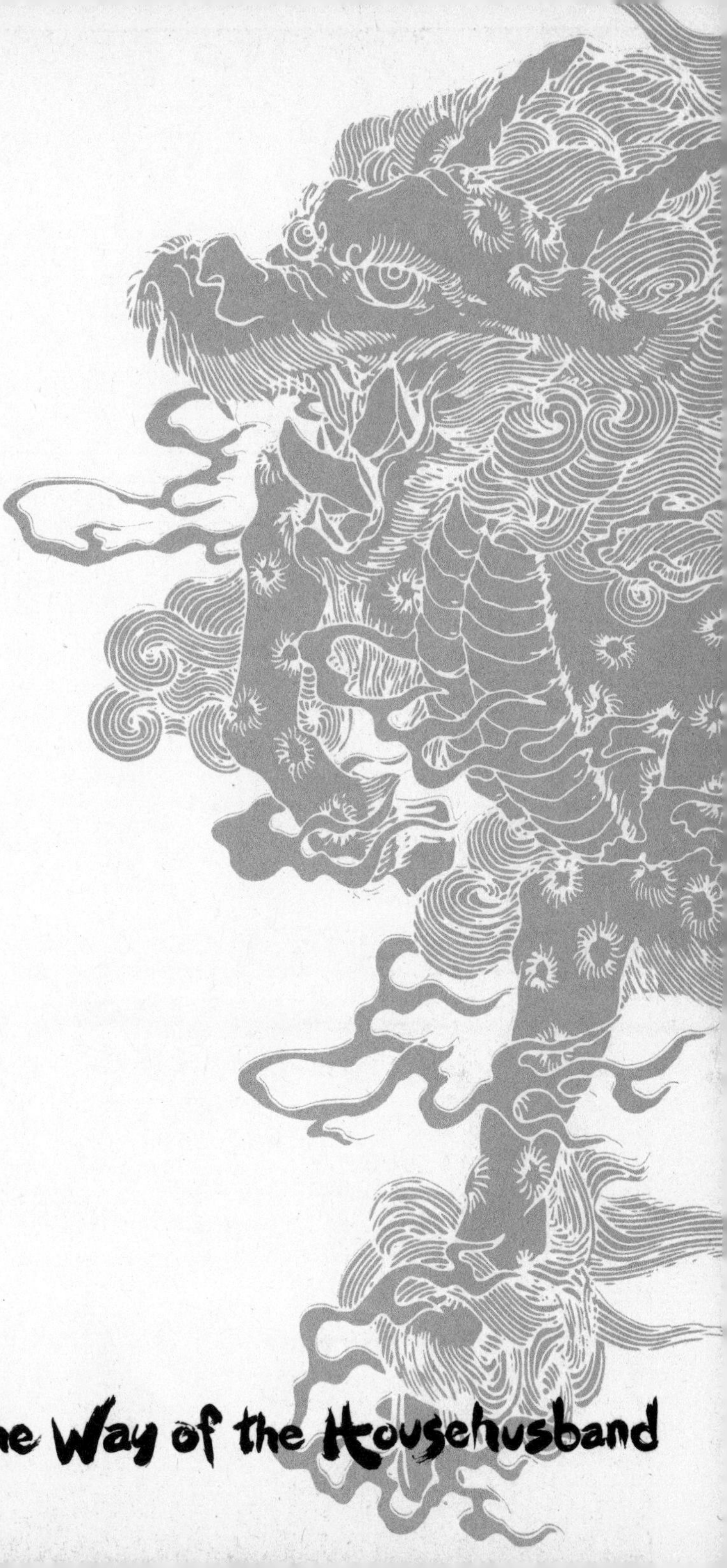

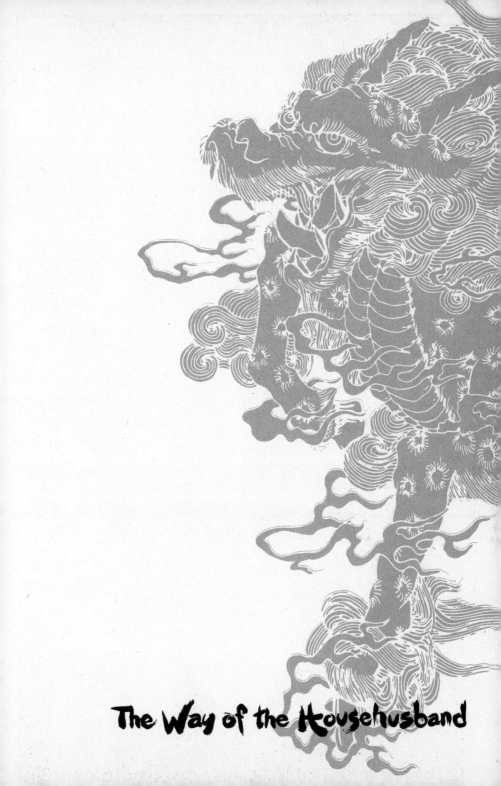

The Way of the Househusband

CHAPTER 11

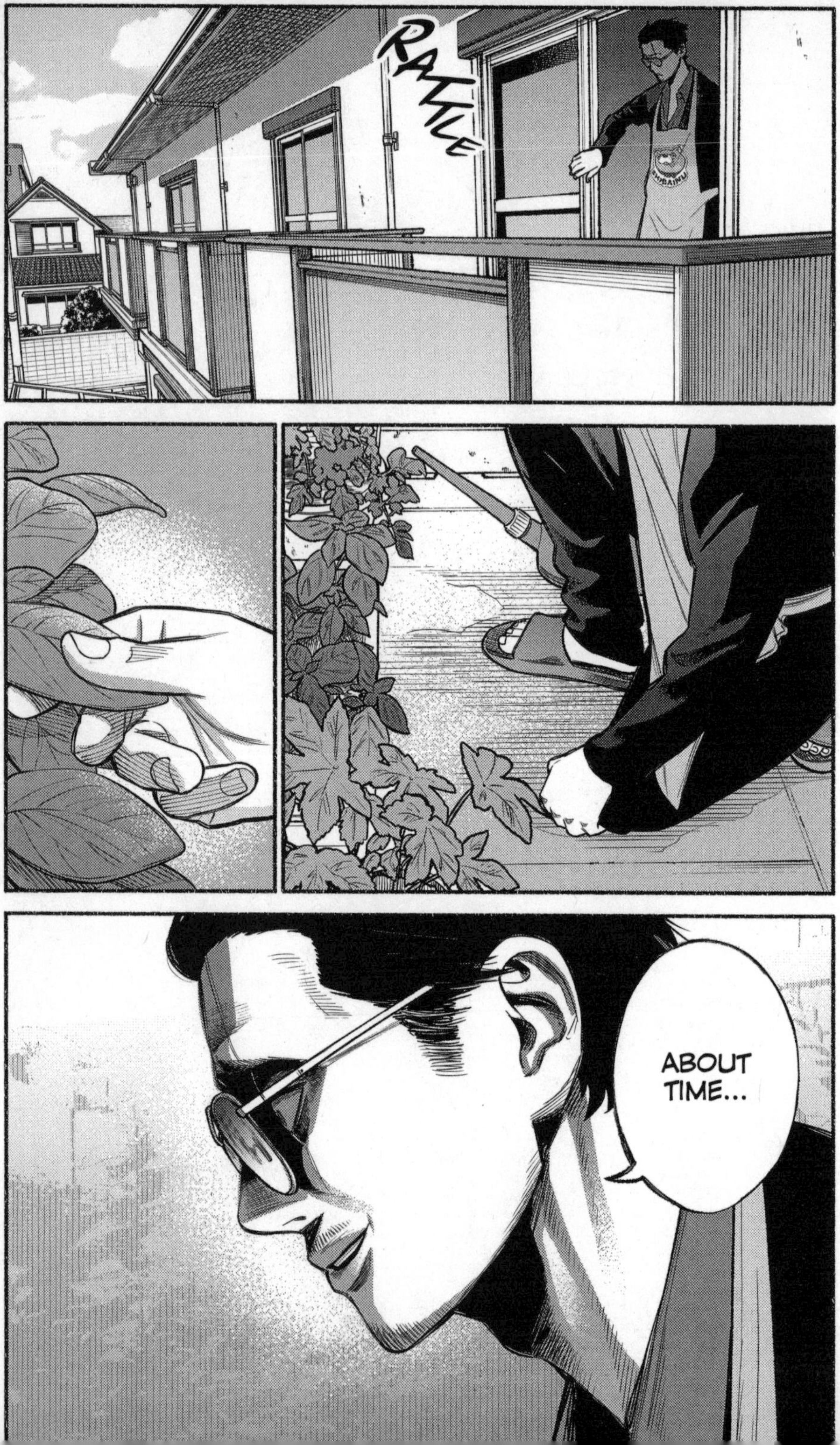
RATTLE
ABOUT TIME...

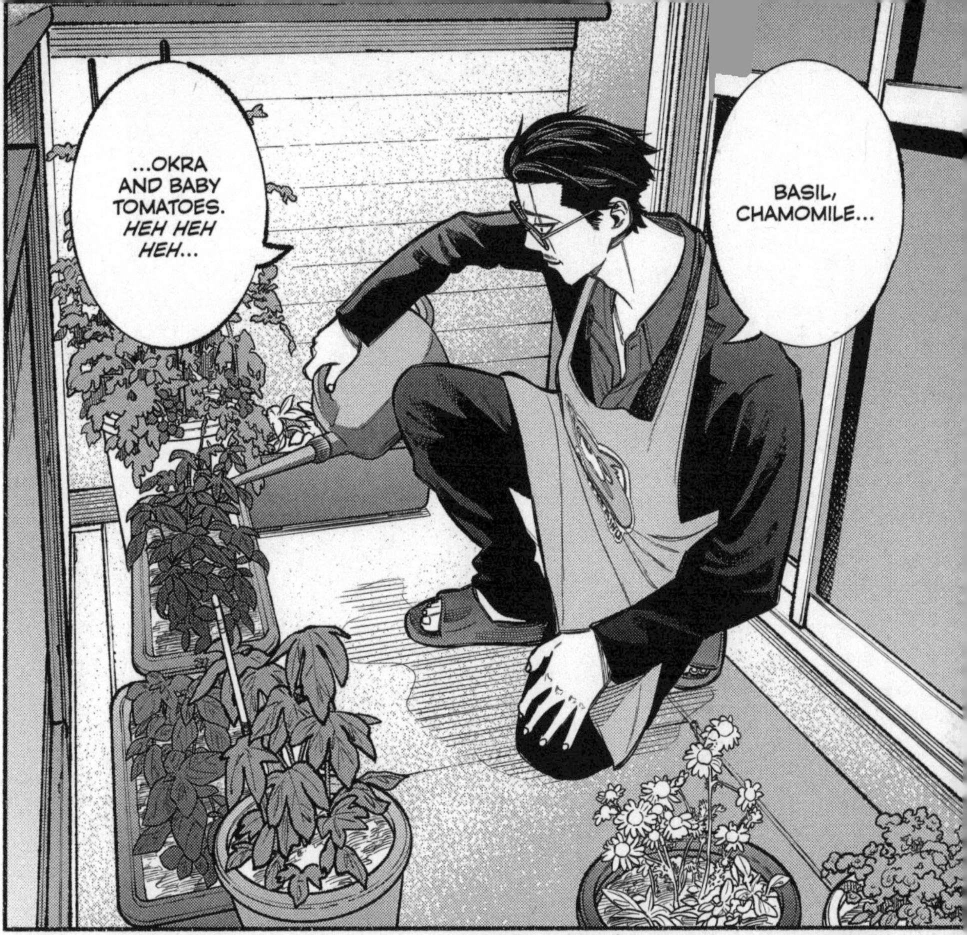
BASIL, CHAMOMILE...
...OKRA AND BABY TOMATOES. *HEH HEH HEH*...

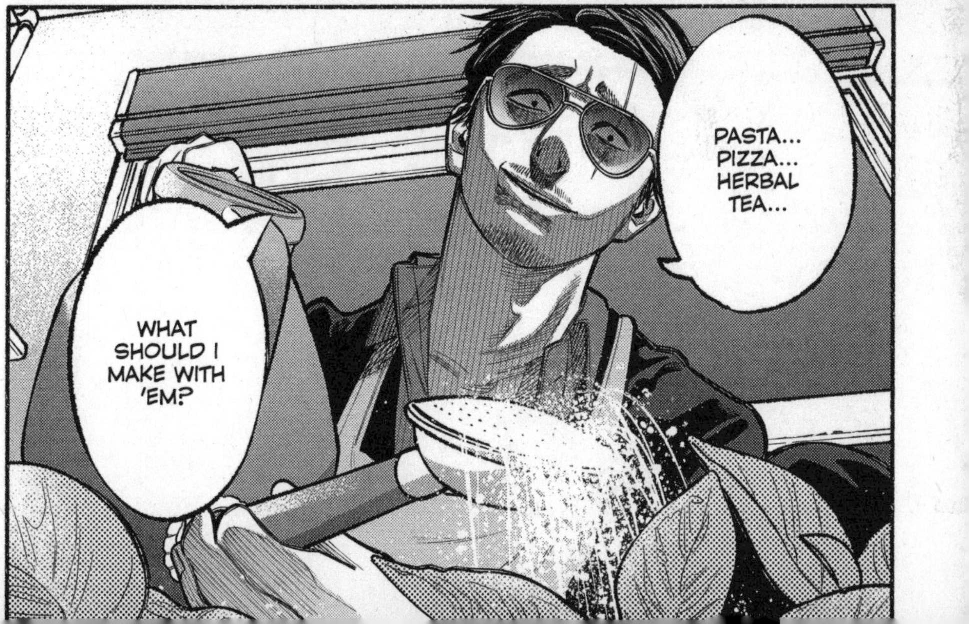
PASTA... PIZZA... HERBAL TEA...
WHAT SHOULD I MAKE WITH 'EM?

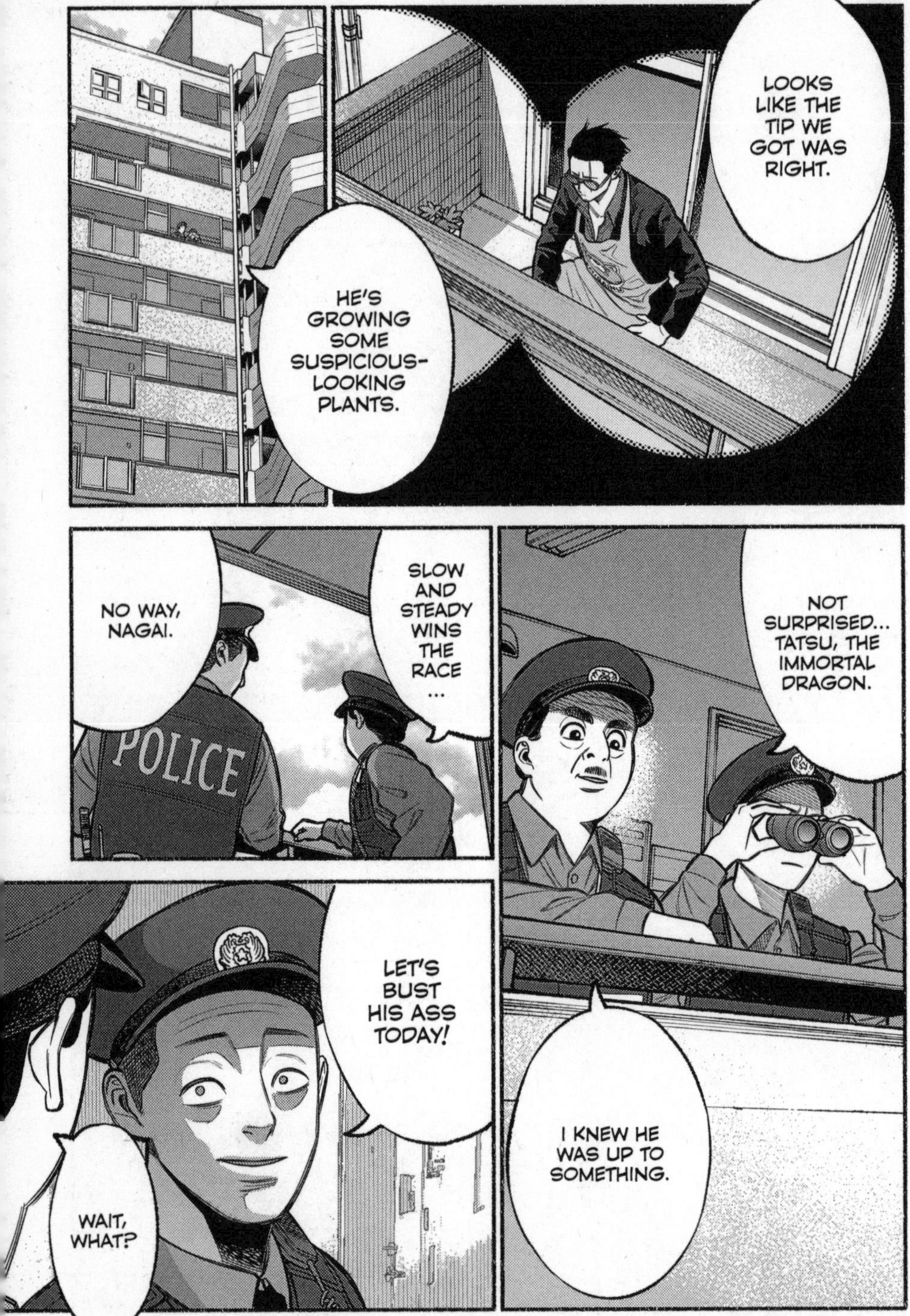
LOOKS LIKE THE TIP WE GOT WAS RIGHT.
HE'S GROWING SOME SUSPICIOUS-LOOKING PLANTS.
NOT SURPRISED... TATSU, THE IMMORTAL DRAGON.
I KNEW HE WAS UP TO SOMETHING.
SLOW AND STEADY WINS THE RACE ...
NO WAY, NAGAI.
POLICE
LET'S BUST HIS ASS TODAY!
WAIT, WHAT?

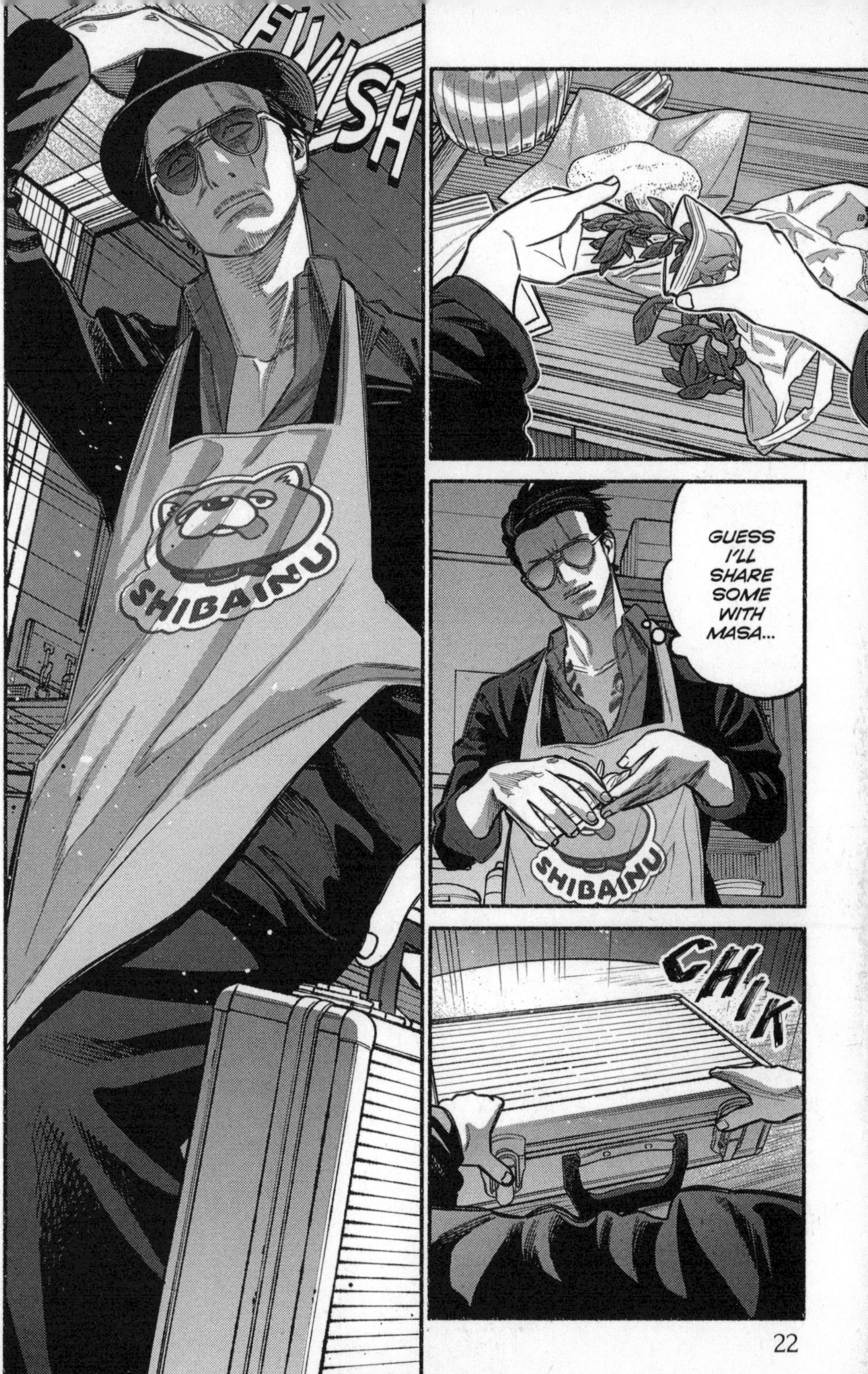
GUESS I'LL SHARE SOME WITH MASA...
CHIK
FWISH

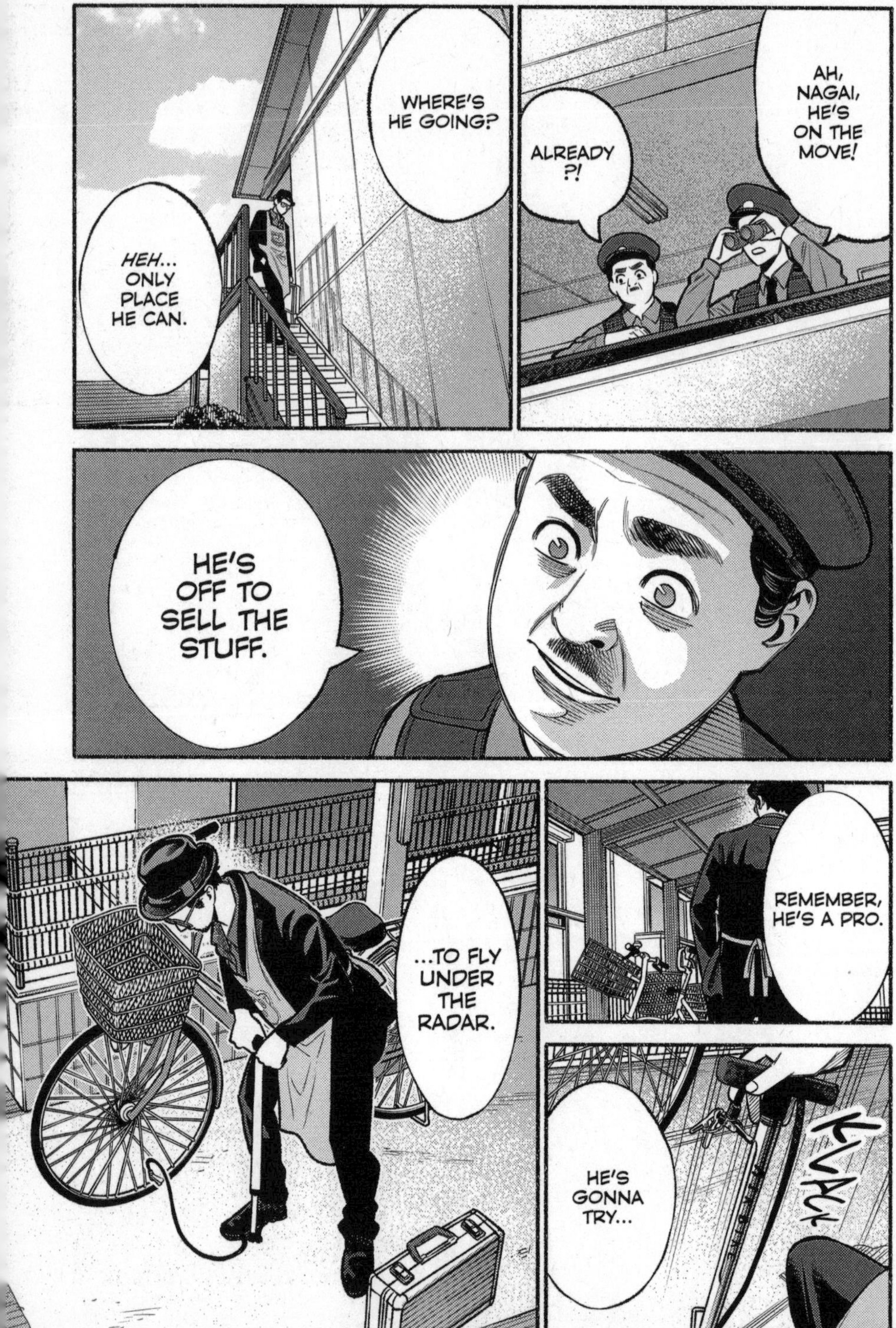
AH, NAGAI, HE'S ON THE MOVE!
ALREADY ?!
WHERE'S HE GOING?
HEH... ONLY PLACE HE CAN.
HE'S OFF TO SELL THE STUFF.
REMEMBER, HE'S A PRO.
KLACK
HE'S GONNA TRY...
...TO FLY UNDER THE RADAR.

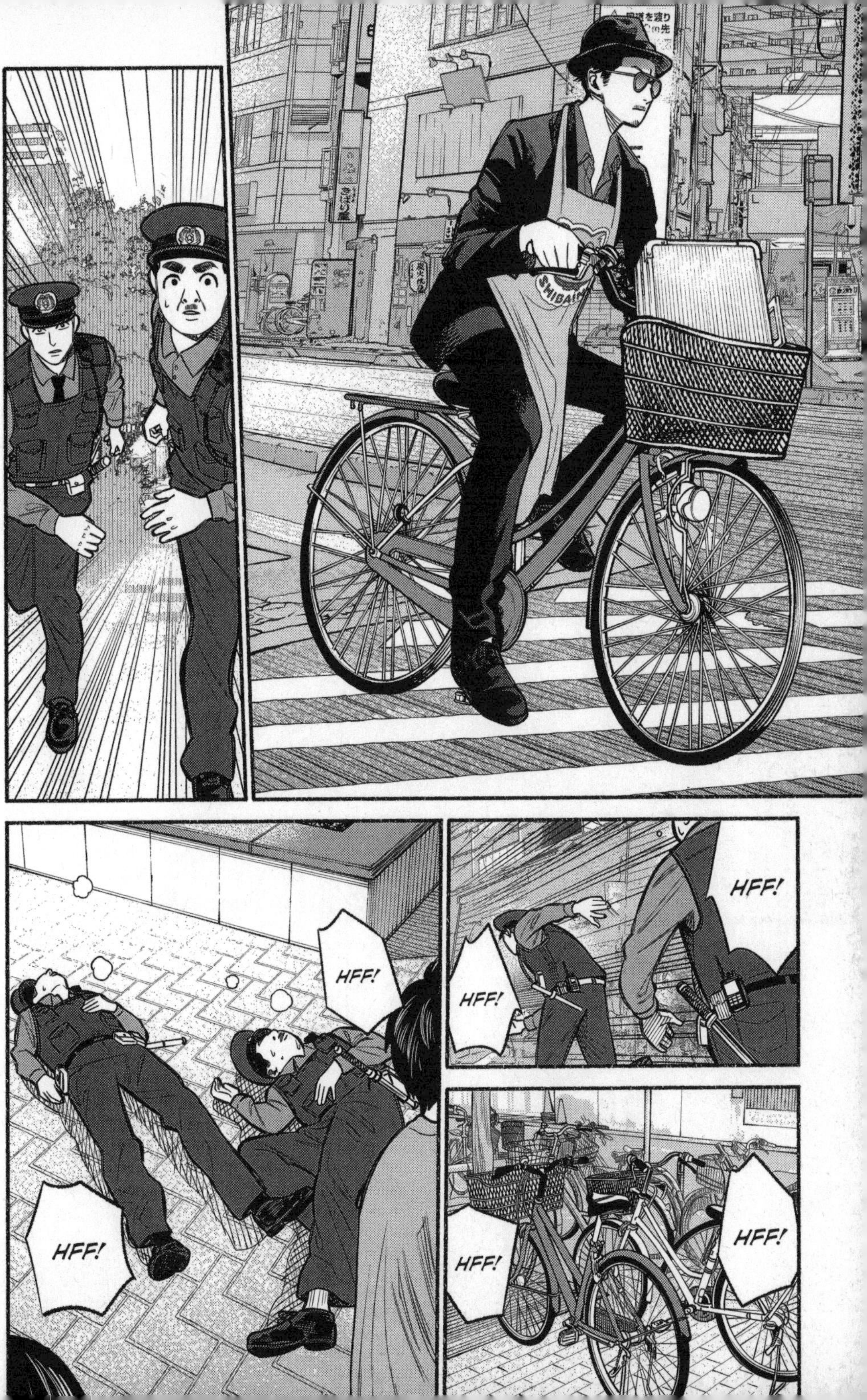
HFF!
HFF!
HFF!
HFF!
HFF!
HFF!

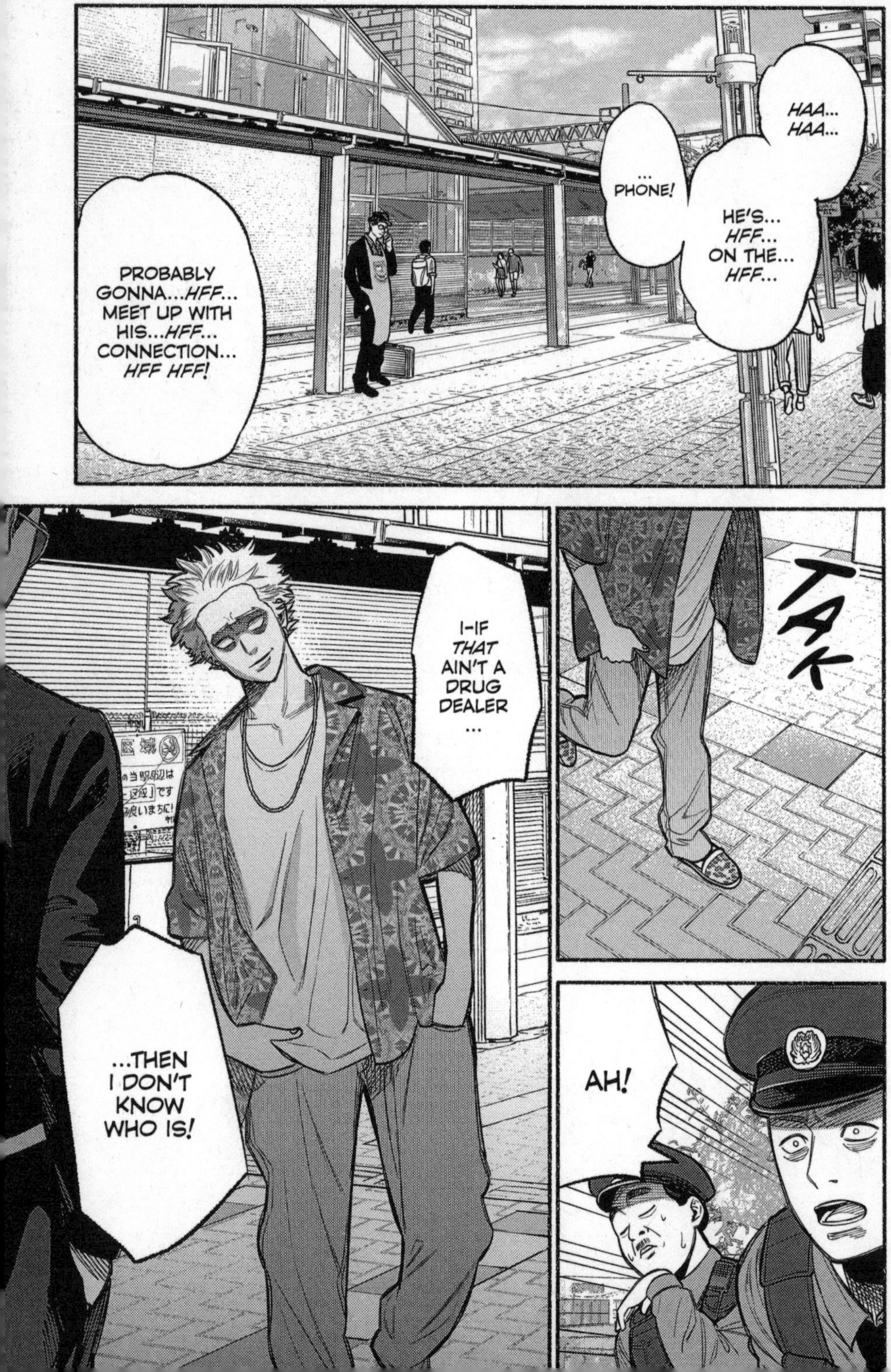
HAA... HAA...
HE'S... HFF... ON THE... HFF...
...PHONE!
PROBABLY GONNA...HFF... MEET UP WITH HIS...HFF... CONNECTION... HFF HFF!
TAK
AH!
I-IF THAT AIN'T A DRUG DEALER ...
...THEN I DON'T KNOW WHO IS!

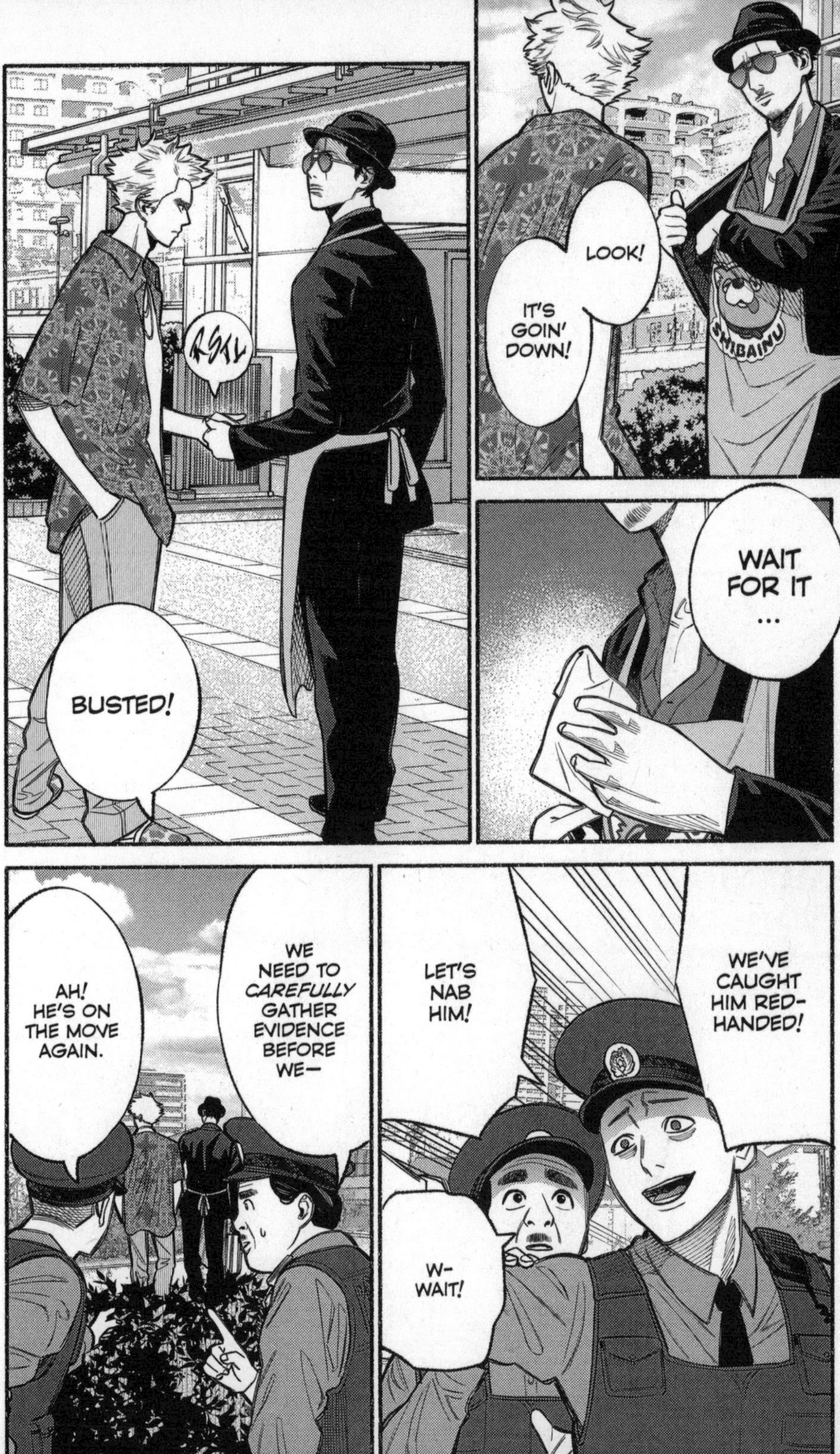
LOOK!
IT'S GOIN' DOWN!
WAIT FOR IT ...
BUSTED!
WE'VE CAUGHT HIM RED-HANDED!
LET'S NAB HIM!
W-WAIT!
WE NEED TO *CAREFULLY* GATHER EVIDENCE BEFORE WE—
AH! HE'S ON THE MOVE AGAIN.

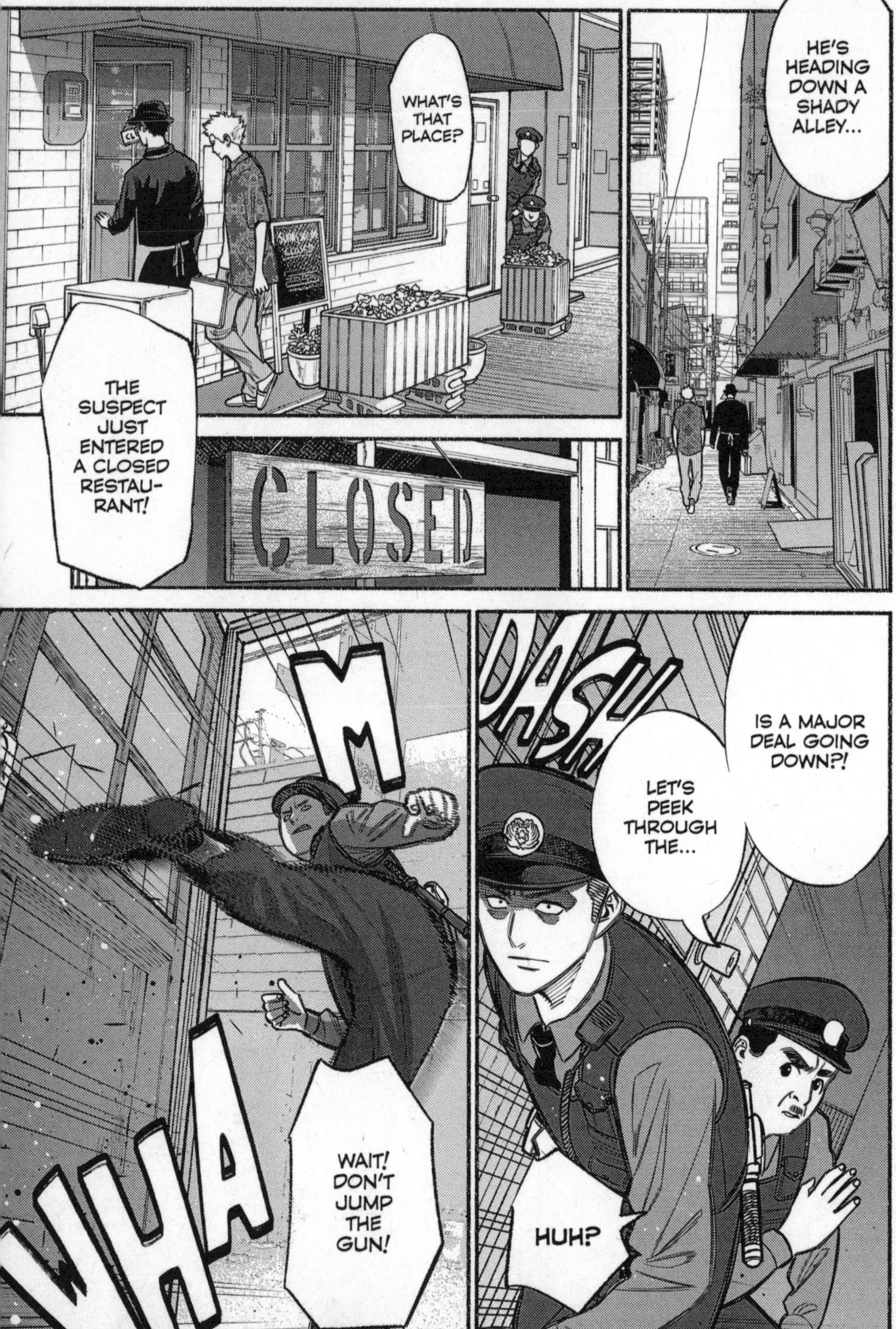
HE'S HEADING DOWN A SHADY ALLEY...
WHAT'S THAT PLACE?
THE SUSPECT JUST ENTERED A CLOSED RESTAU-RANT!
CLOSED
DASH
IS A MAJOR DEAL GOING DOWN?!
LET'S PEEK THROUGH THE...
HUH?
WHAM
WAIT! DON'T JUMP THE GUN!

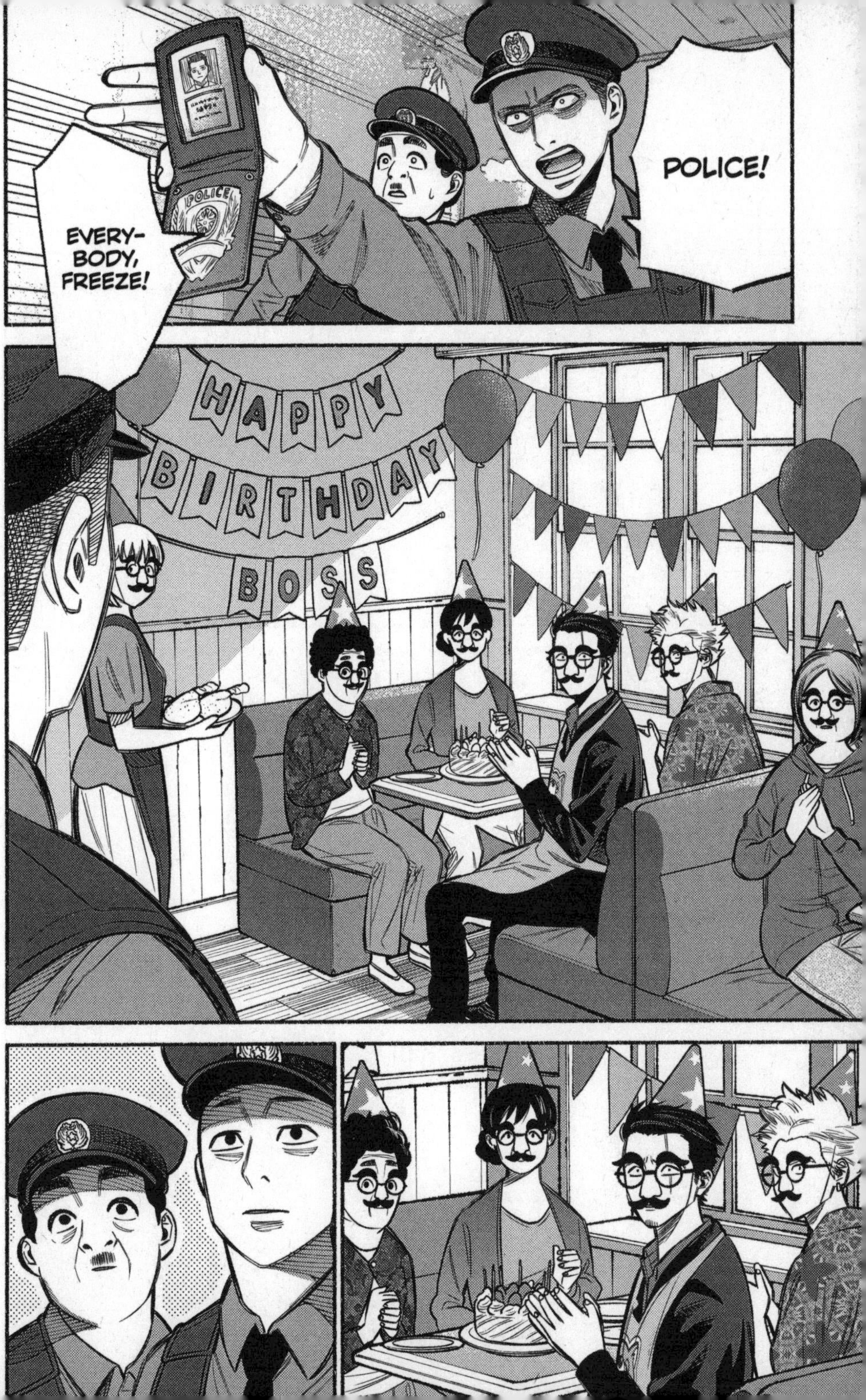
POLICE!
EVERY-BODY, FREEZE!
HAPPY BIRTHDAY BOSS

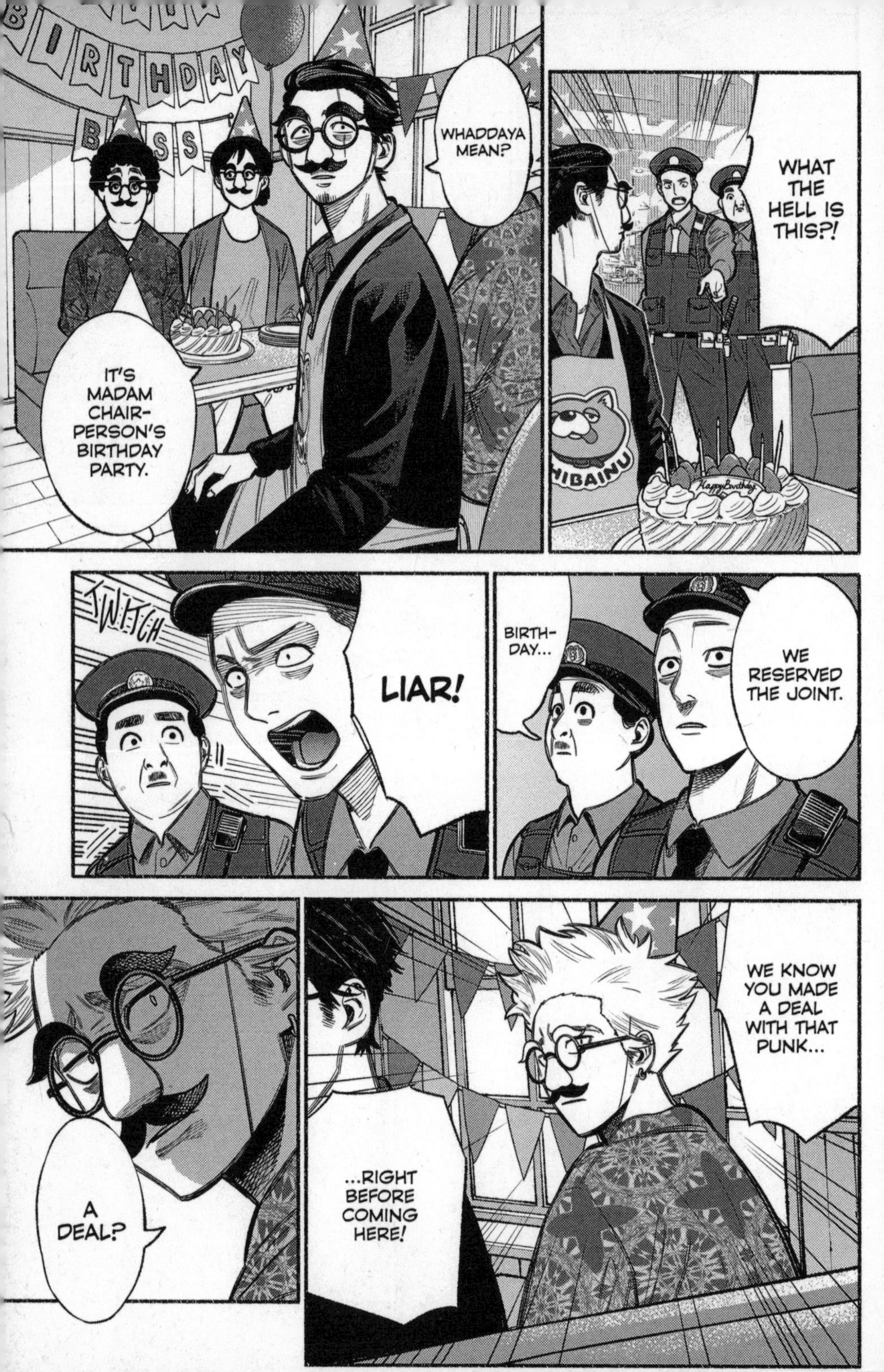
WHAT THE HELL IS THIS?!
Happy Birthday
WHADDAYA MEAN?
IT'S MADAM CHAIR-PERSON'S BIRTHDAY PARTY.
WE RESERVED THE JOINT.
BIRTH-DAY...
SWITCH
LIAR!
WE KNOW YOU MADE A DEAL WITH THAT PUNK...
...RIGHT BEFORE COMING HERE!
A DEAL?

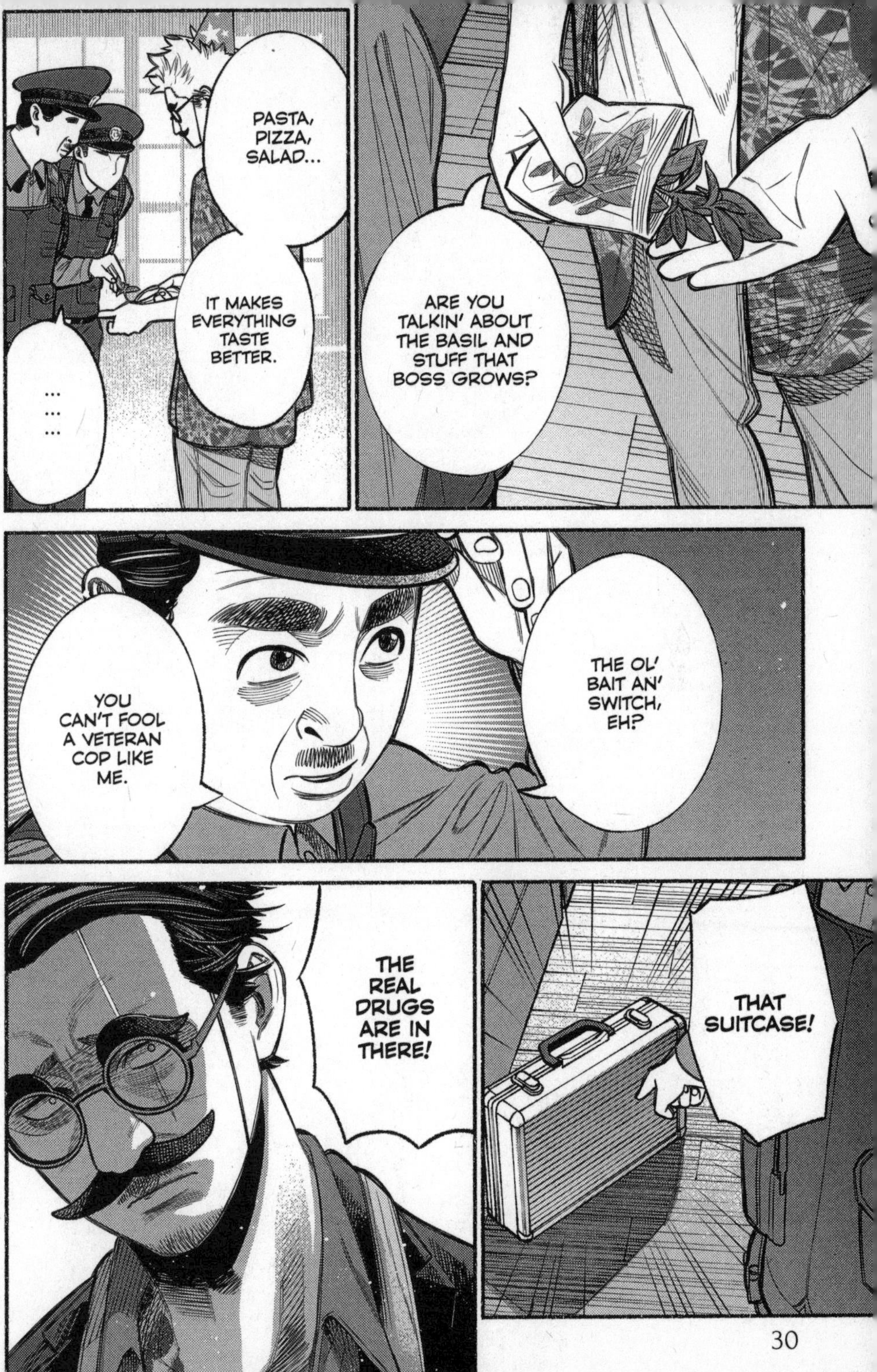
ARE YOU TALKIN' ABOUT THE BASIL AND STUFF THAT BOSS GROWS?
PASTA, PIZZA, SALAD...
IT MAKES EVERYTHING TASTE BETTER.
... ...
THE OL' BAIT AN' SWITCH, EH?
YOU CAN'T FOOL A VETERAN COP LIKE ME.
THAT SUITCASE!
THE REAL DRUGS ARE IN THERE!

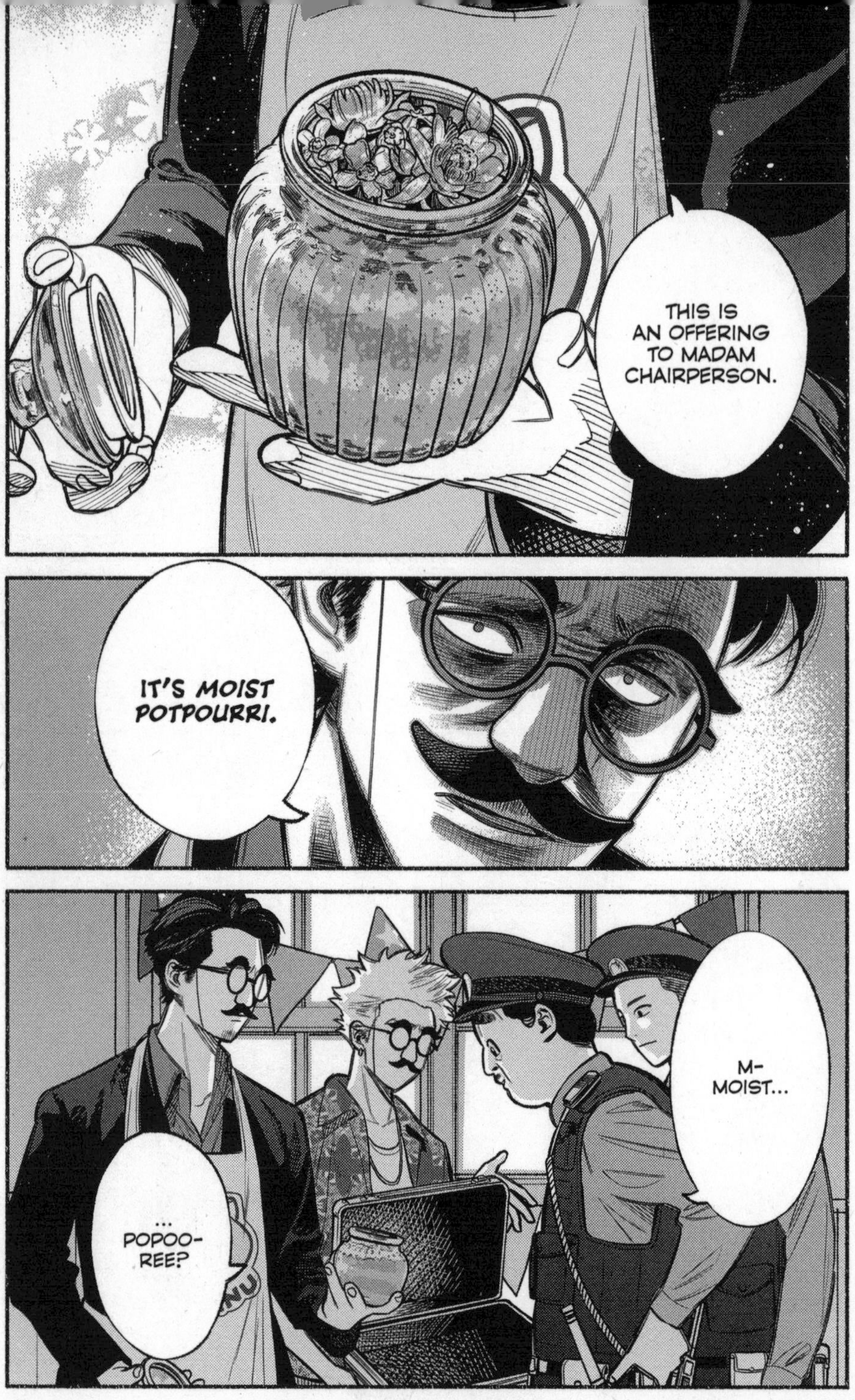
THIS IS AN OFFERING TO MADAM CHAIRPERSON.
IT'S MOIST POTPOURRI.
M-MOIST...
...POPOO-REE?

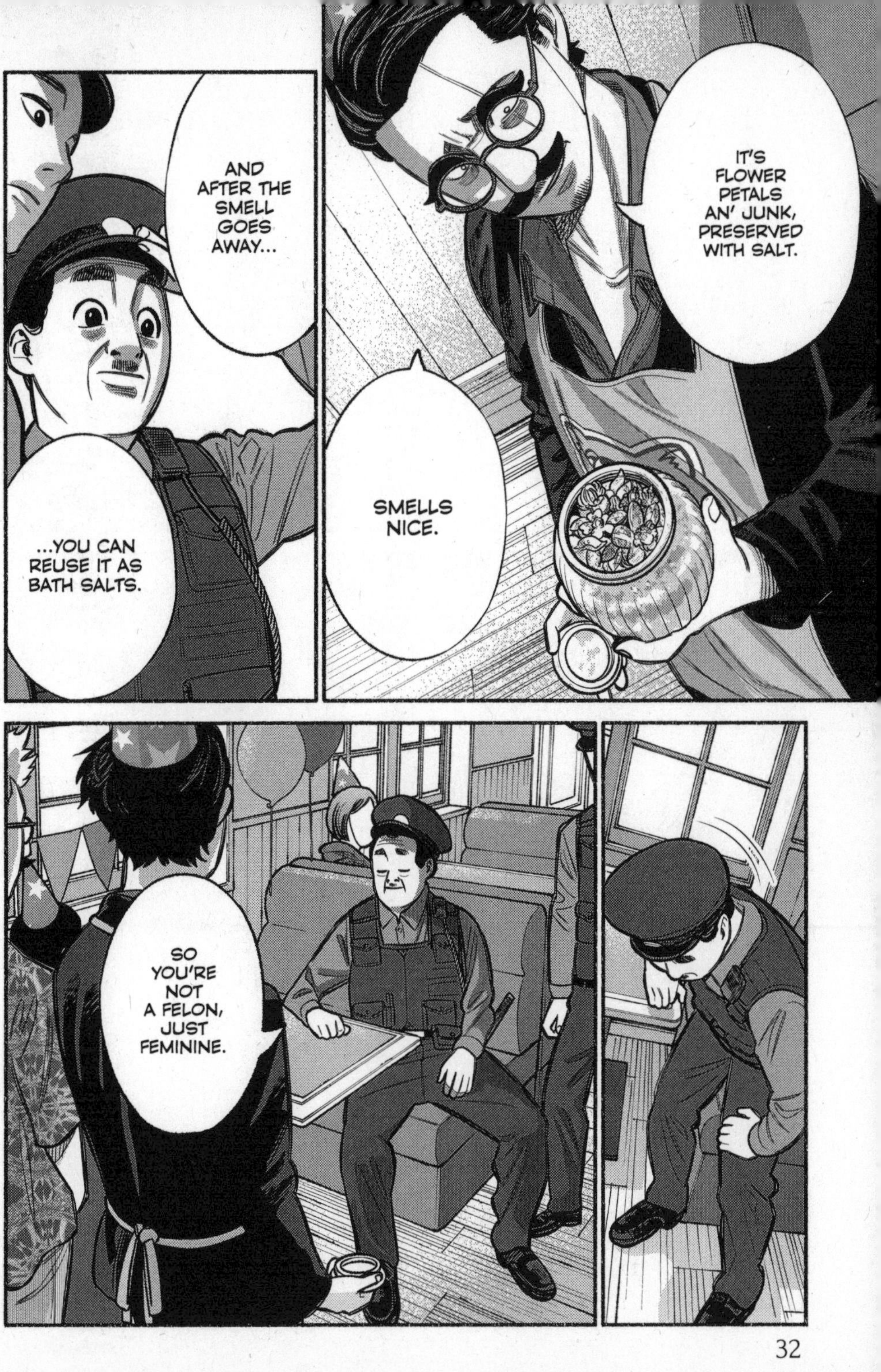
IT'S FLOWER PETALS AN' JUNK, PRESERVED WITH SALT.
SMELLS NICE.
AND AFTER THE SMELL GOES AWAY...
...YOU CAN REUSE IT AS BATH SALTS.
SO YOU'RE NOT A FELON, JUST FEMININE.

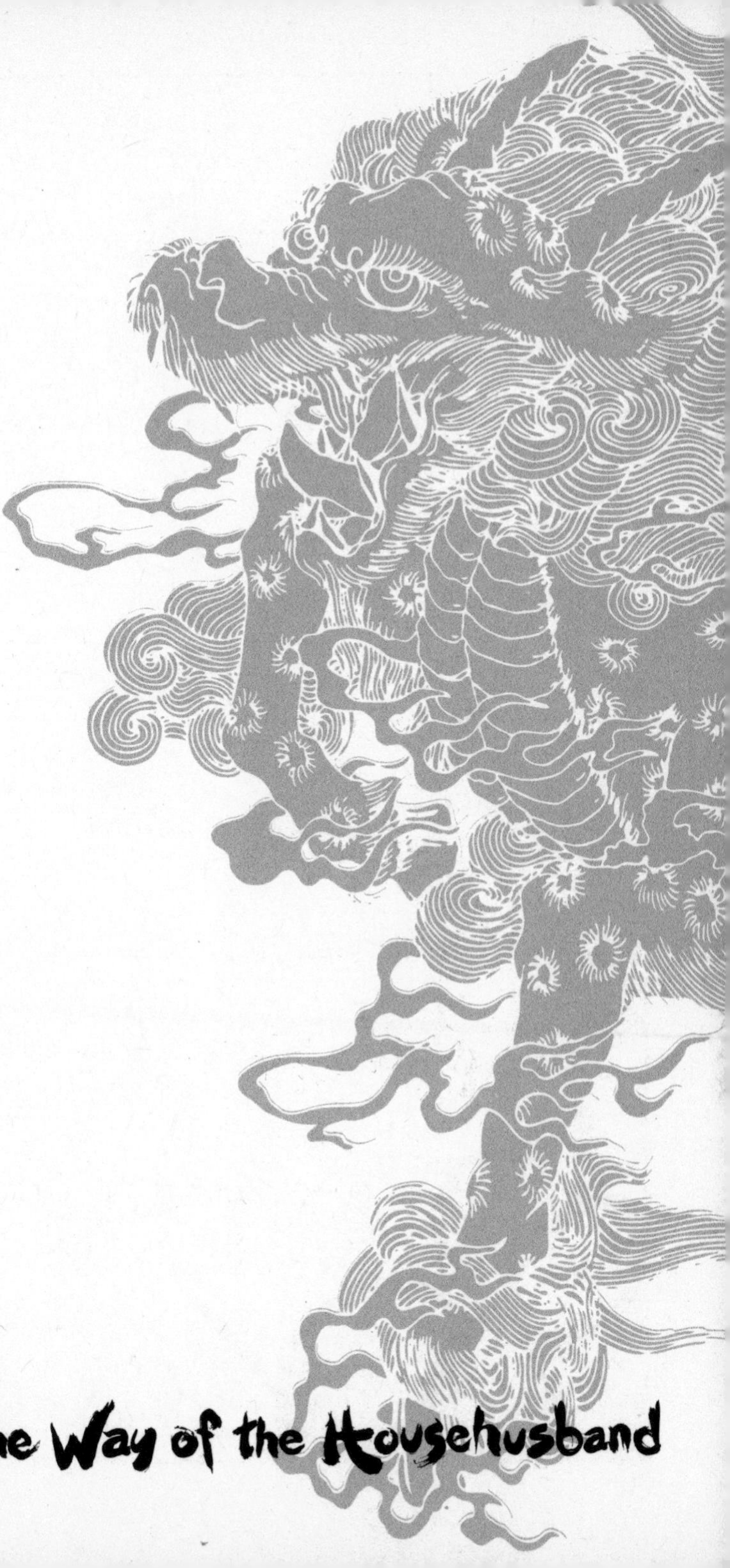

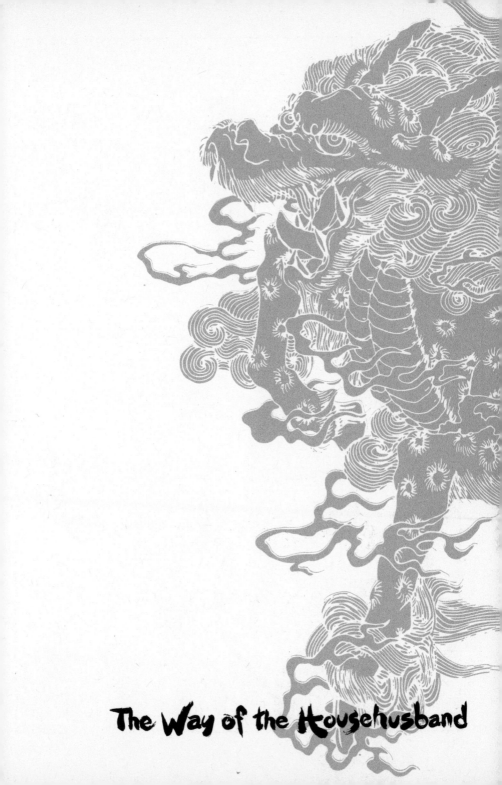

The Way of the Househusband

CHAPTER 12

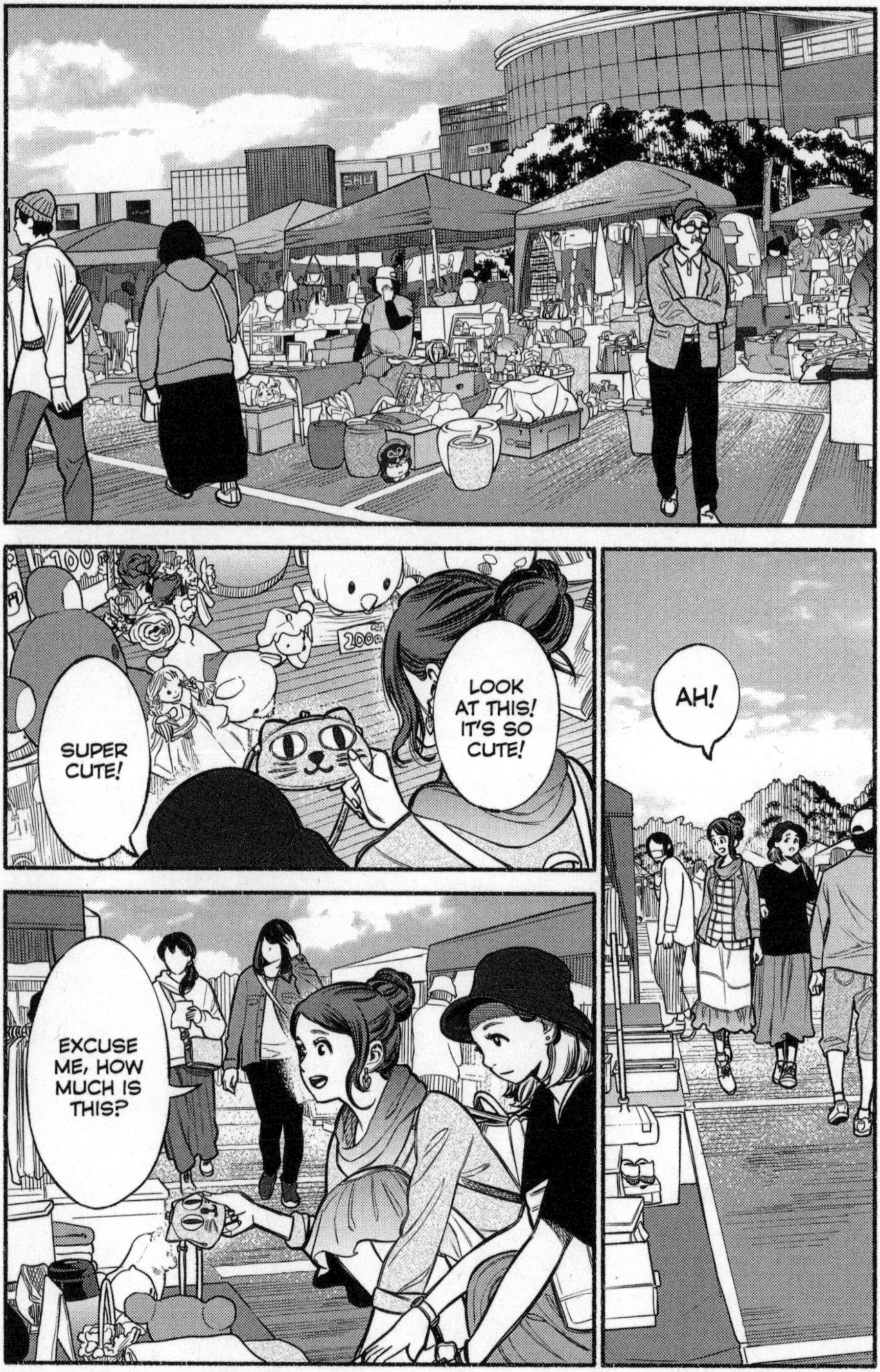
AH!
LOOK AT THIS! IT'S SO CUTE!
SUPER CUTE!
EXCUSE ME, HOW MUCH IS THIS?

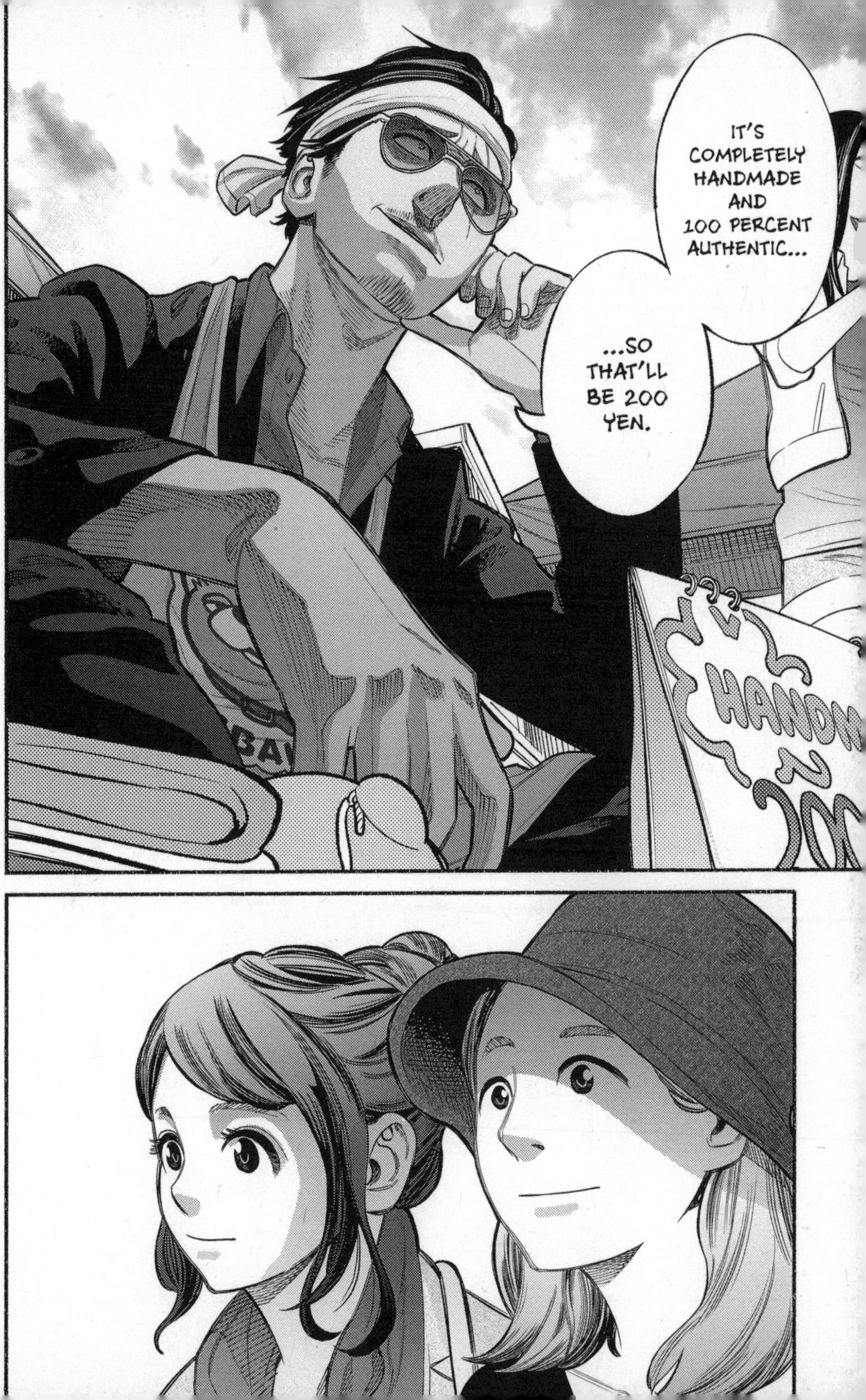
IT'S COMPLETELY HANDMADE AND 100 PERCENT AUTHENTIC...
...SO THAT'LL BE 200 YEN.

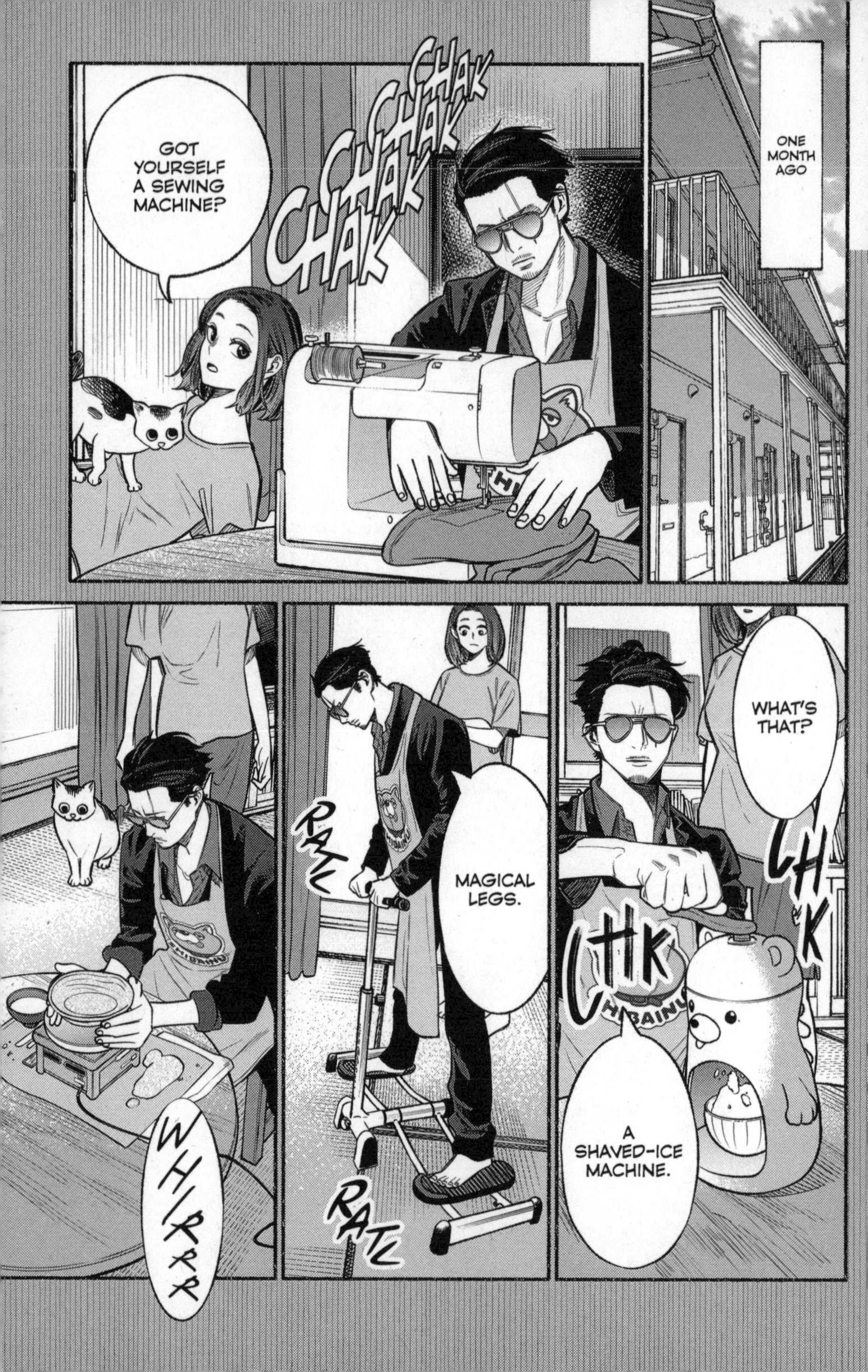
ONE MONTH AGO
GOT YOURSELF A SEWING MACHINE?
CHAK CHAK CHAK CHAK
WHAT'S THAT?
CHK
CHK
A SHAVED-ICE MACHINE.
RATL
MAGICAL LEGS.
RATL
WHIRRR

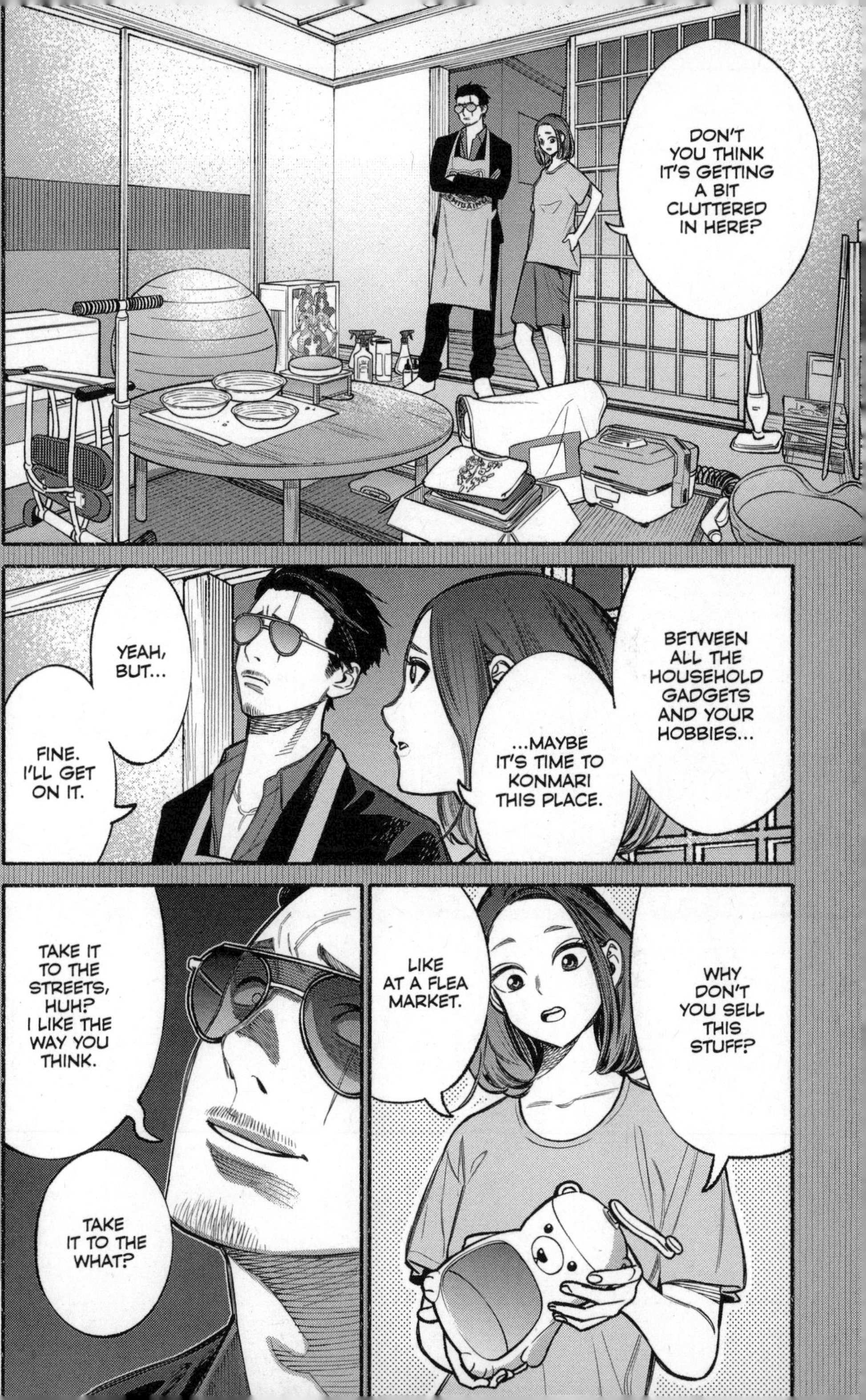
DON'T YOU THINK IT'S GETTING A BIT CLUTTERED IN HERE?
BETWEEN ALL THE HOUSEHOLD GADGETS AND YOUR HOBBIES...
...MAYBE IT'S TIME TO KONMARI THIS PLACE.
YEAH, BUT...
FINE. I'LL GET ON IT.
WHY DON'T YOU SELL THIS STUFF?
LIKE AT A FLEA MARKET.
TAKE IT TO THE STREETS, HUH? I LIKE THE WAY YOU THINK.
TAKE IT TO THE WHAT?

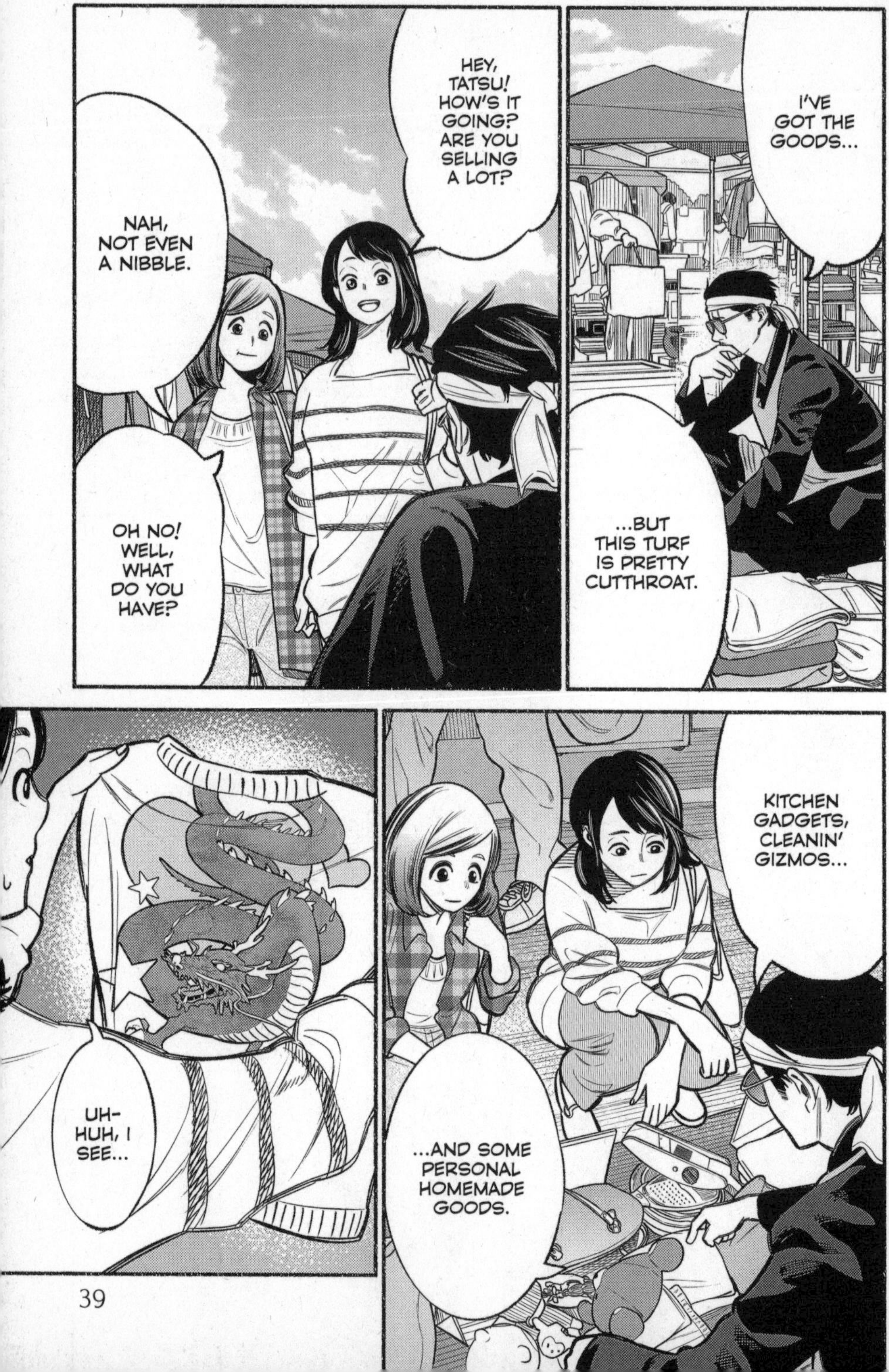
HEY, TATSU! HOW'S IT GOING? ARE YOU SELLING A LOT?
NAH, NOT EVEN A NIBBLE.
OH NO! WELL, WHAT DO YOU HAVE?
I'VE GOT THE GOODS...
...BUT THIS TURF IS PRETTY CUTTHROAT.
KITCHEN GADGETS, CLEANIN' GIZMOS...
...AND SOME PERSONAL HOMEMADE GOODS.
UH-HUH, I SEE...

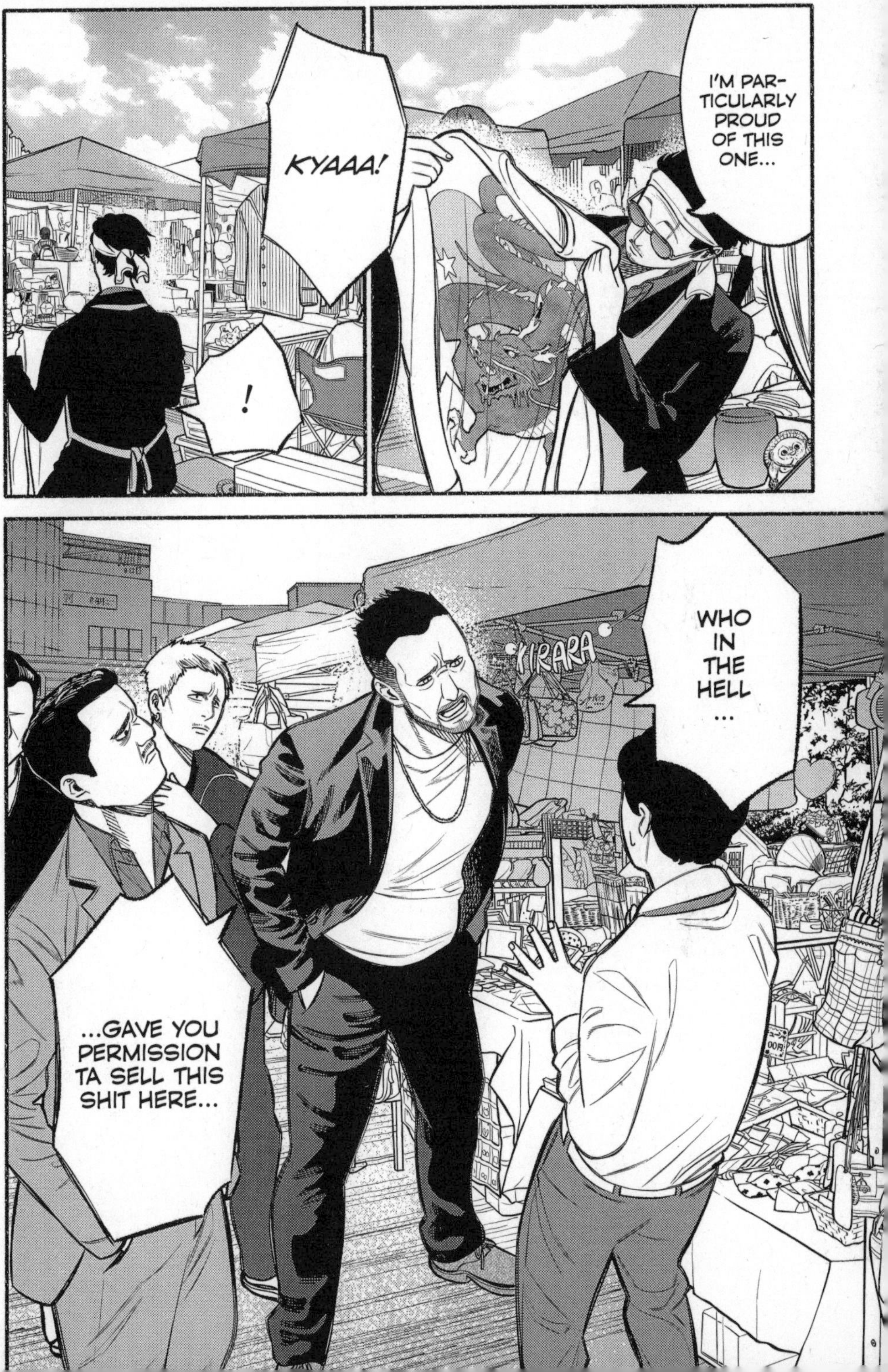
I'M PAR-TICULARLY PROUD OF THIS ONE...
KYAAA!
!
WHO IN THE HELL...
KIRARA
...GAVE YOU PERMISSION TA SELL THIS SHIT HERE...

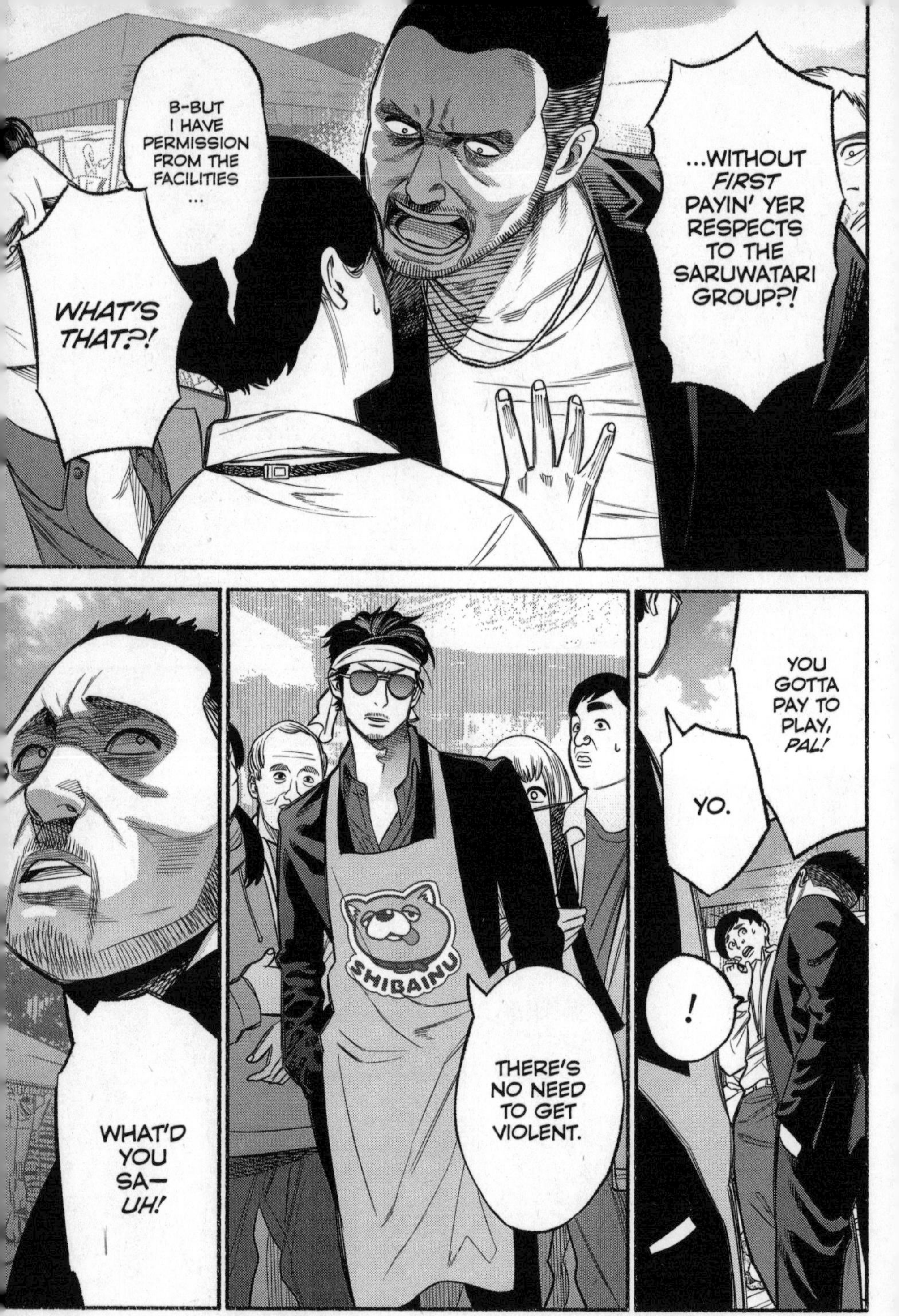
...WITHOUT *FIRST* PAYIN' YER RESPECTS TO THE SARUWATARI GROUP?!
B-BUT I HAVE PERMISSION FROM THE FACILITIES ...
WHAT'S THAT?!
YOU GOTTA PAY TO PLAY, *PAL!*
YO.
!
THERE'S NO NEED TO GET VIOLENT.
WHAT'D YOU SA— *UH!*

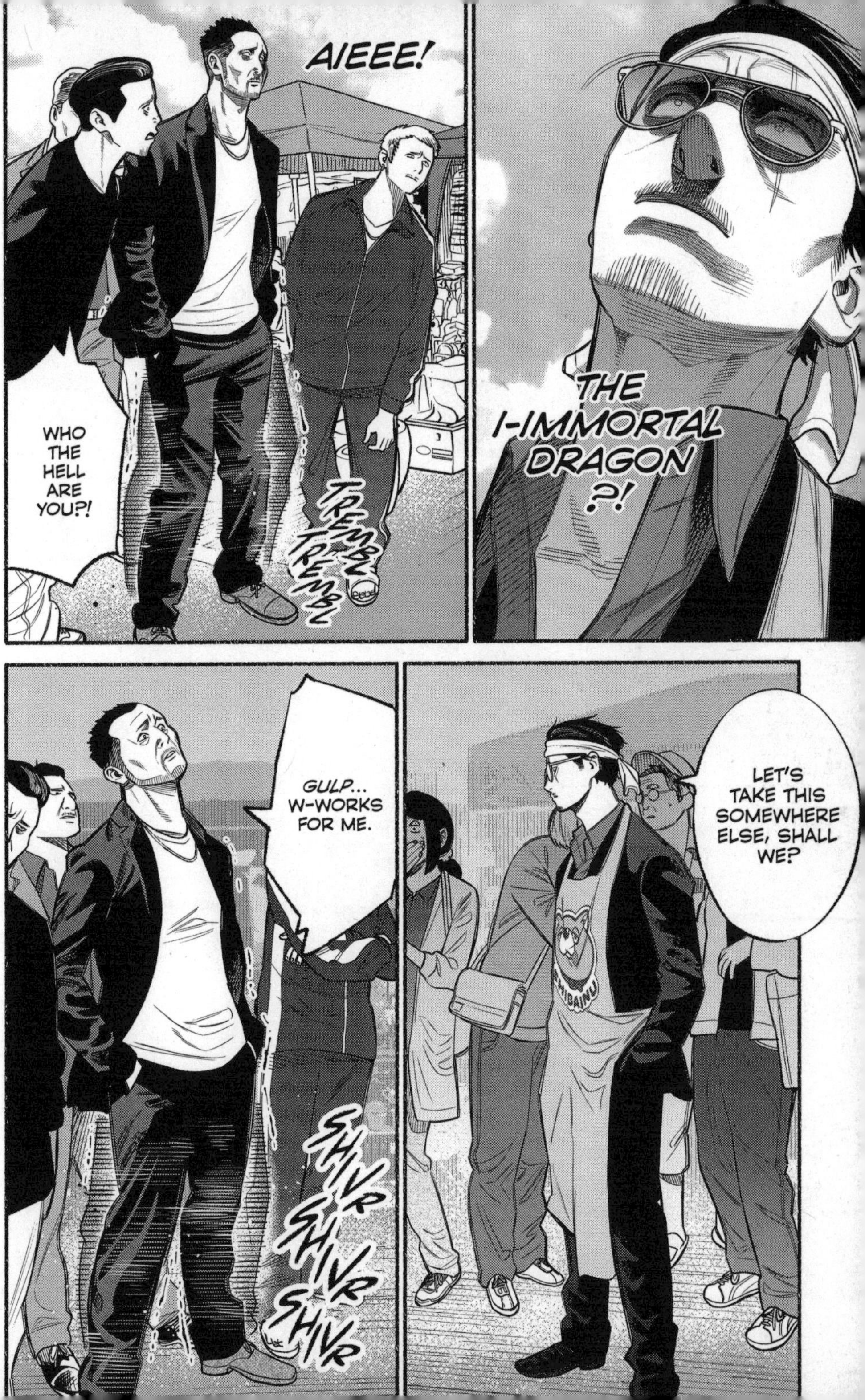
THE I-IMMORTAL DRAGON ?!
AIEEE!
WHO THE HELL ARE YOU?!
TREMBL TREMBL
LET'S TAKE THIS SOMEWHERE ELSE, SHALL WE?
GULP... W-WORKS FOR ME.
SHIVR SHIVR SHIVR SHIVR

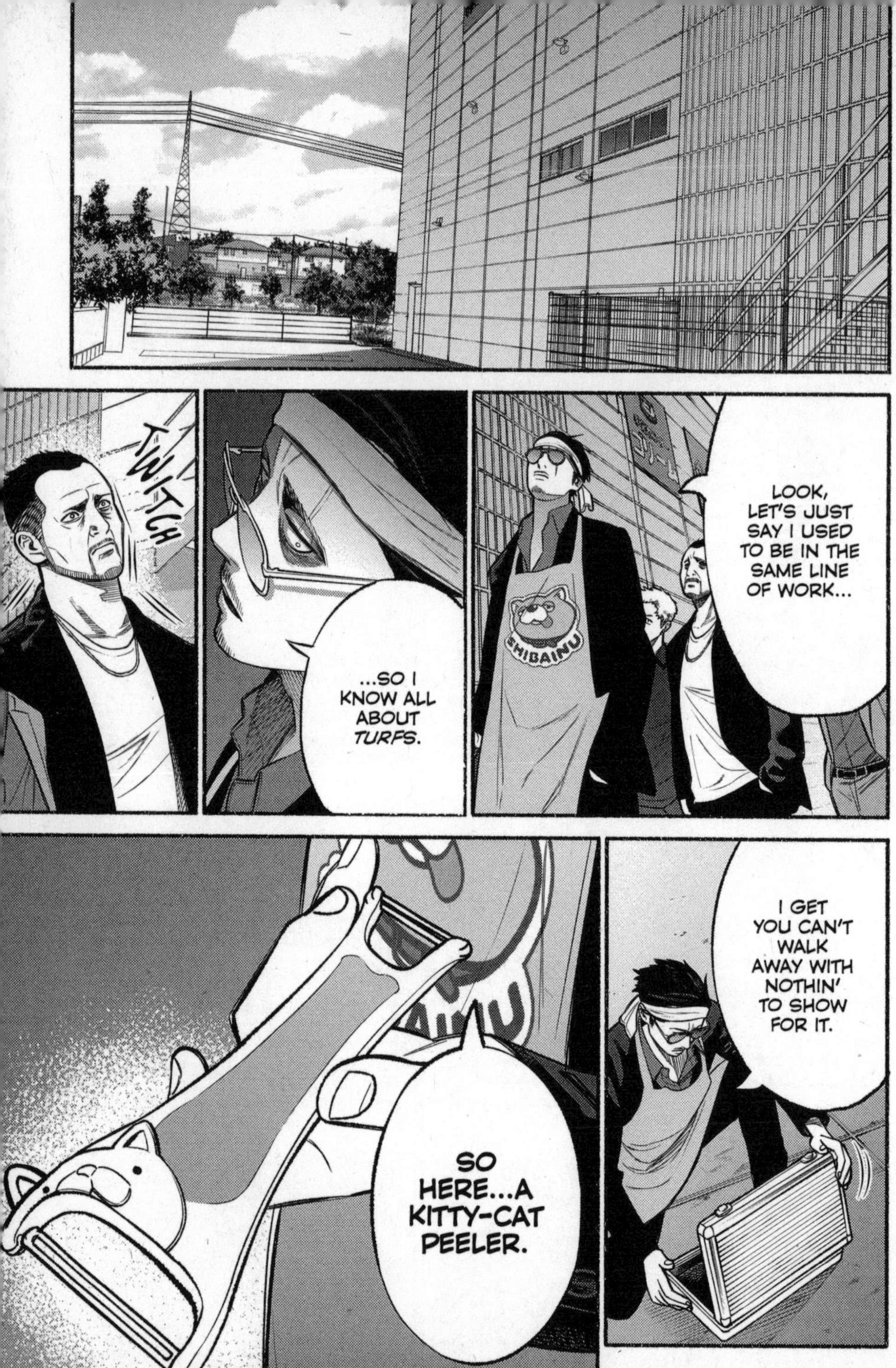
LOOK, LET'S JUST SAY I USED TO BE IN THE SAME LINE OF WORK...
SHIBAINU
...SO I KNOW ALL ABOUT *TURFS.*
TWITCH
I GET YOU CAN'T WALK AWAY WITH NOTHIN' TO SHOW FOR IT.
SO HERE...A KITTY-CAT PEELER.

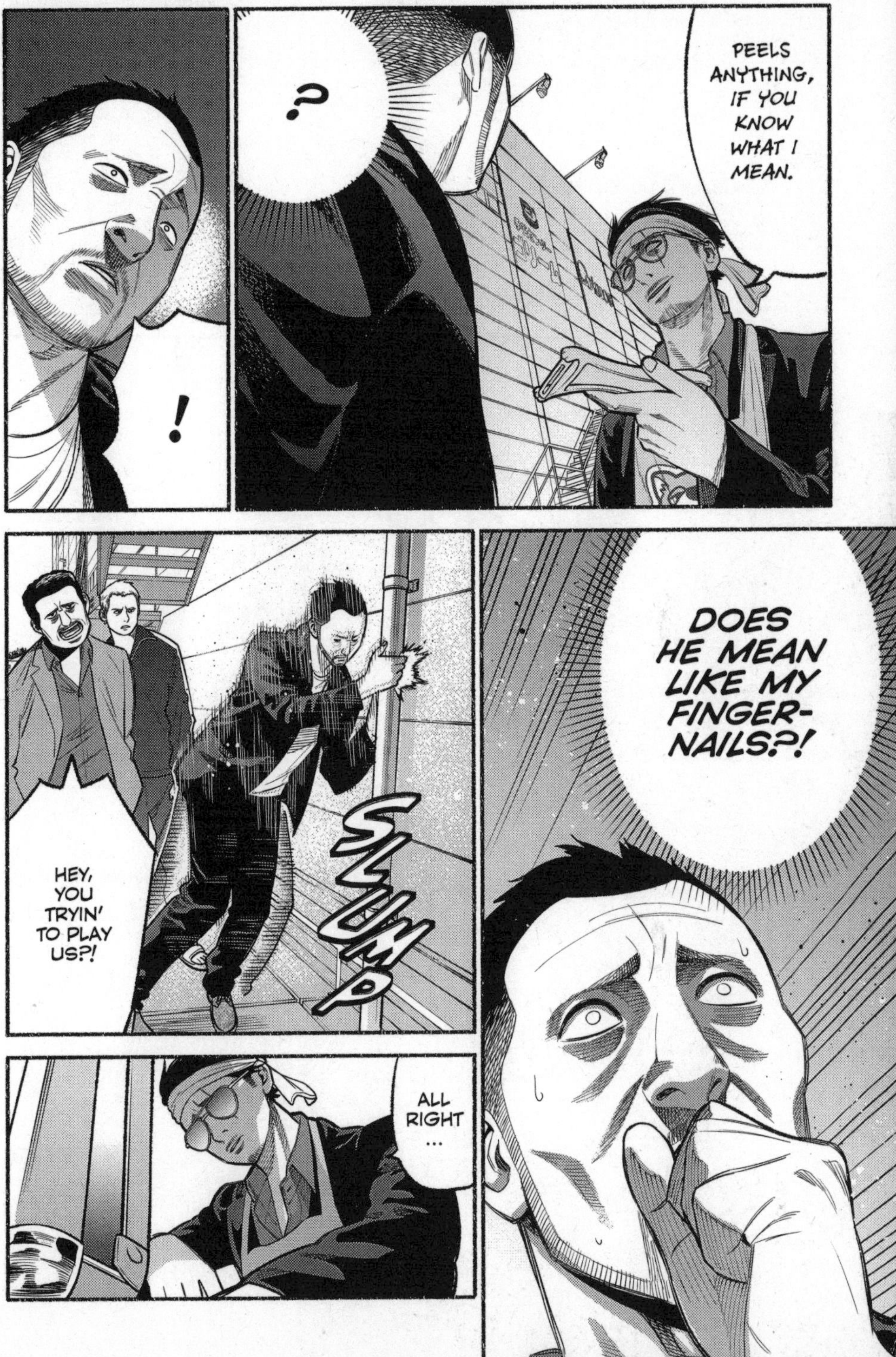
PEELS ANYTHING, IF YOU KNOW WHAT I MEAN.
?
!
DOES HE MEAN LIKE MY FINGER-NAILS?!
SLUMP
HEY, YOU TRYIN' TO PLAY US?!
ALL RIGHT ...

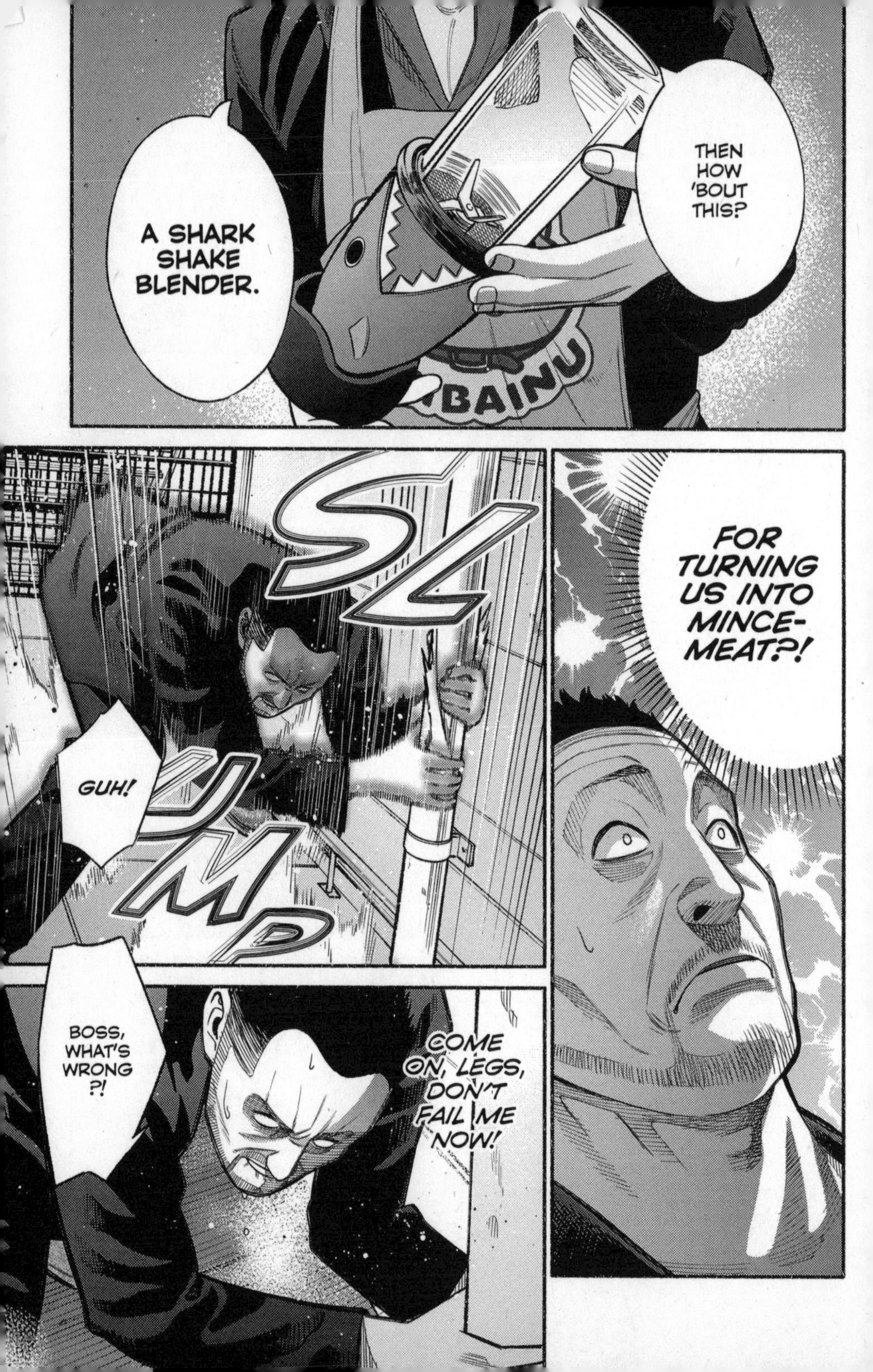
THEN HOW 'BOUT THIS?
A SHARK SHAKE BLENDER.
BAINU
FOR TURNING US INTO MINCE-MEAT?!
SLUMP
GUH!
BOSS, WHAT'S WRONG?!
COME ON, LEGS, DON'T FAIL ME NOW!

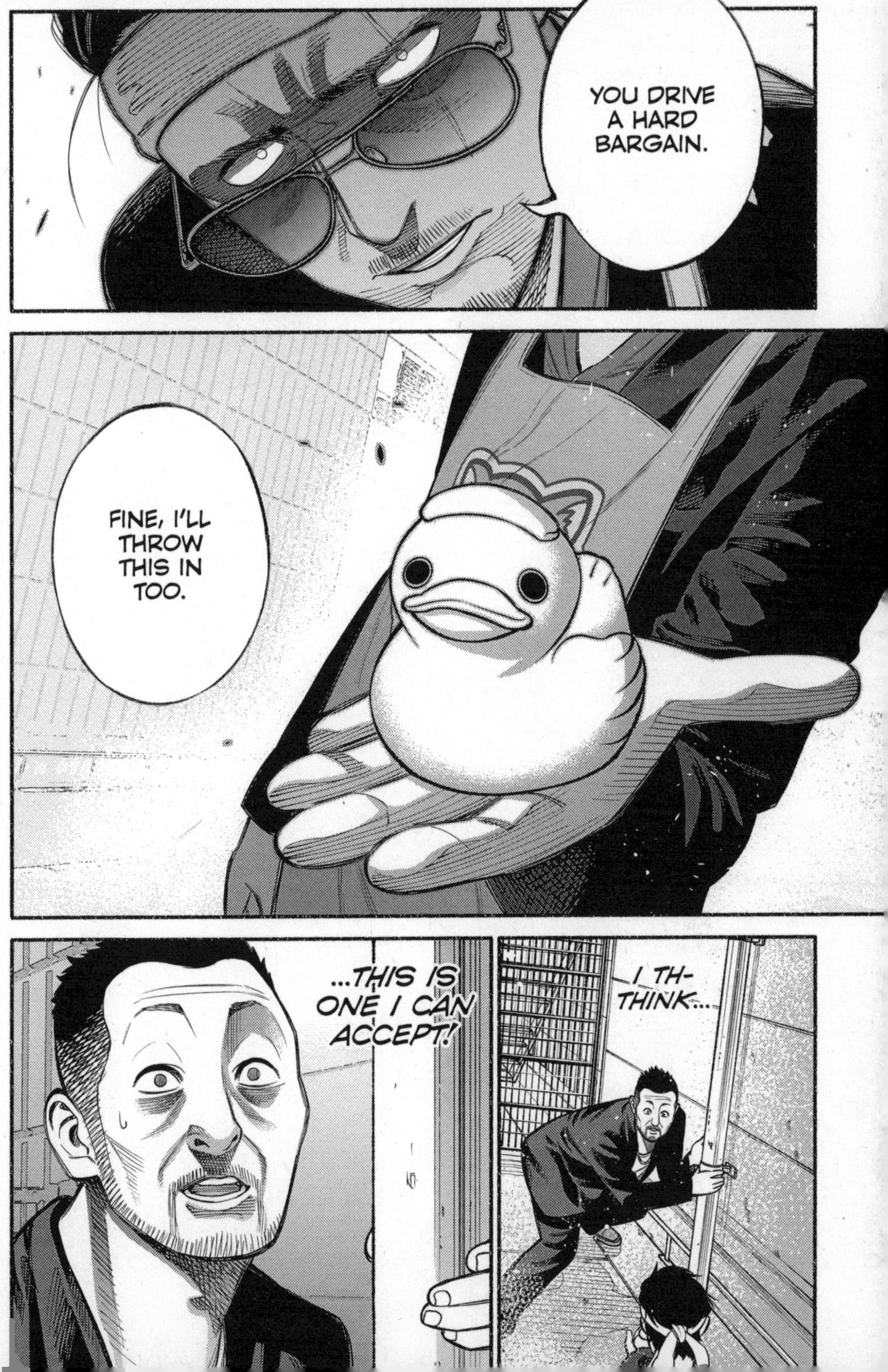
YOU DRIVE A HARD BARGAIN.
FINE, I'LL THROW THIS IN TOO.
I TH- THINK...
...THIS IS ONE I CAN ACCEPT!

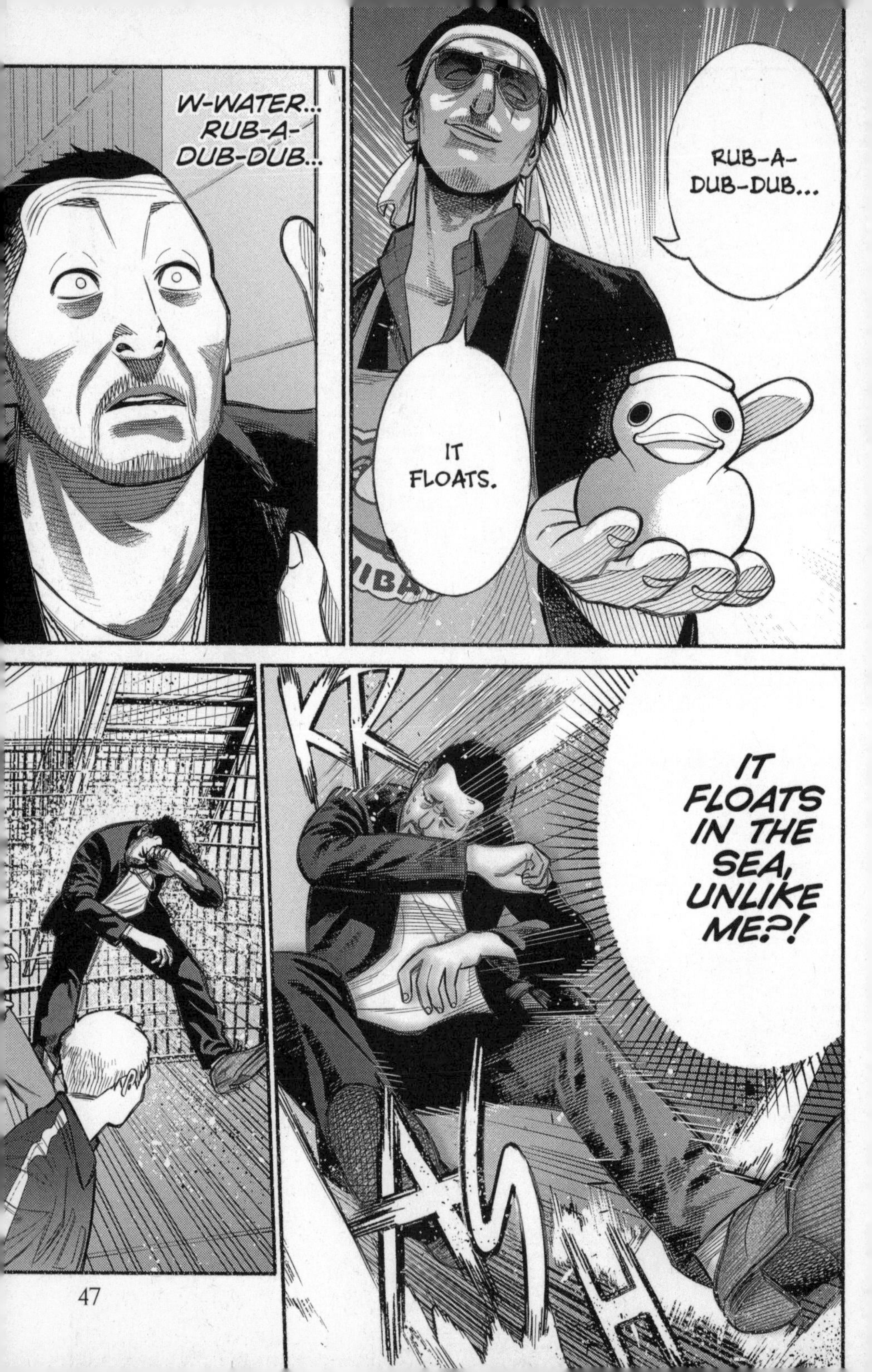
RUB-A-DUB-DUB...
IT FLOATS.
W-WATER... RUB-A-DUB-DUB...
IT FLOATS IN THE SEA, UNLIKE ME?!

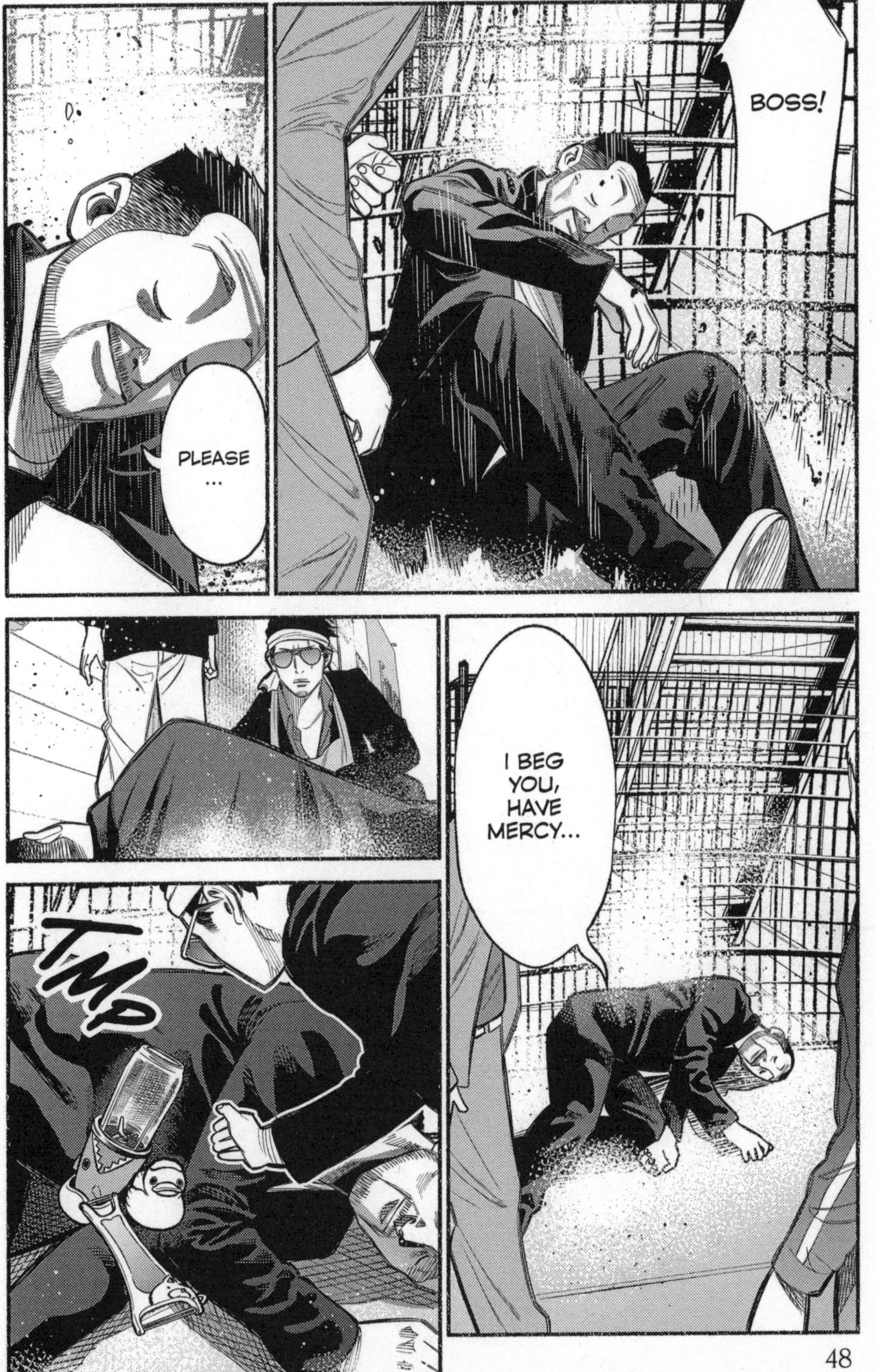
BOSS!
PLEASE ...
I BEG YOU, HAVE MERCY...
TMP

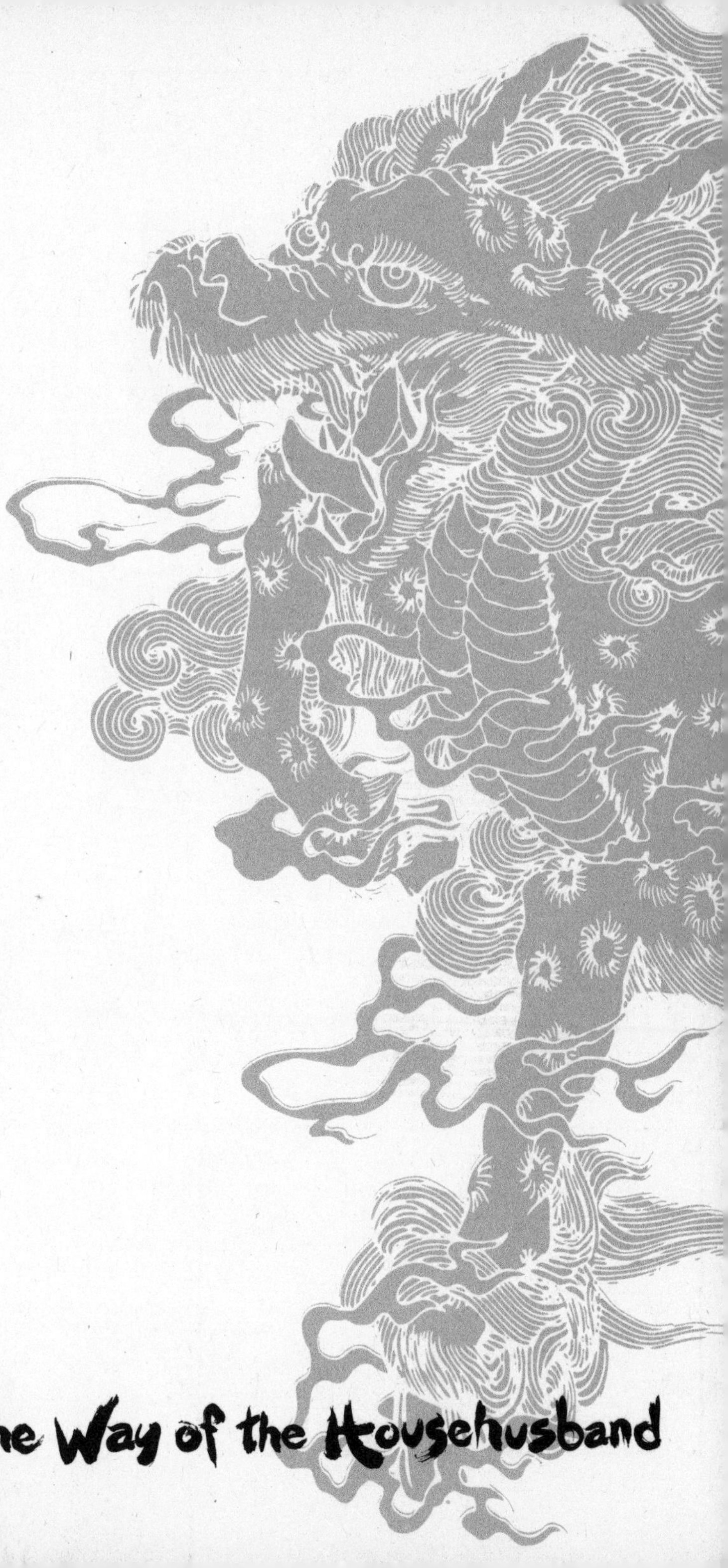

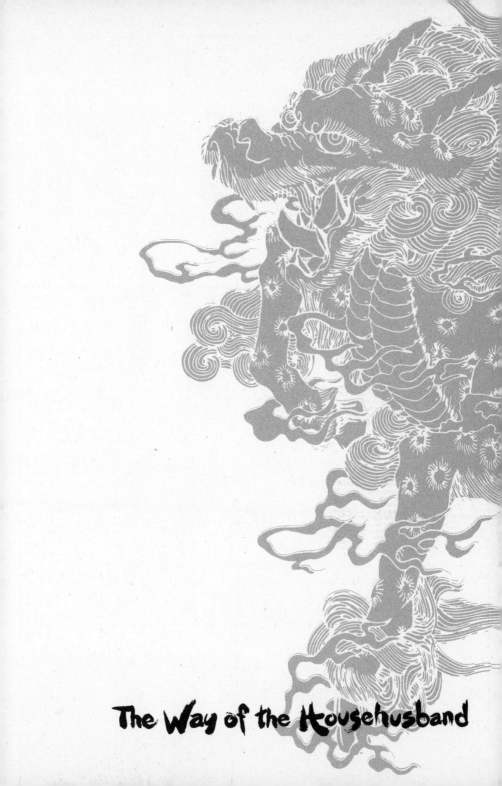

The Way of the Househusband

CHAPTER 13

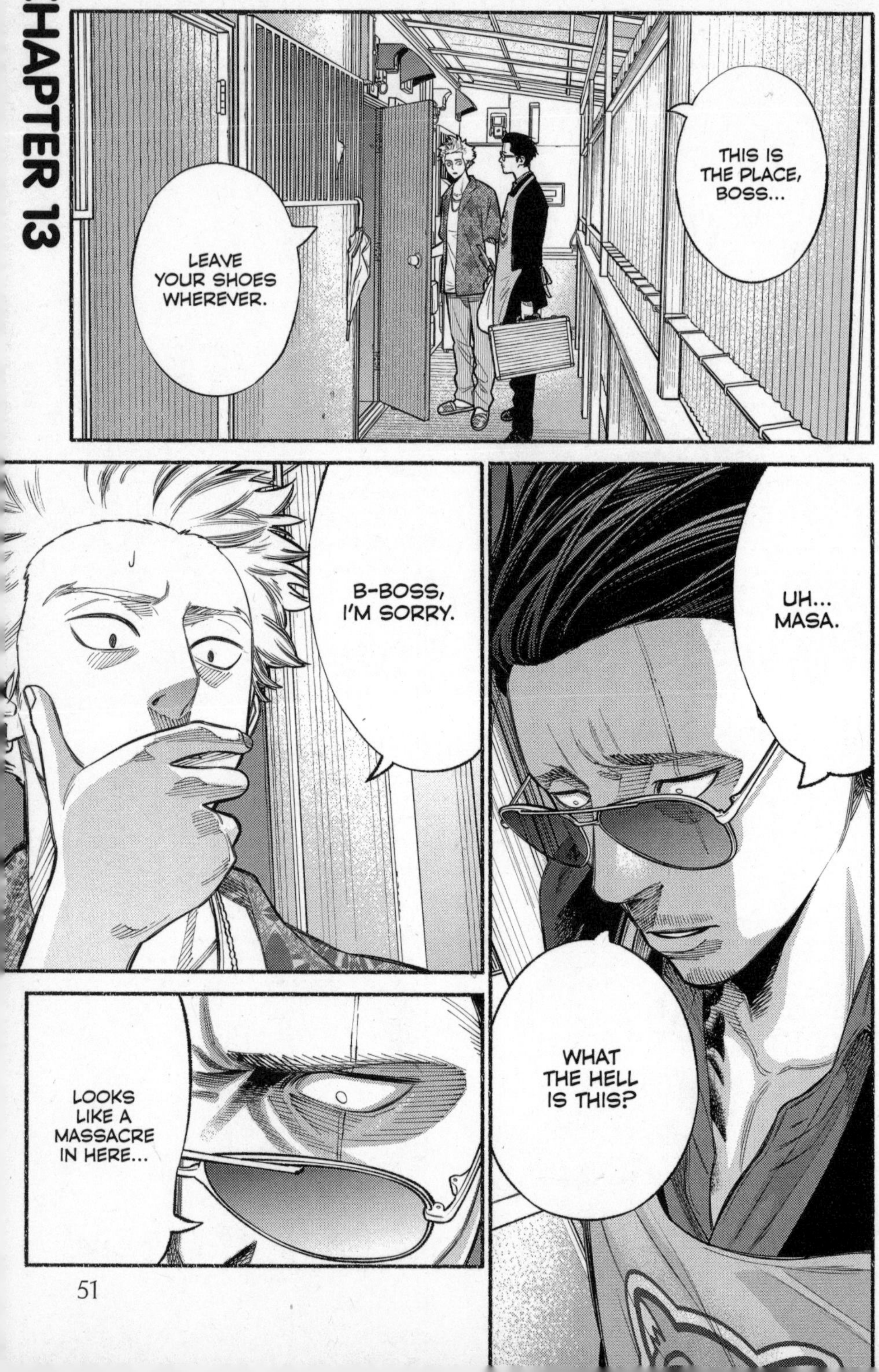
THIS IS THE PLACE, BOSS...
LEAVE YOUR SHOES WHEREVER.
UH... MASA.
WHAT THE HELL IS THIS?
B-BOSS, I'M SORRY.
LOOKS LIKE A MASSACRE IN HERE...

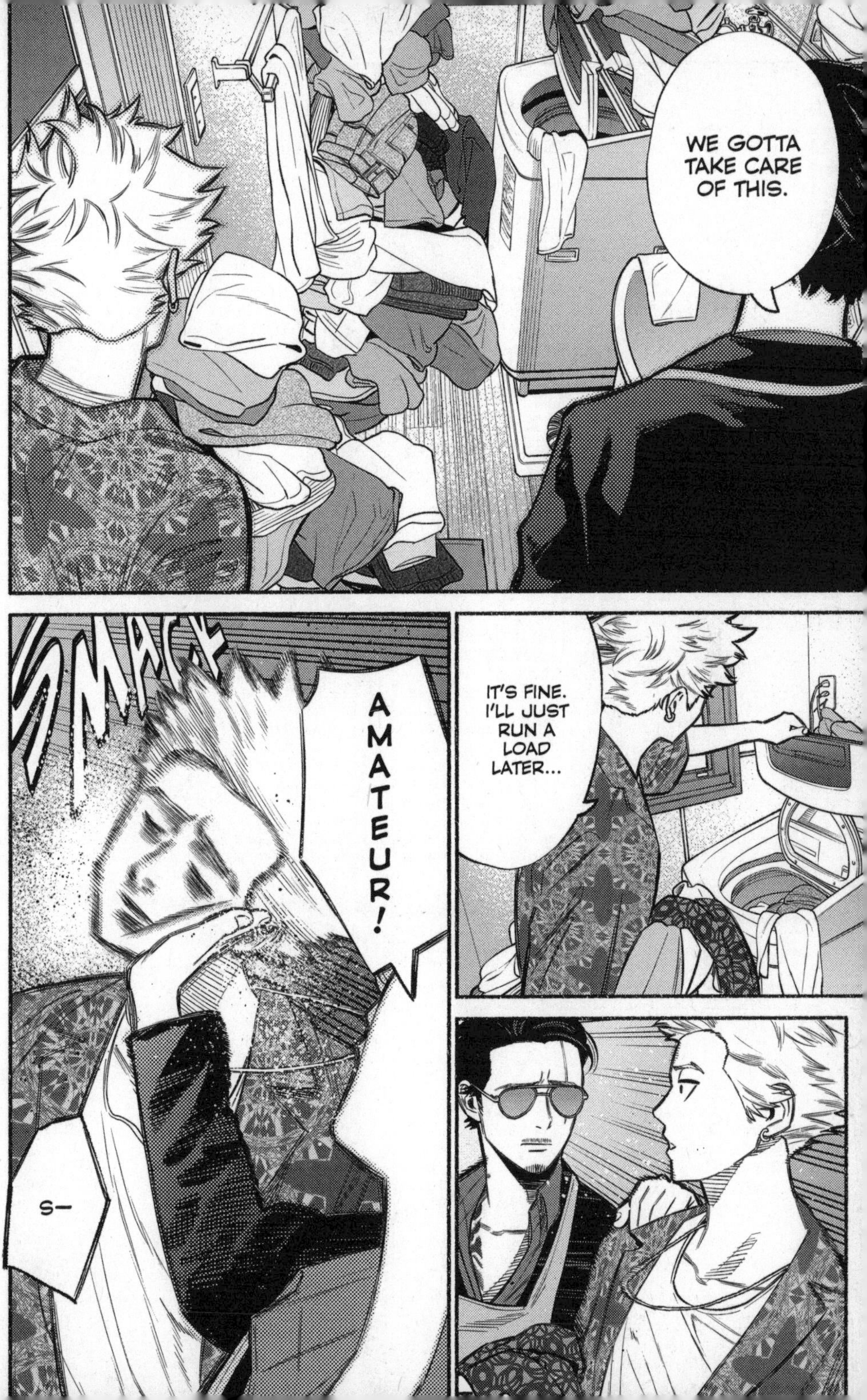
WE GOTTA TAKE CARE OF THIS.
IT'S FINE. I'LL JUST RUN A LOAD LATER...
SMACK
AMATEUR!
S—

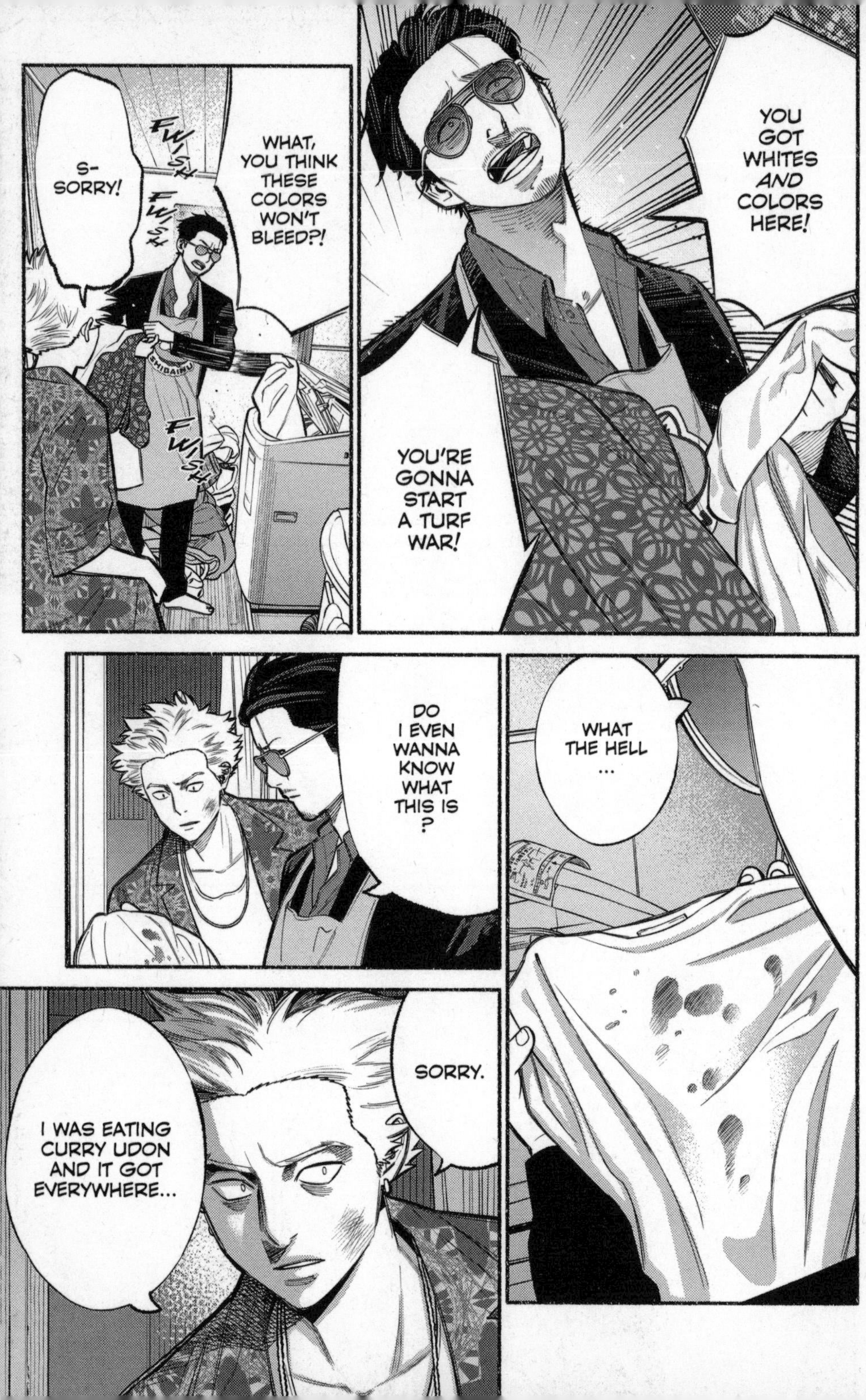
YOU GOT WHITES AND COLORS HERE!
YOU'RE GONNA START A TURF WAR!
WHAT, YOU THINK THESE COLORS WON'T BLEED?!
FWISH
FWISH
FWISH
S-SORRY!
WHAT THE HELL ...
DO I EVEN WANNA KNOW WHAT THIS IS ?
SORRY.
I WAS EATING CURRY UDON AND IT GOT EVERYWHERE...

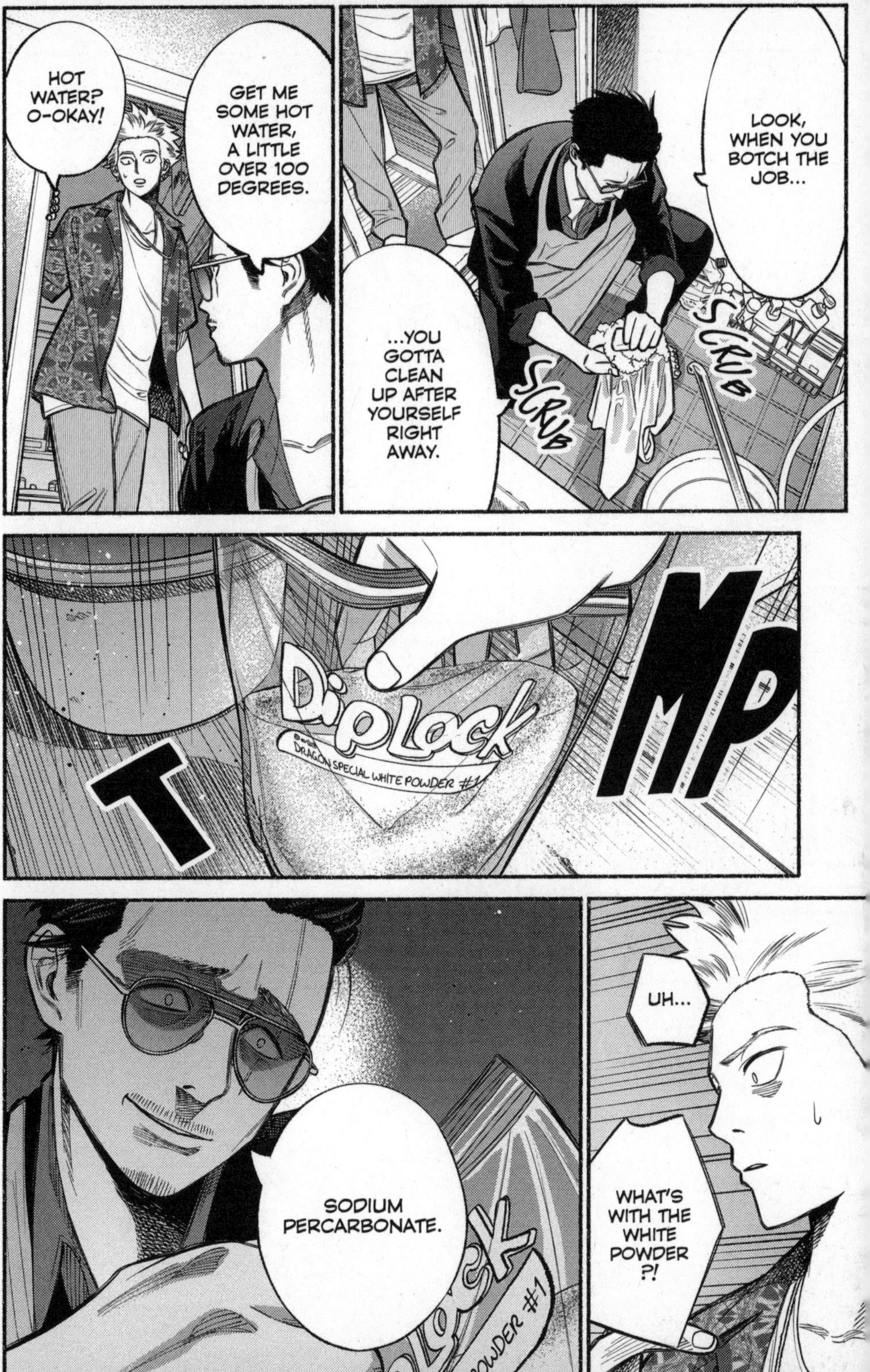
LOOK, WHEN YOU BOTCH THE JOB...
SCRUB
SCRUB
...YOU GOTTA CLEAN UP AFTER YOURSELF RIGHT AWAY.
GET ME SOME HOT WATER, A LITTLE OVER 100 DEGREES.
HOT WATER? O-OKAY!
T
MP
DipLock
DRAGON SPECIAL WHITE POWDER #1
UH...
WHAT'S WITH THE WHITE POWDER?!
SODIUM PERCARBONATE.

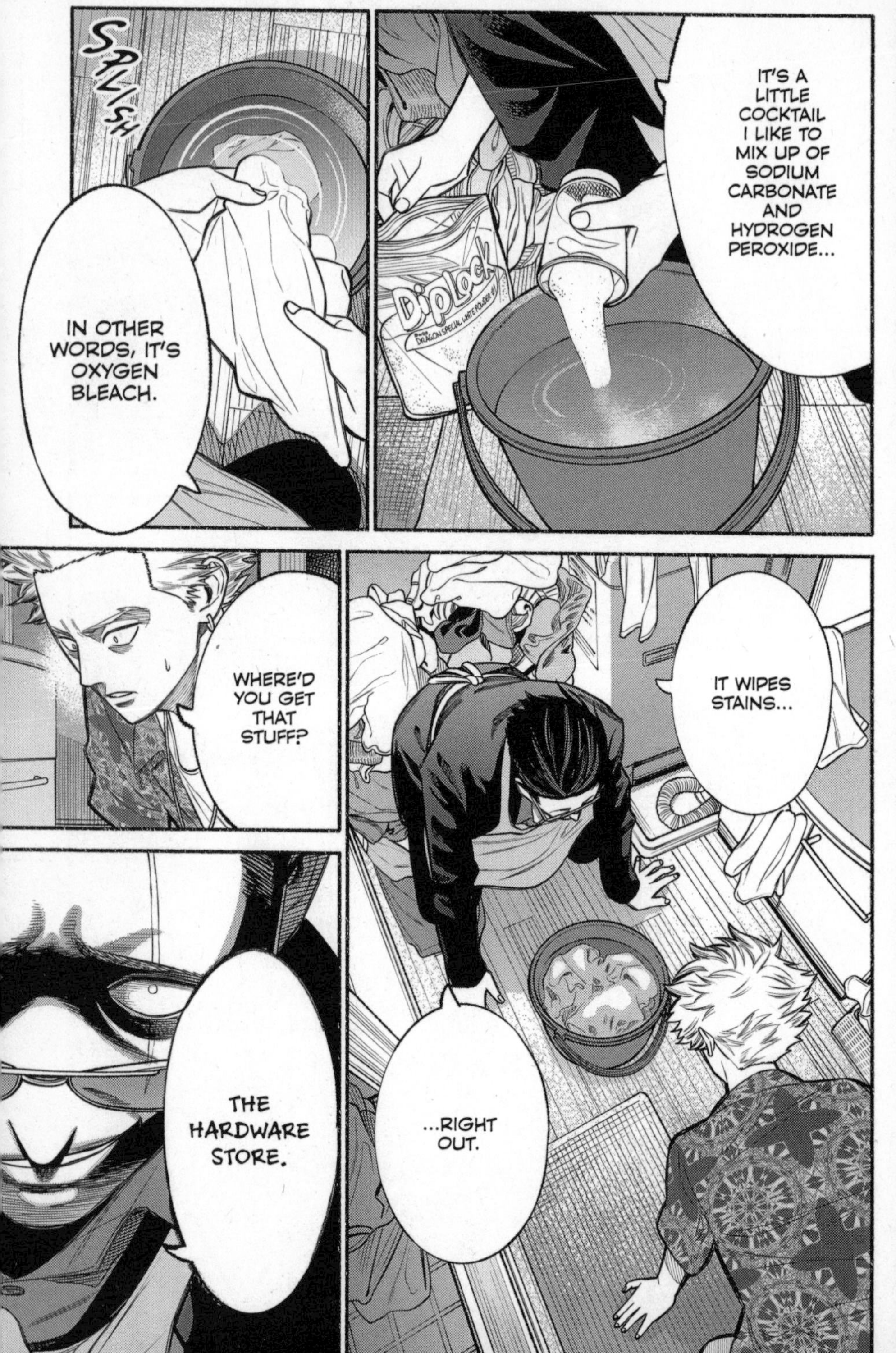
IT'S A LITTLE COCKTAIL I LIKE TO MIX UP OF SODIUM CARBONATE AND HYDROGEN PEROXIDE...
DipLock
SPLISH
IN OTHER WORDS, IT'S OXYGEN BLEACH.
IT WIPES STAINS...
...RIGHT OUT.
WHERE'D YOU GET THAT STUFF?
THE HARDWARE STORE.

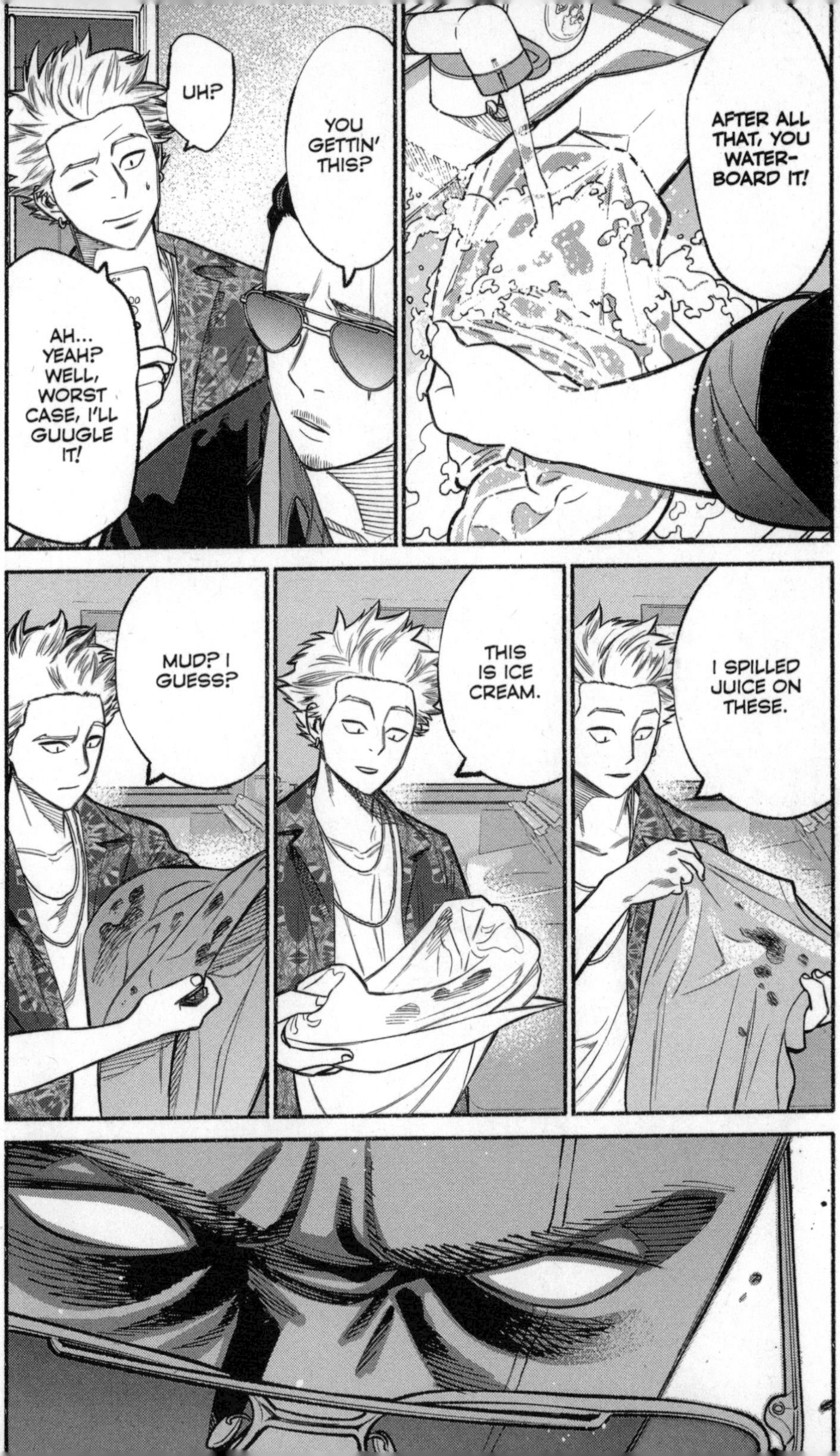
AFTER ALL THAT, YOU WATER-BOARD IT!
YOU GETTIN' THIS?
UH?
AH... YEAH? WELL, WORST CASE, I'LL GUUGLE IT!
I SPILLED JUICE ON THESE.
THIS IS ICE CREAM.
MUD? I GUESS?

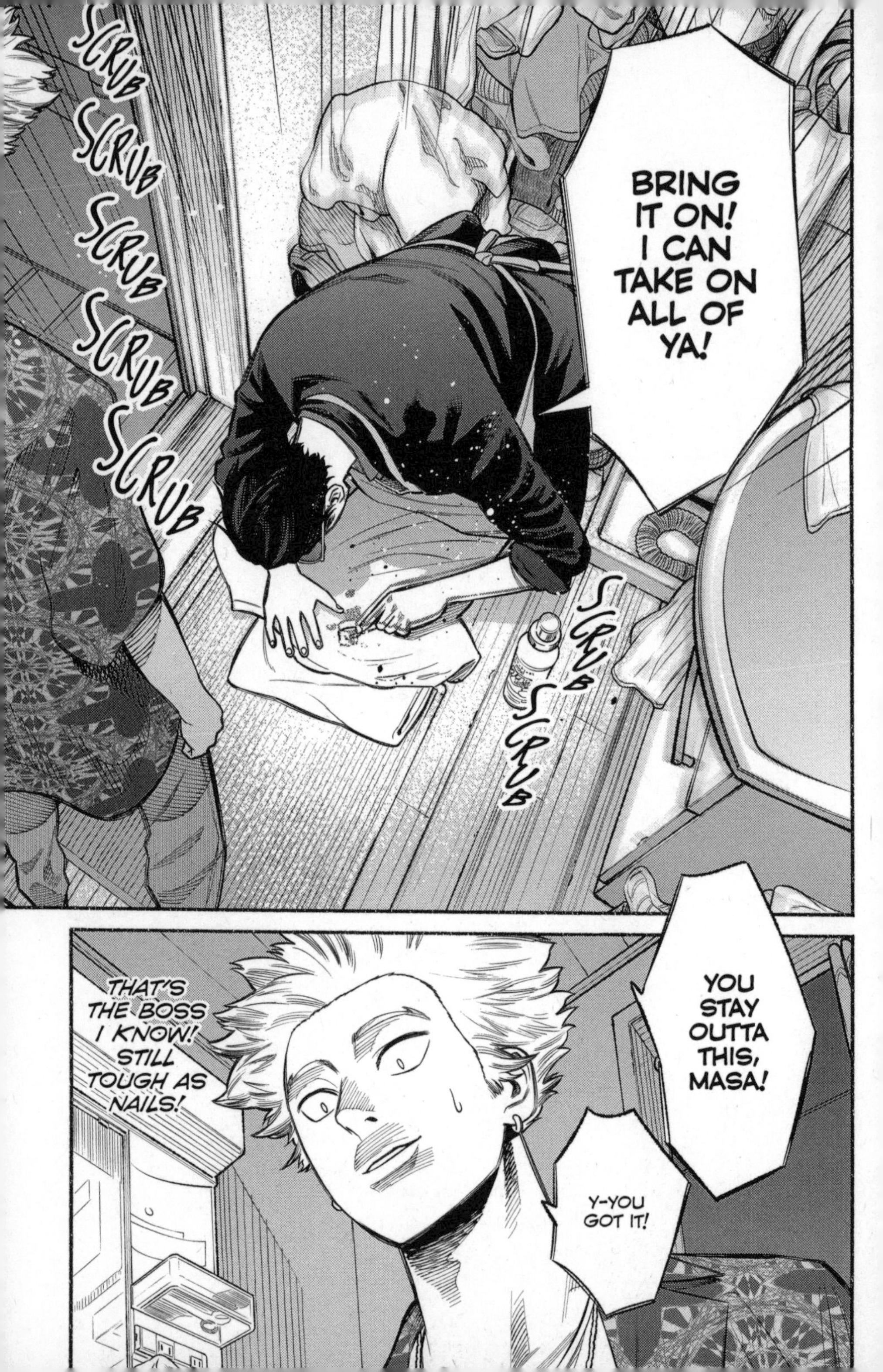
BRING IT ON! I CAN TAKE ON ALL OF YA!
SCRUB SCRUB
SCRUB SCRUB SCRUB SCRUB SCRUB
YOU STAY OUTTA THIS, MASA!
Y-YOU GOT IT!
THAT'S THE BOSS I KNOW! STILL TOUGH AS NAILS!

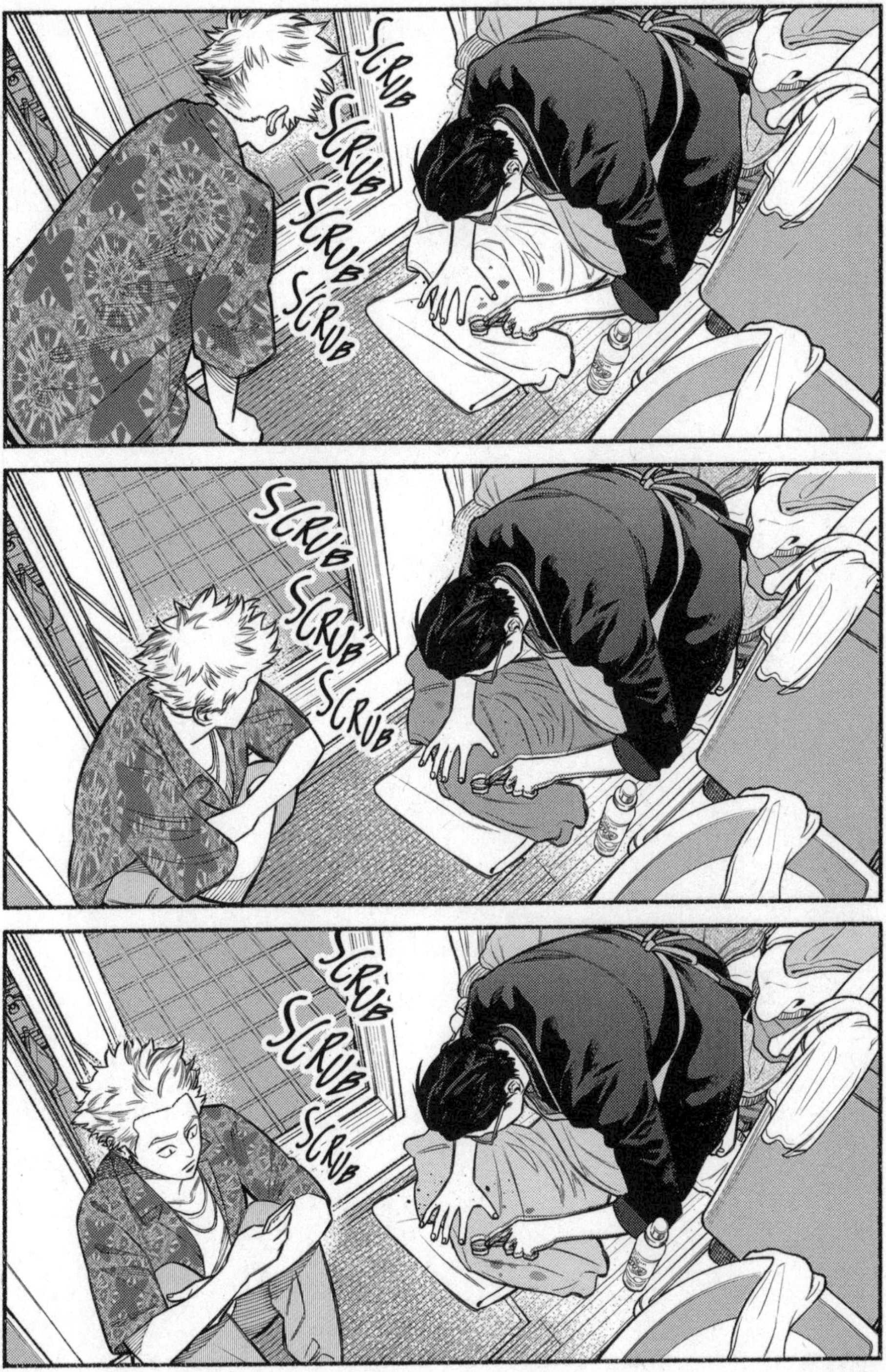
SCRUB
SCRUB
SCRUB
SCRUB
SCRUB
SCRUB
SCRUB
SCRUB
SCRUB
SCRUB

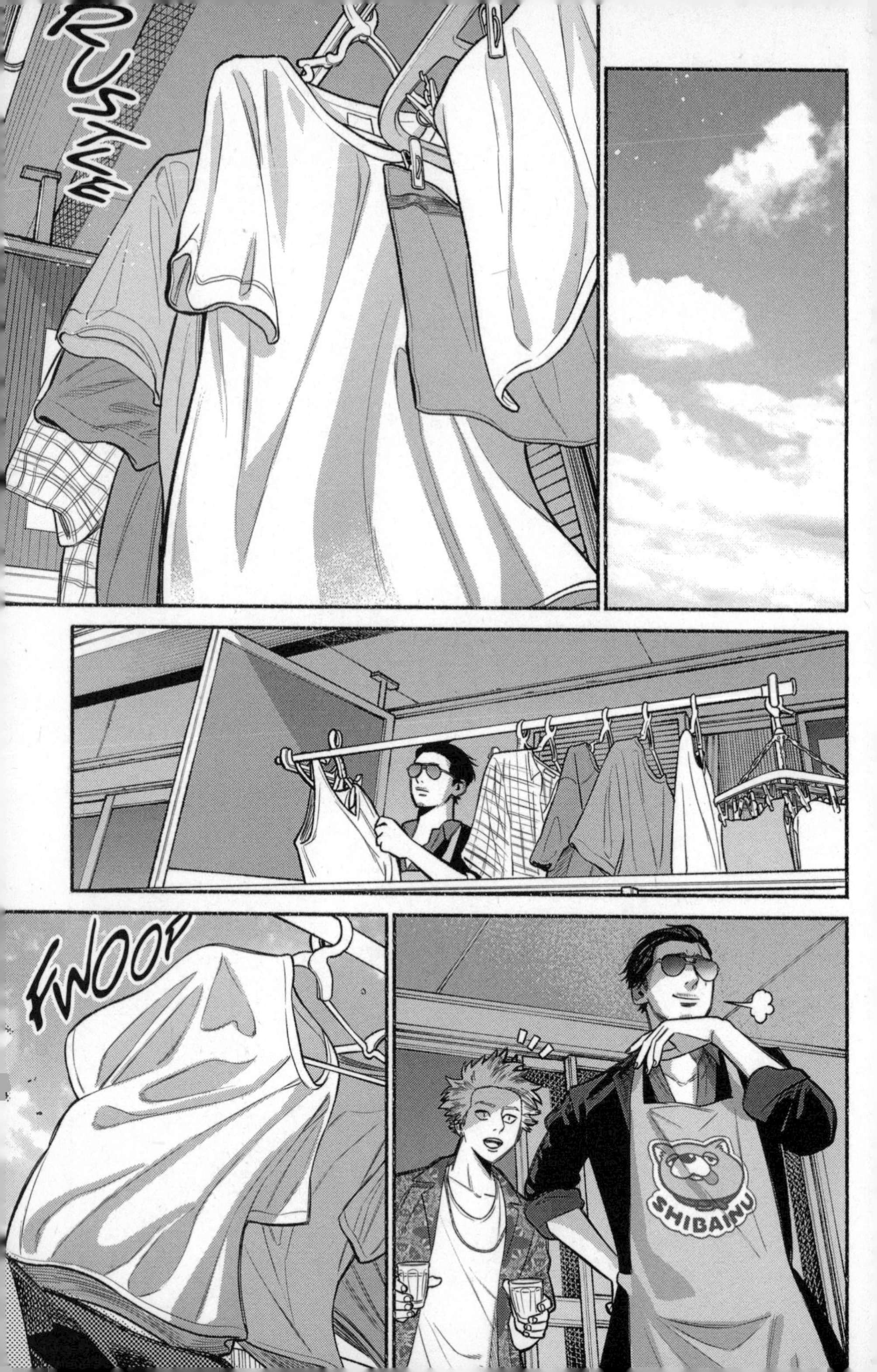
RUSTLE
SHIBAINU
FWOOP

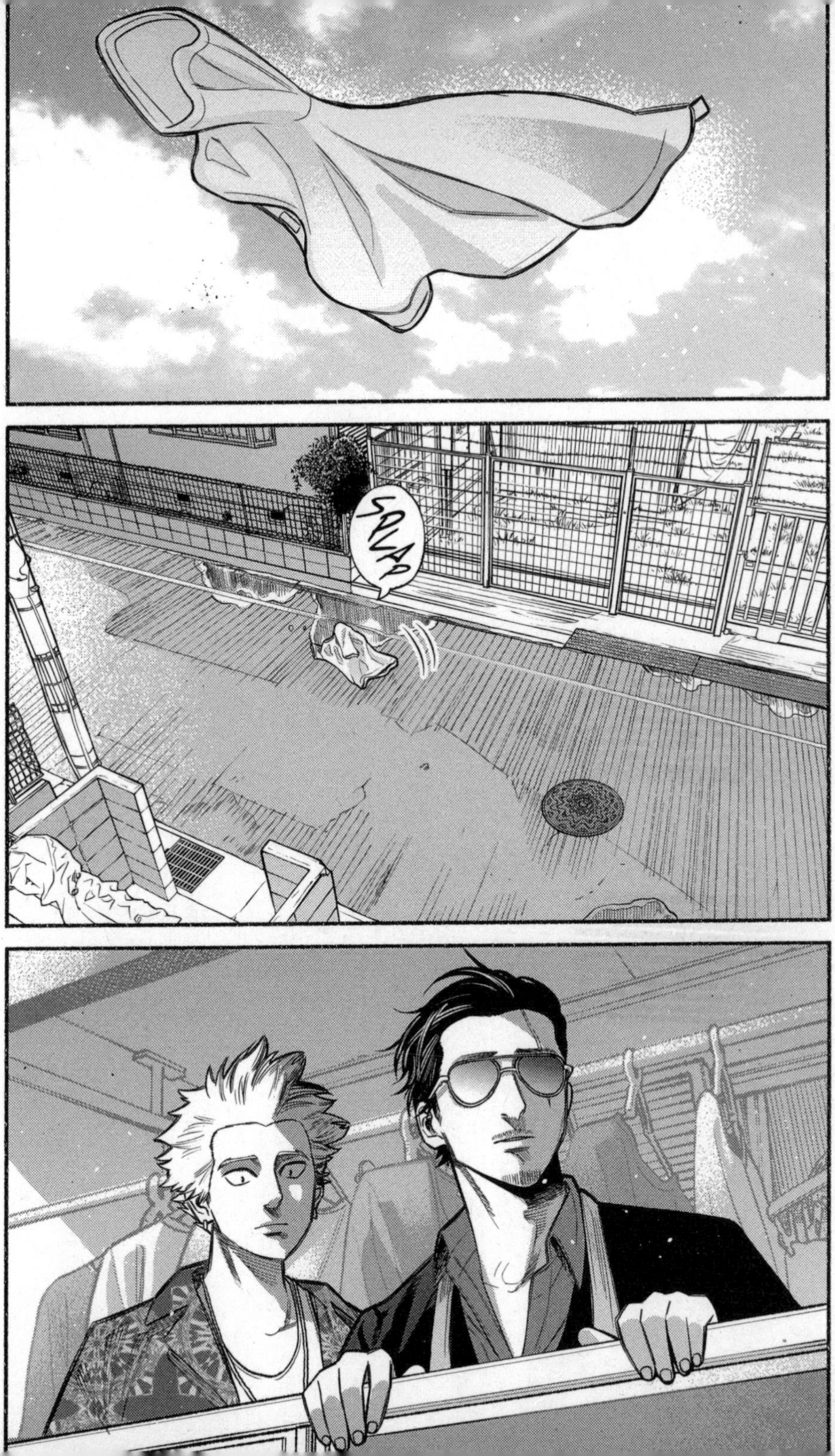
SPLAP

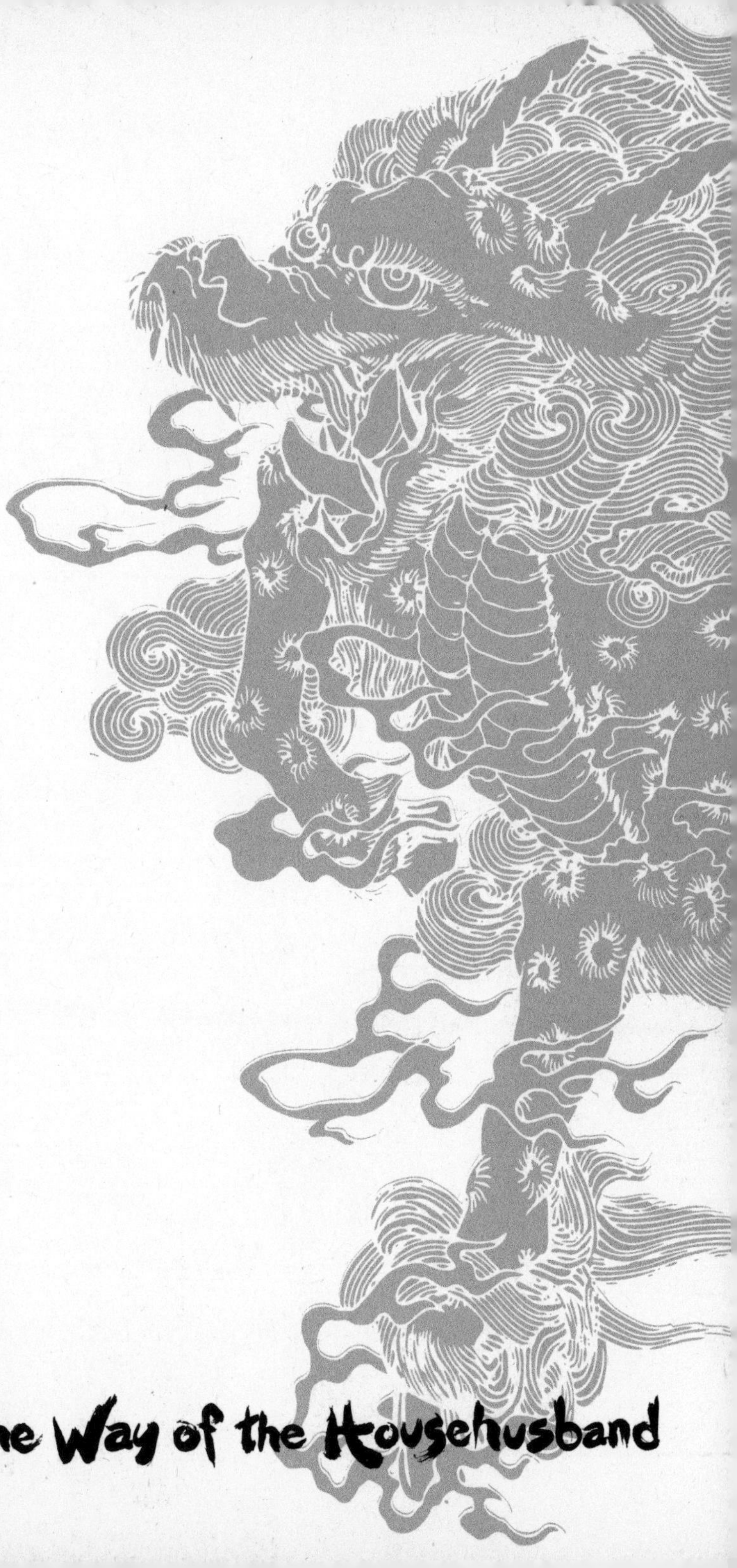

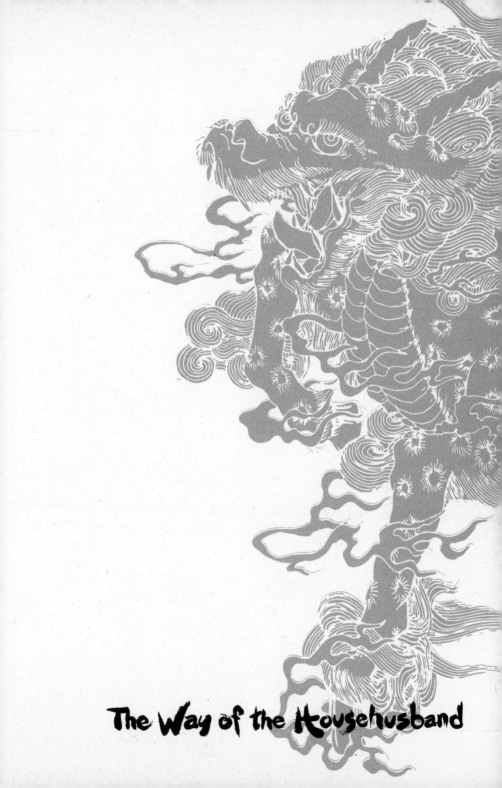

The Way of the Househusband

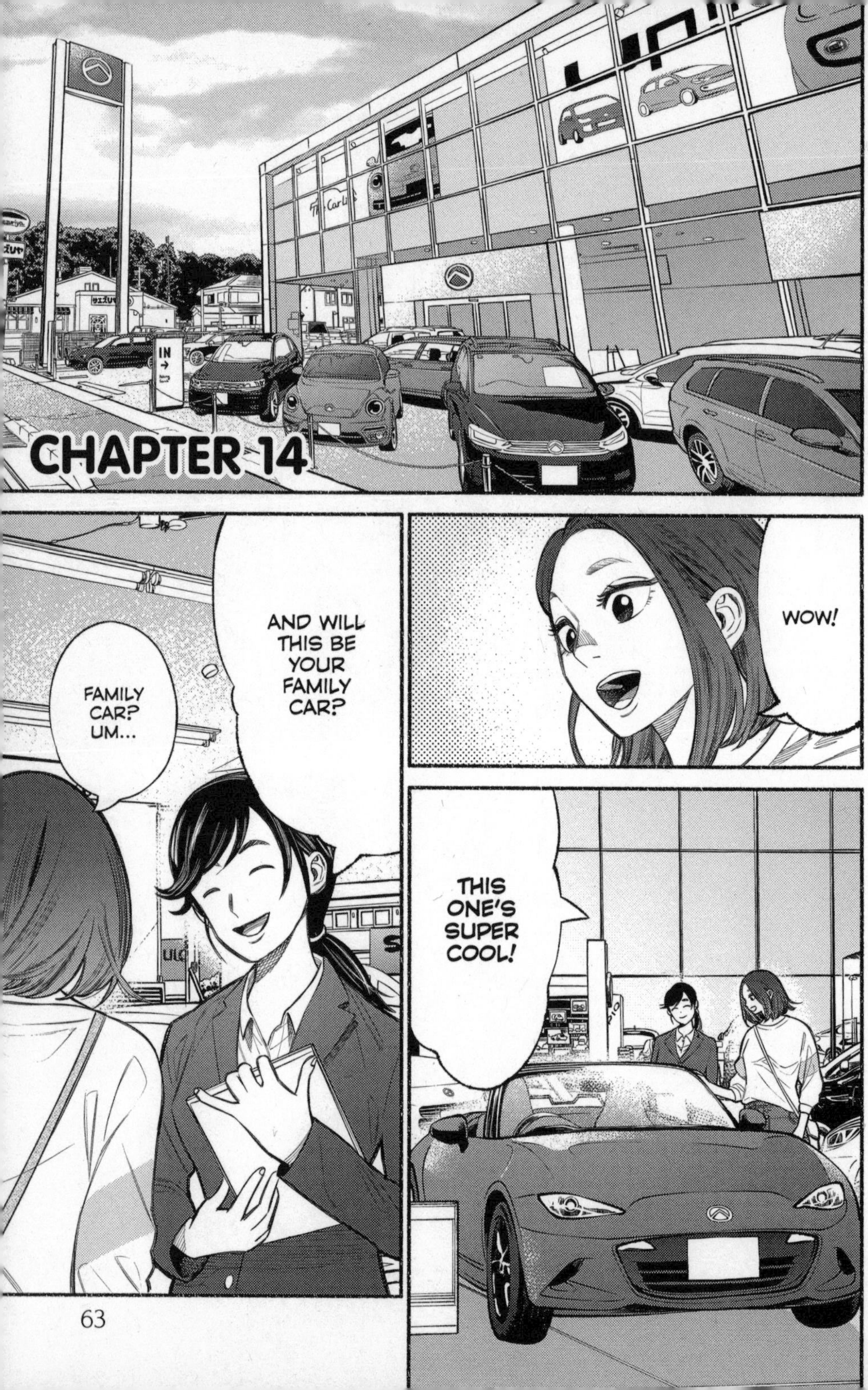
CHAPTER 14
IN →
WOW!
THIS ONE'S SUPER COOL!
AND WILL THIS BE YOUR FAMILY CAR?
FAMILY CAR? UM...

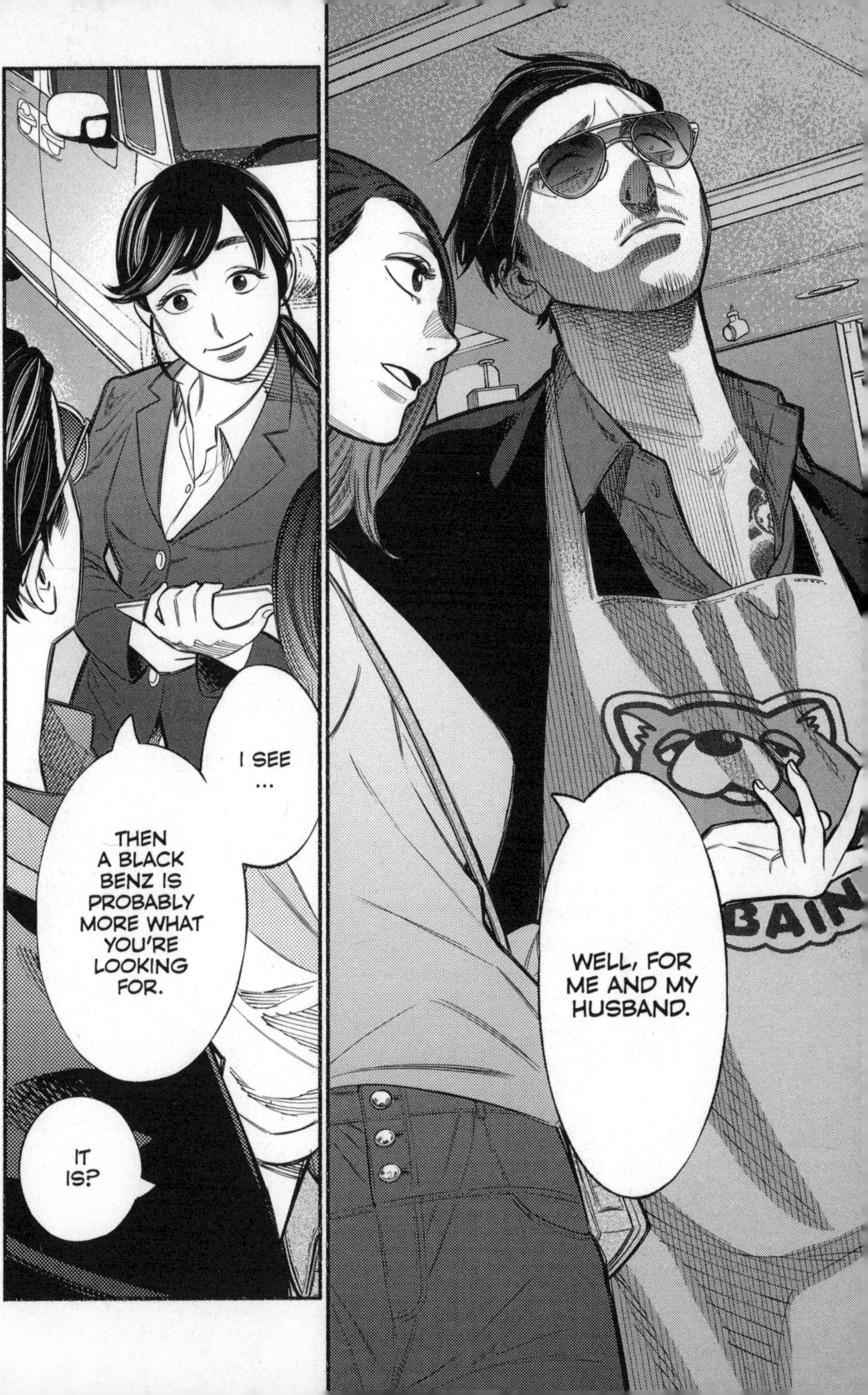
BAIN
WELL, FOR ME AND MY HUSBAND.
I SEE ...
THEN A BLACK BENZ IS PROBABLY MORE WHAT YOU'RE LOOKING FOR.
IT IS?

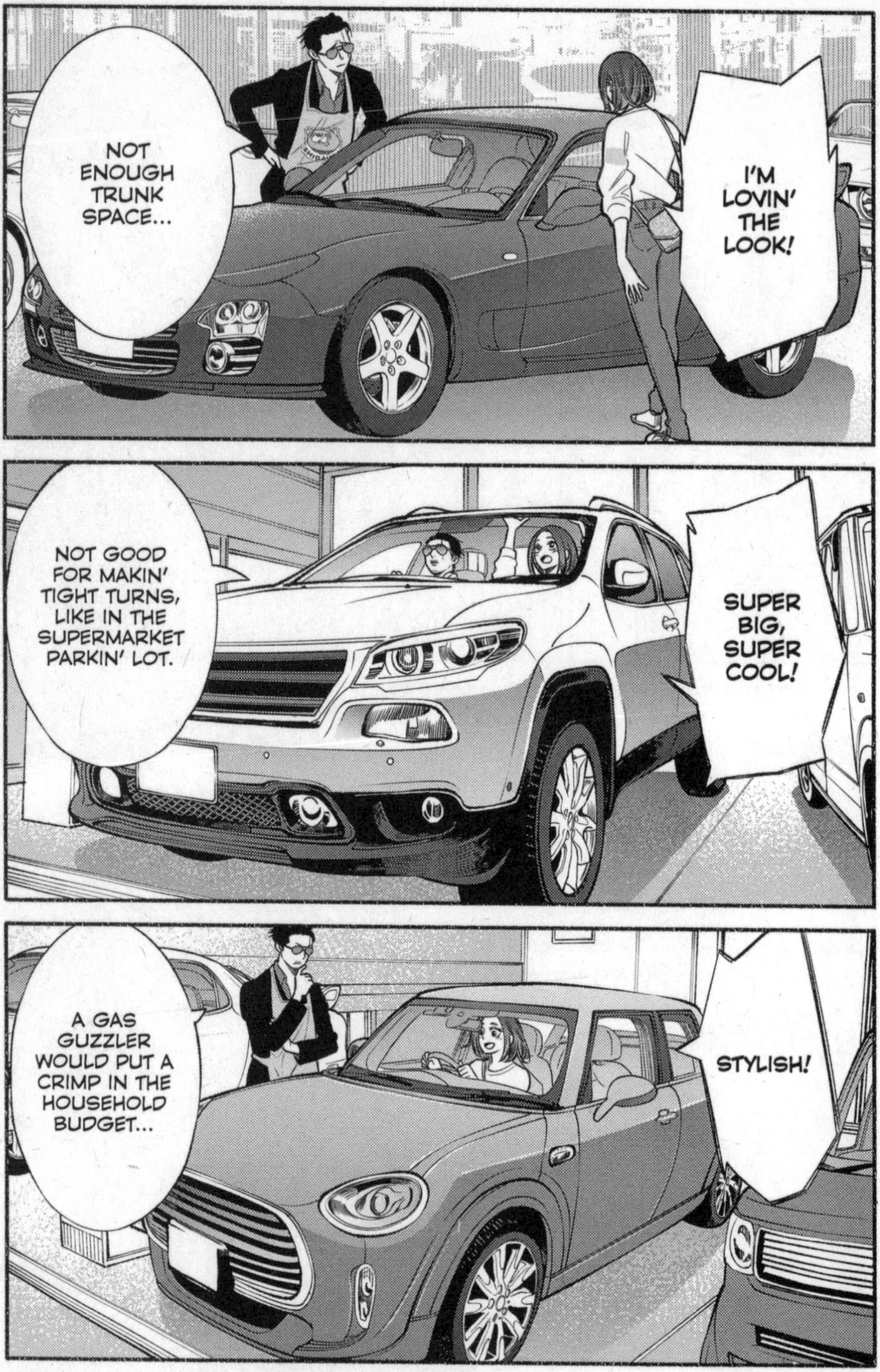
I'M LOVIN' THE LOOK!
NOT ENOUGH TRUNK SPACE...
SUPER BIG, SUPER COOL!
NOT GOOD FOR MAKIN' TIGHT TURNS, LIKE IN THE SUPERMARKET PARKIN' LOT.
STYLISH!
A GAS GUZZLER WOULD PUT A CRIMP IN THE HOUSEHOLD BUDGET...

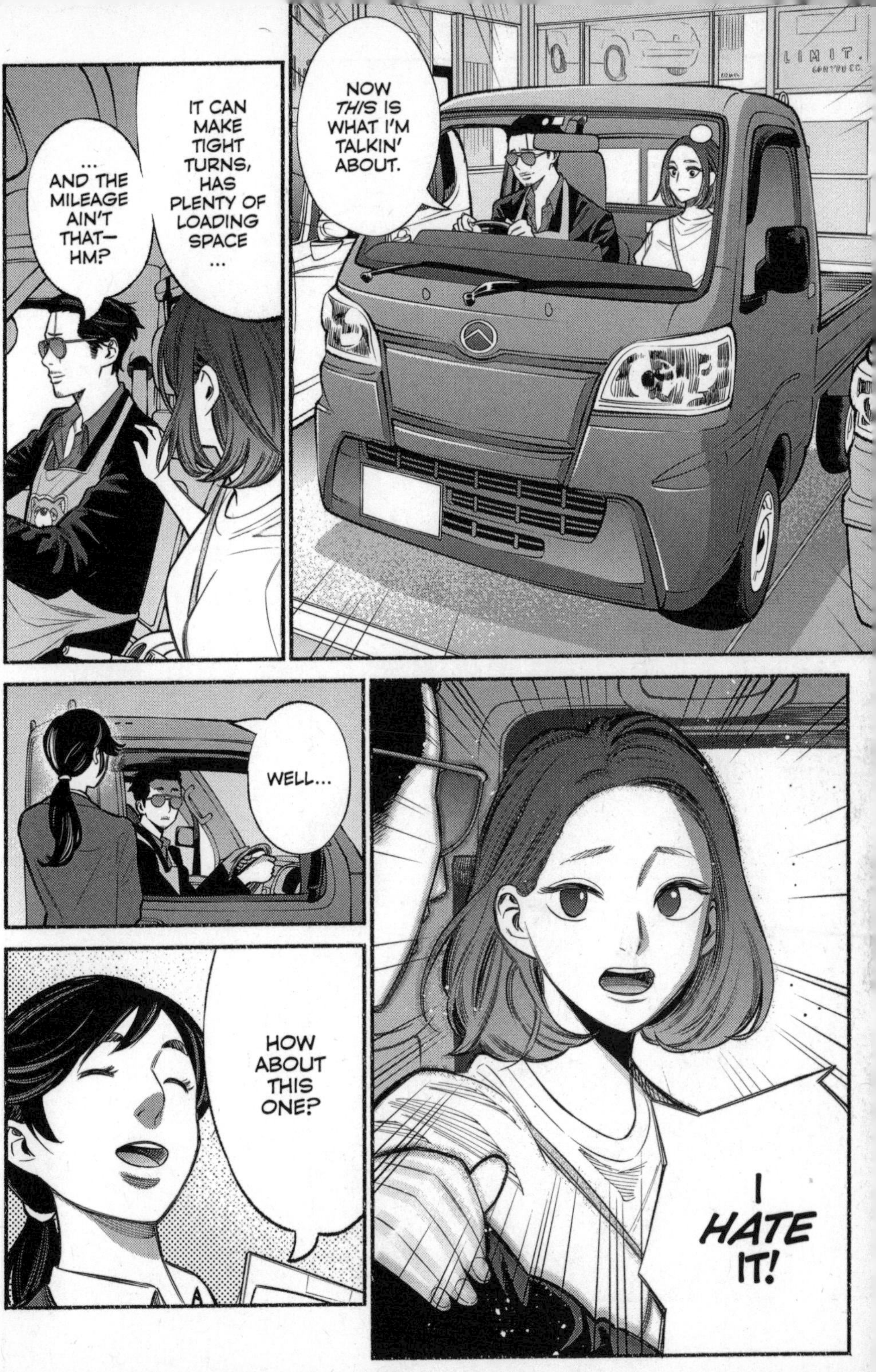
LIMIT.
NOW *THIS* IS WHAT I'M TALKIN' ABOUT.
IT CAN MAKE TIGHT TURNS, HAS PLENTY OF LOADING SPACE ...
... AND THE MILEAGE AIN'T THAT— HM?
I *HATE* IT!
WELL...
HOW ABOUT THIS ONE?

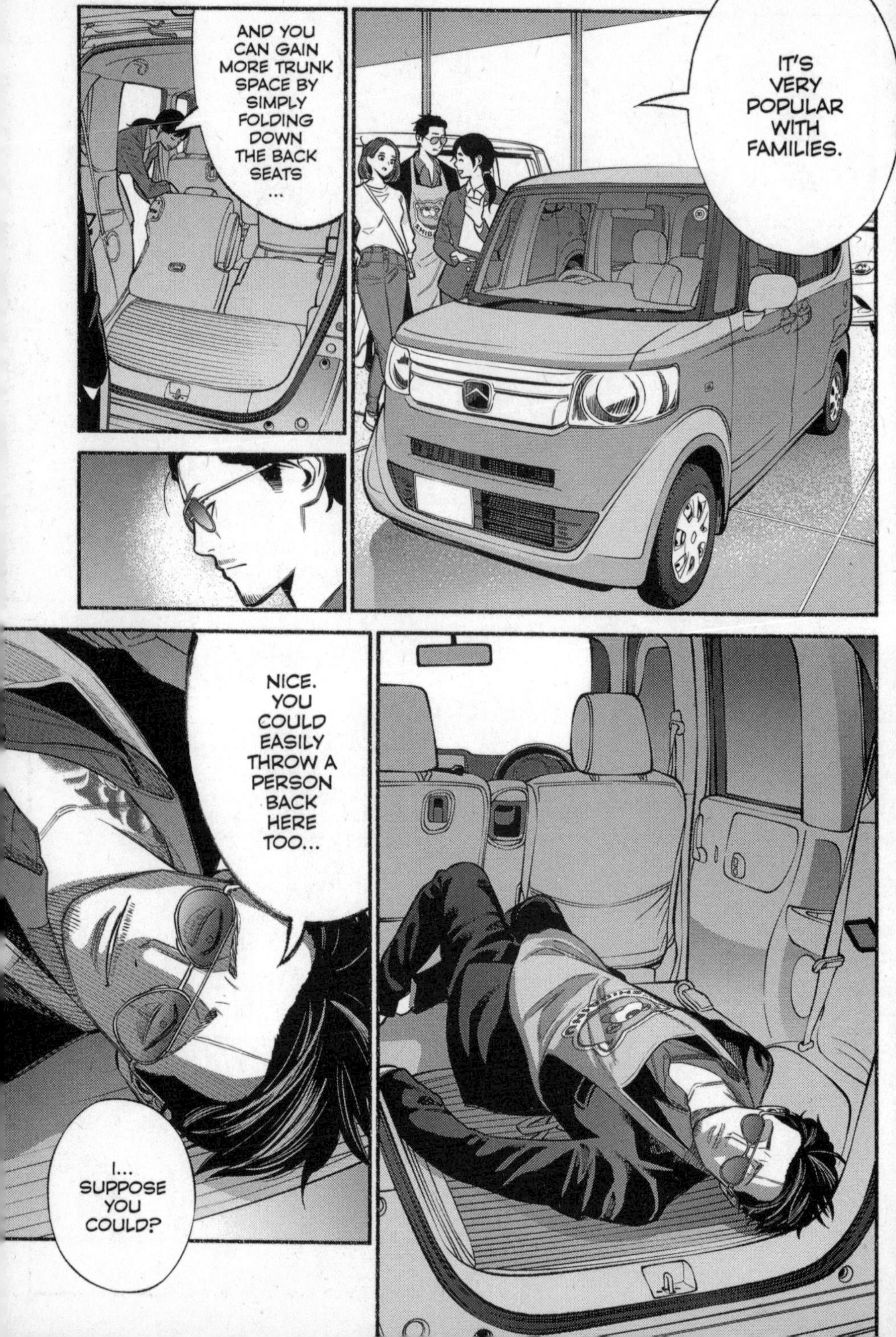
IT'S VERY POPULAR WITH FAMILIES.
AND YOU CAN GAIN MORE TRUNK SPACE BY SIMPLY FOLDING DOWN THE BACK SEATS ...
NICE. YOU COULD EASILY THROW A PERSON BACK HERE TOO...
I... SUPPOSE YOU COULD?

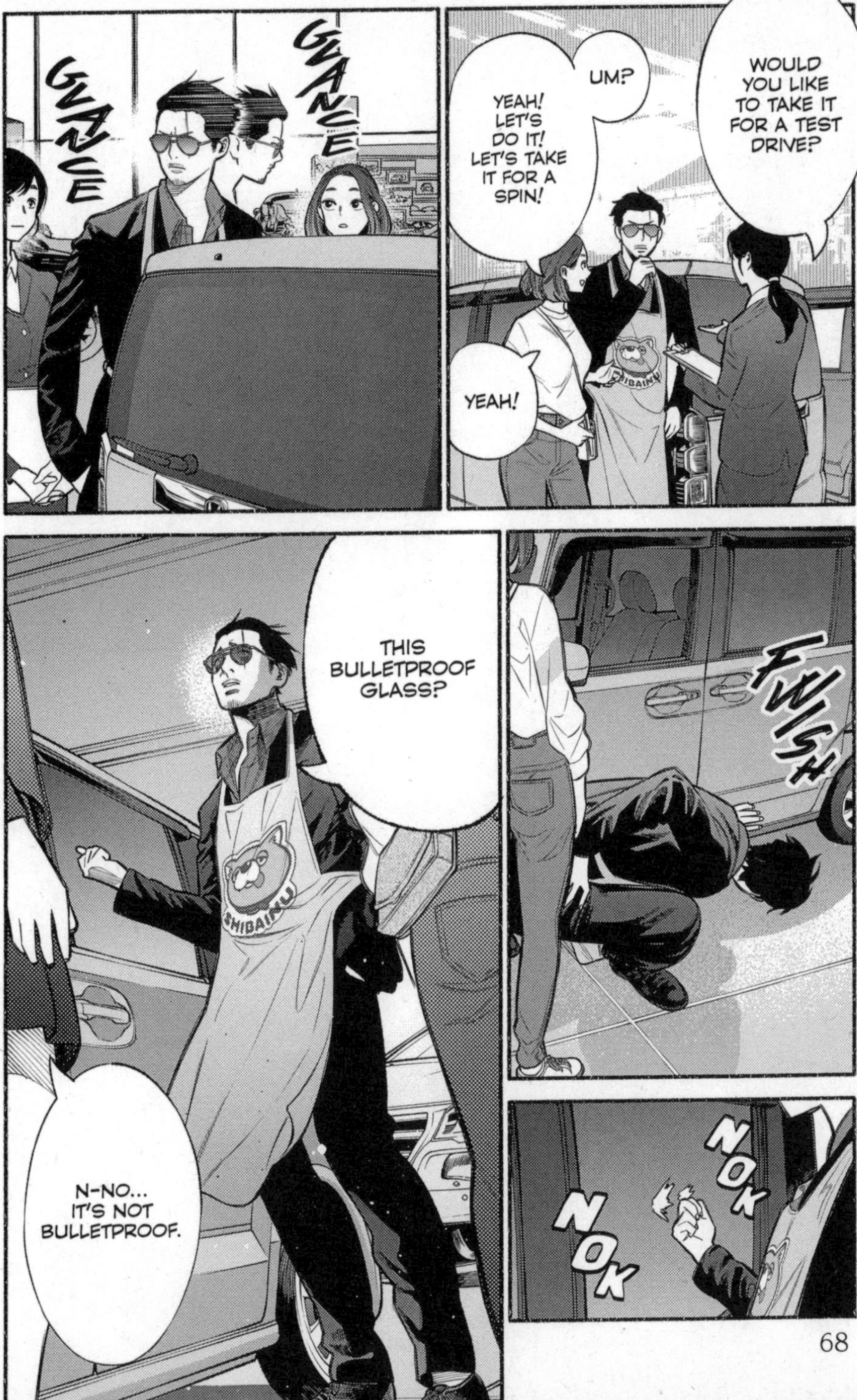
WOULD YOU LIKE TO TAKE IT FOR A TEST DRIVE?
UM?
YEAH! LET'S DO IT! LET'S TAKE IT FOR A SPIN!
YEAH!
GLANCE
GLANCE
FWISH
NOK
NOK
THIS BULLETPROOF GLASS?
N-NO... IT'S NOT BULLETPROOF.

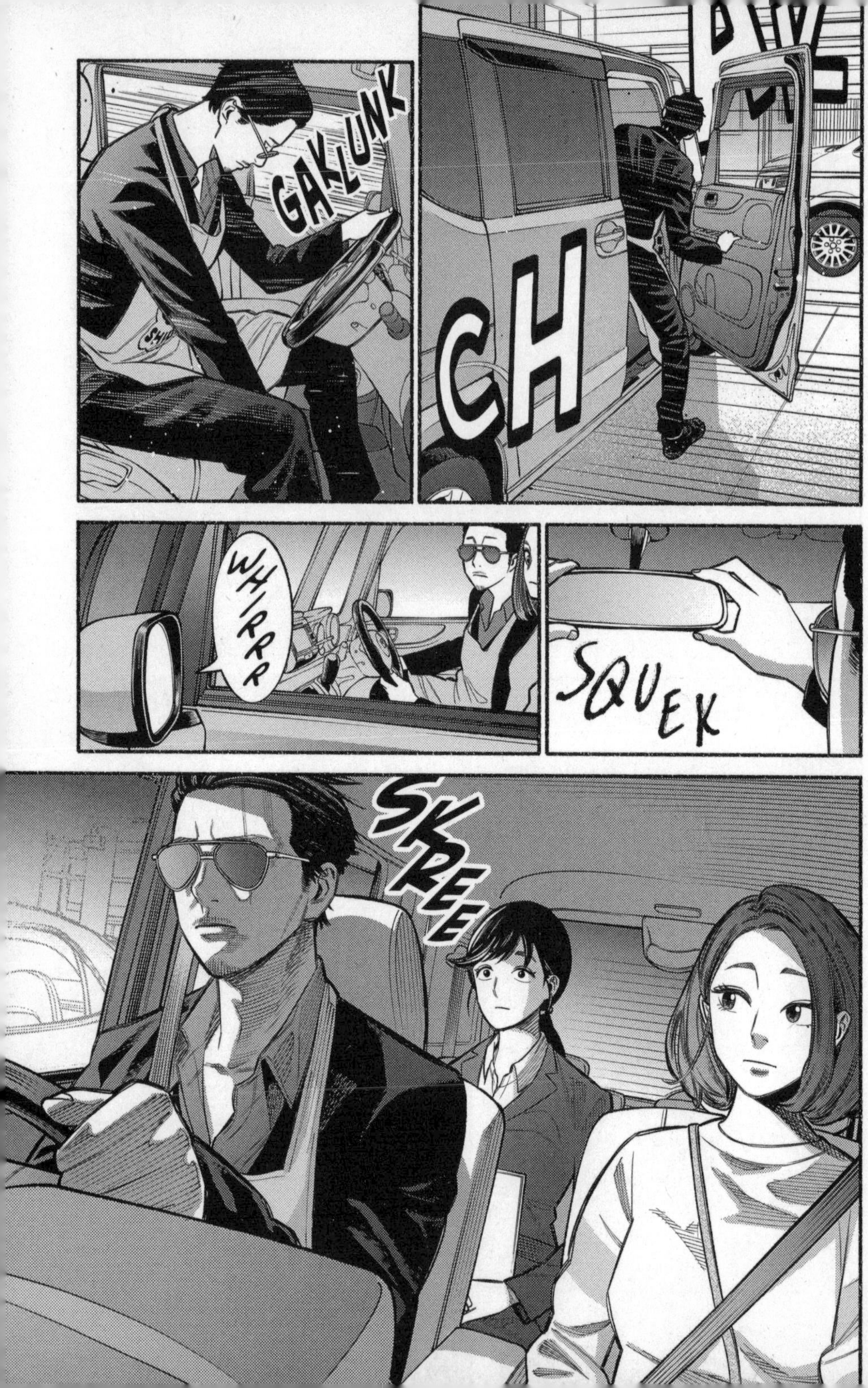
CH
GAKLUNK
SQUEK
WHIRRR
SKREE

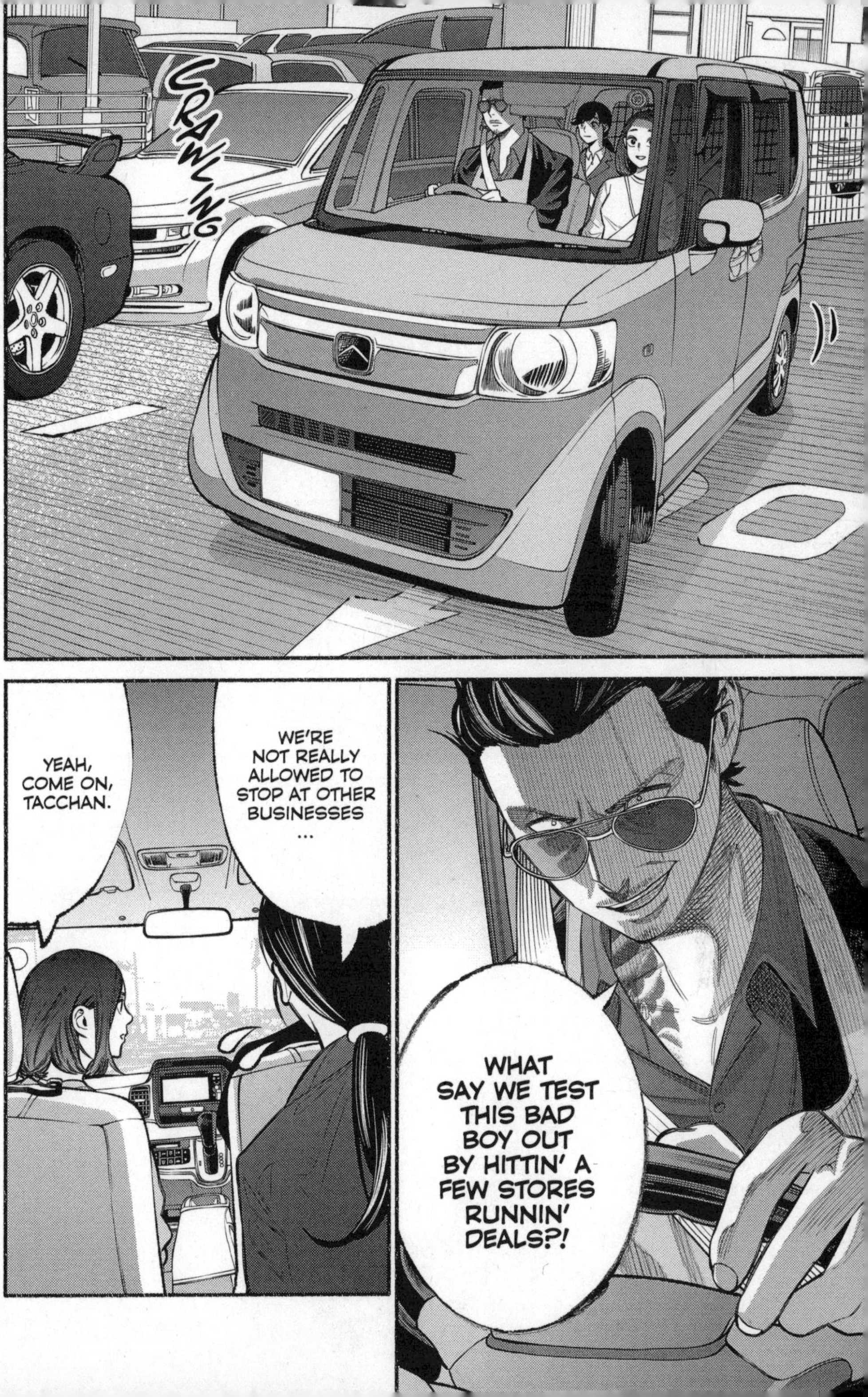
CRAWLING
WHAT SAY WE TEST THIS BAD BOY OUT BY HITTIN' A FEW STORES RUNNIN' DEALS?!
WE'RE NOT REALLY ALLOWED TO STOP AT OTHER BUSINESSES ...
YEAH, COME ON, TACCHAN.

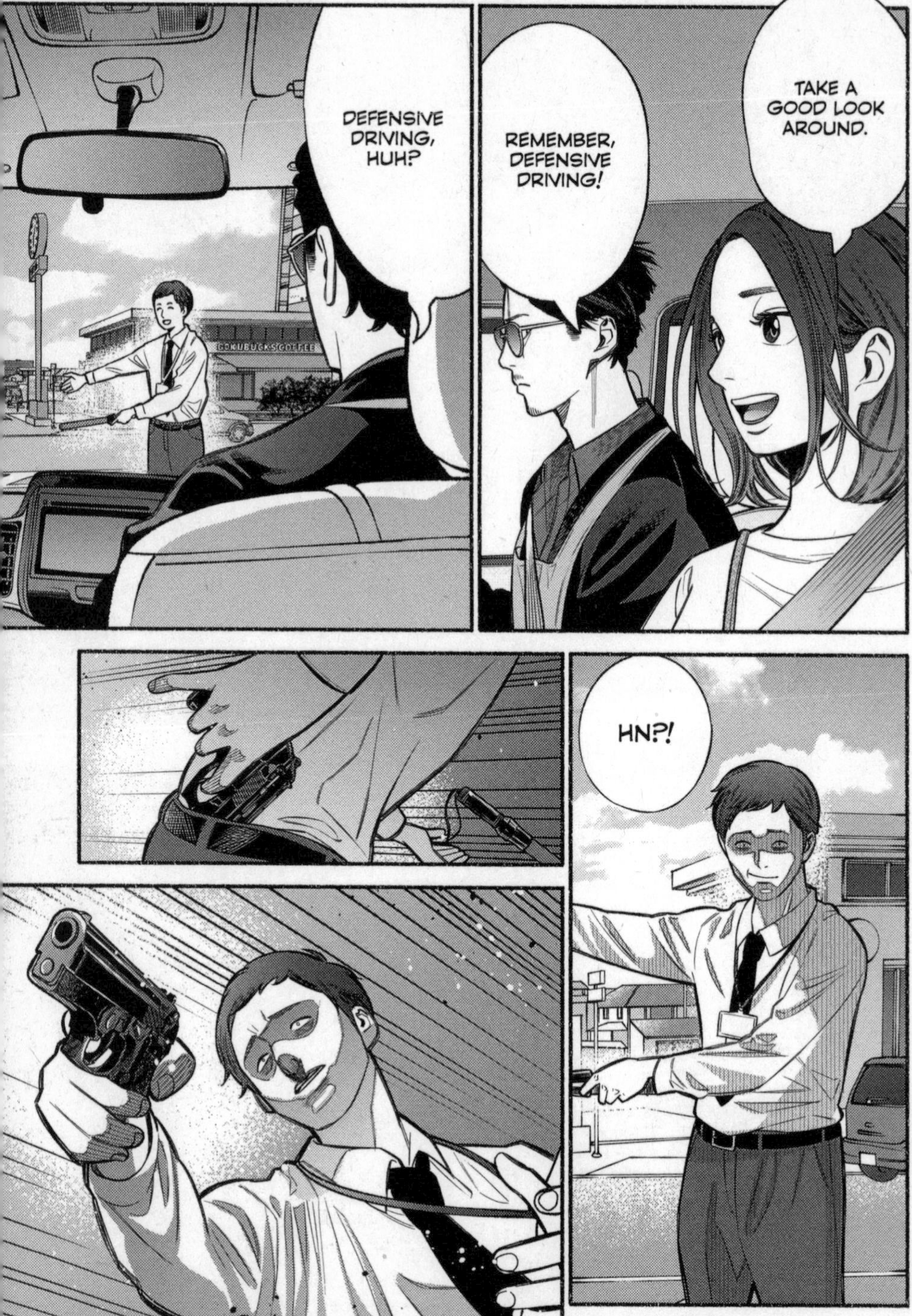
TAKE A GOOD LOOK AROUND.
REMEMBER, DEFENSIVE DRIVING!
DEFENSIVE DRIVING, HUH?
HN?!

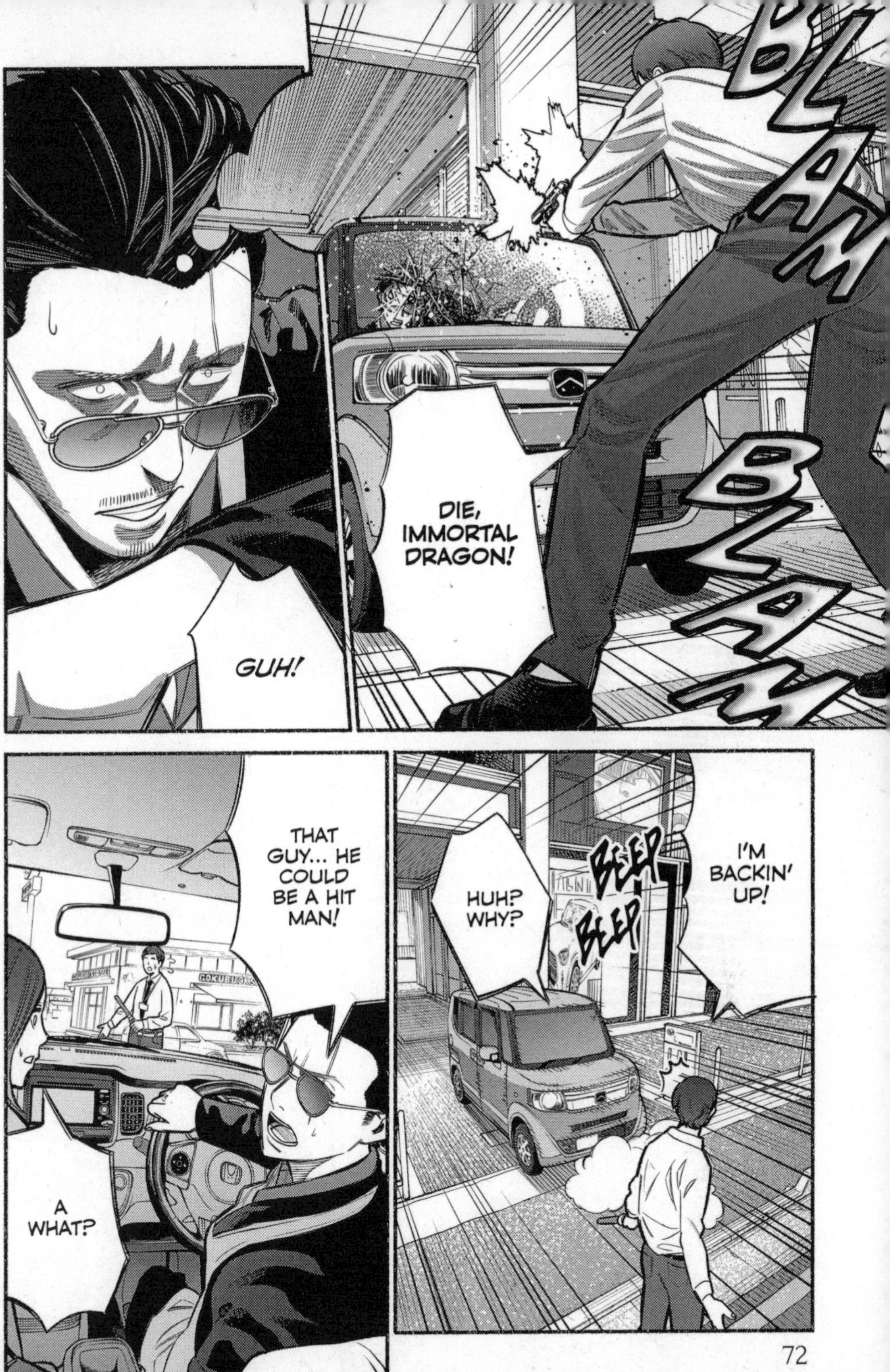
BLAM
BLAM
DIE, IMMORTAL DRAGON!
GUH!
I'M BACKIN' UP!
HUH? WHY?
BEEP BEEP
THAT GUY... HE COULD BE A HIT MAN!
A WHAT?

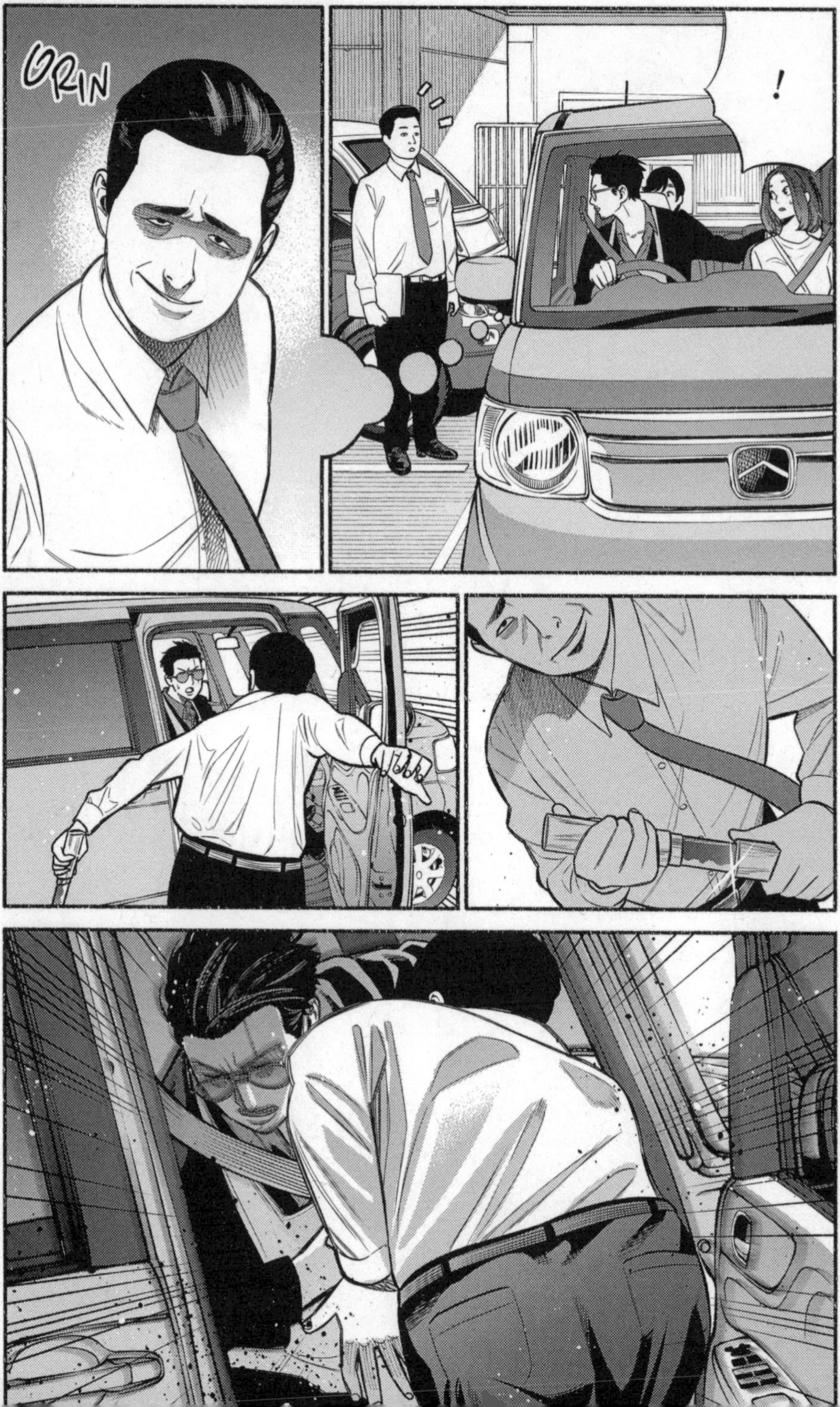
!
GRIN

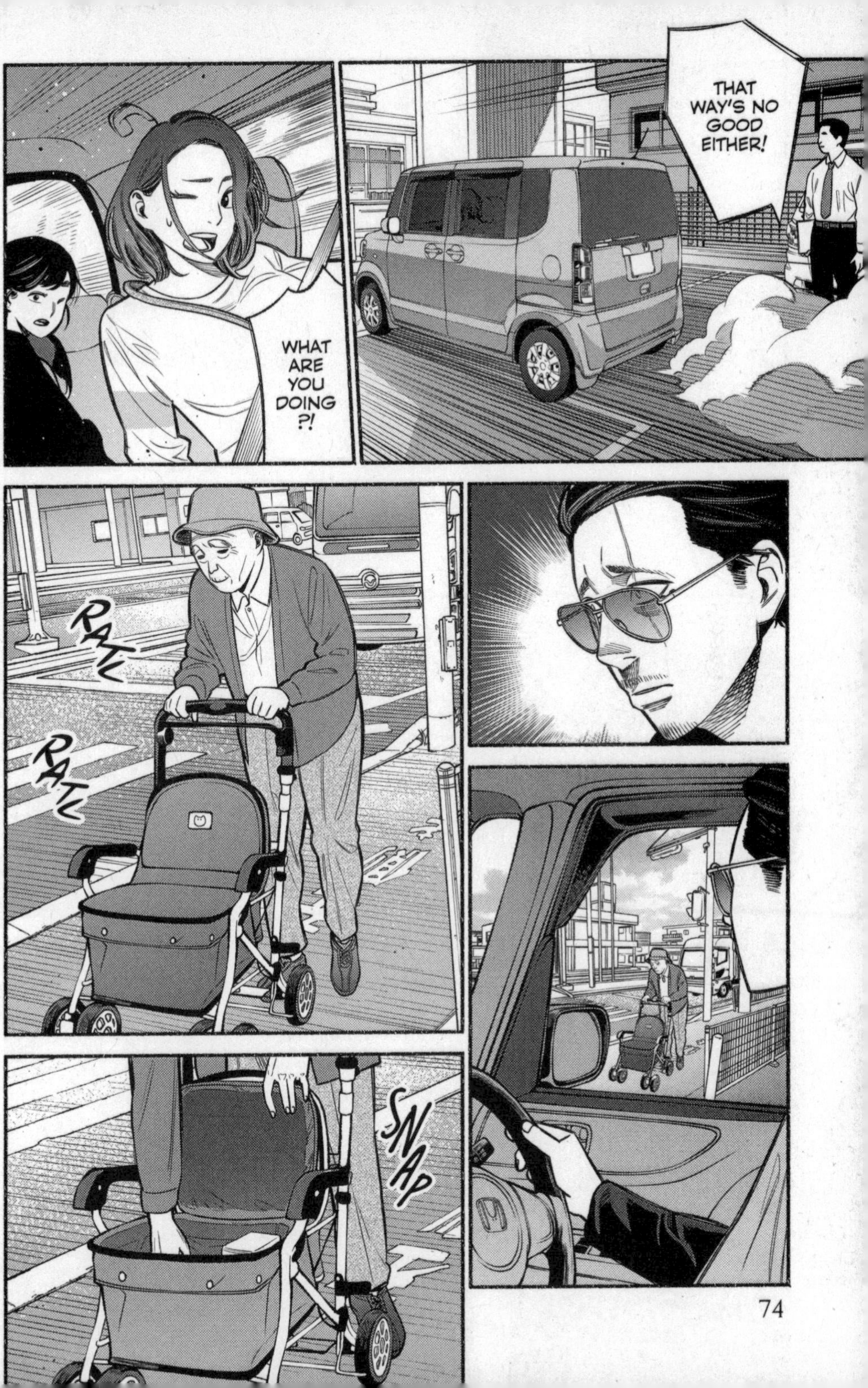
THAT WAY'S NO GOOD EITHER!
WHAT ARE YOU DOING?!
RATTL
RATTL
SNAP

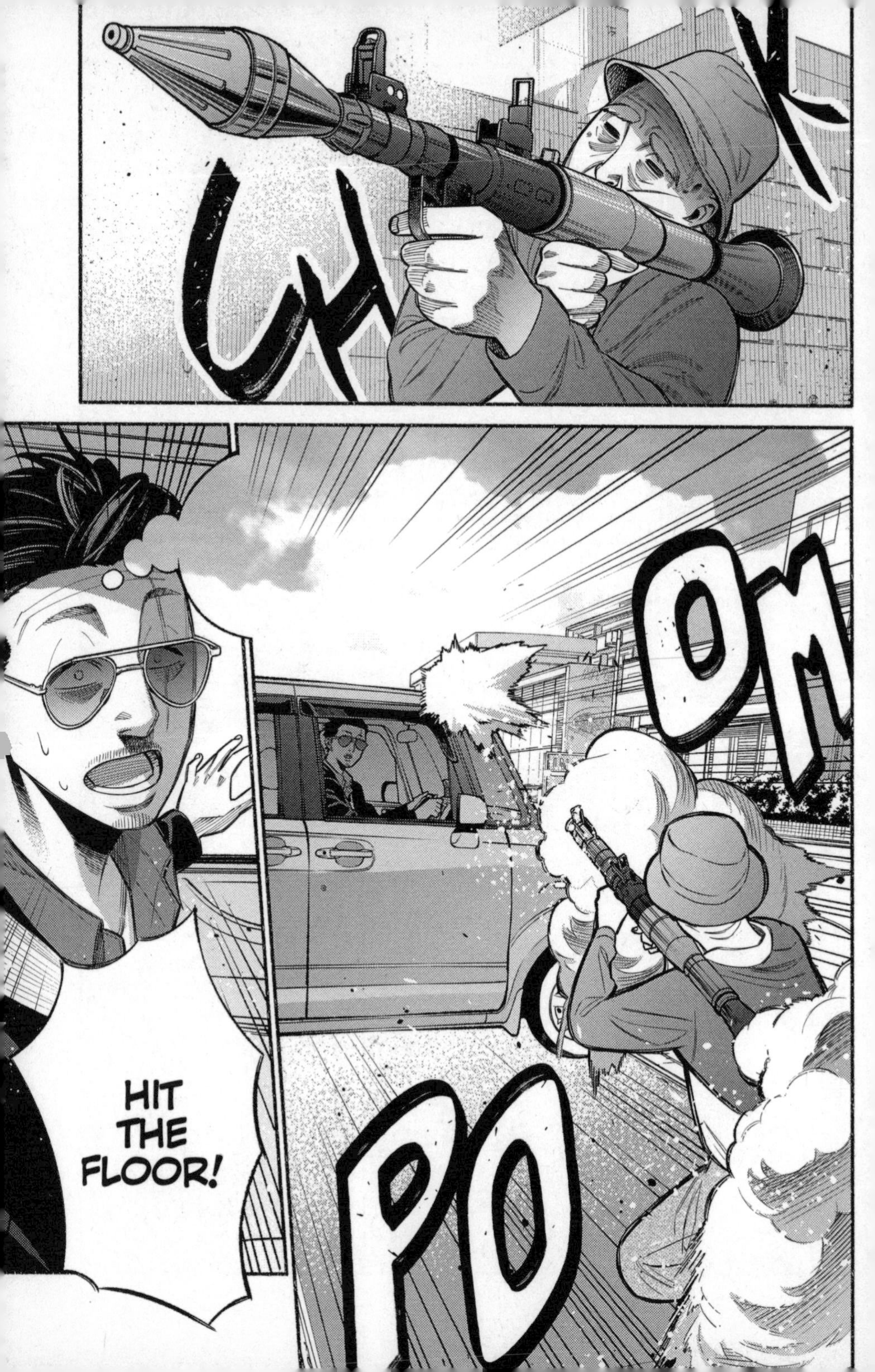
CHK
POOM
HIT THE FLOOR!

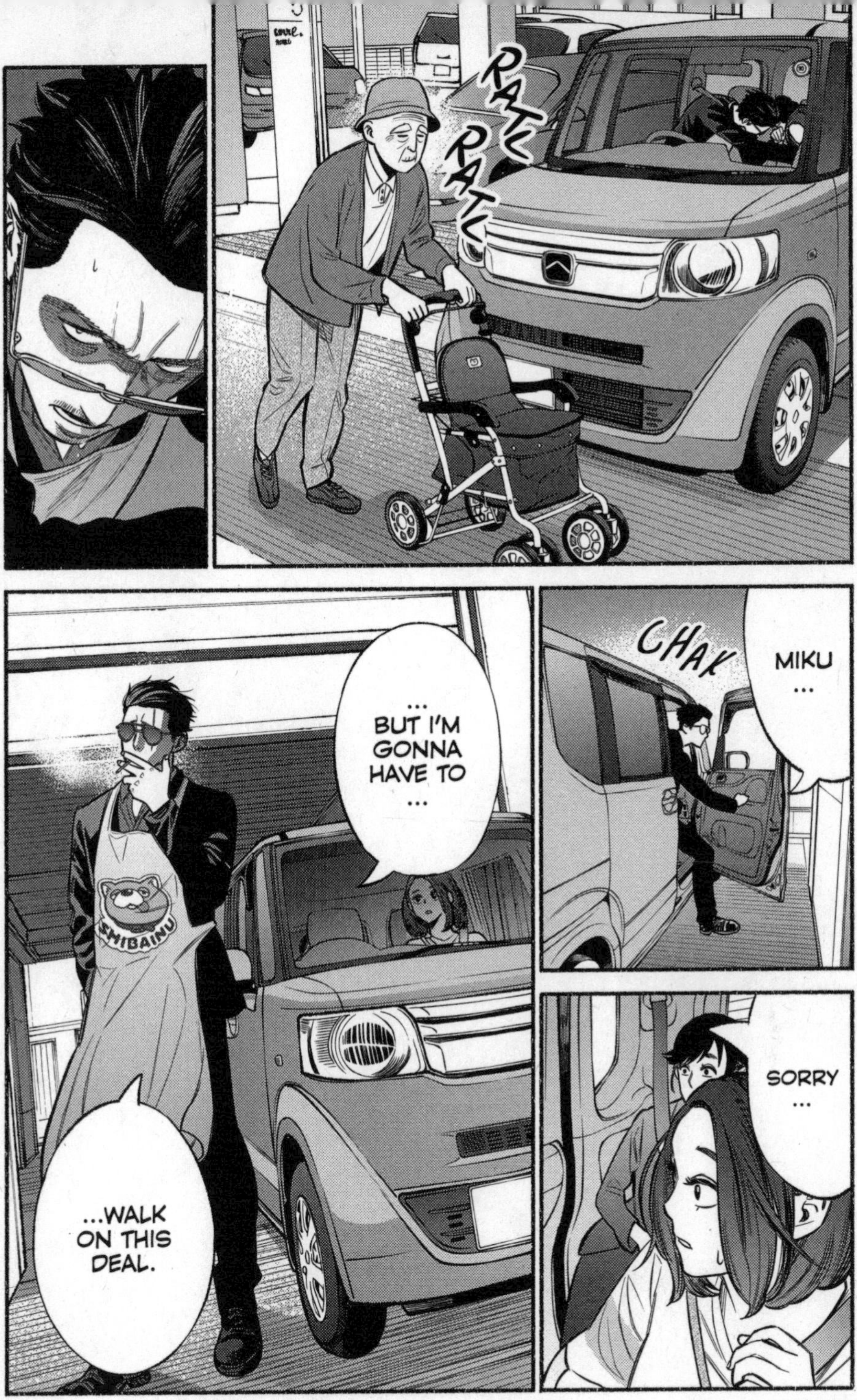
RATK
RATK
CHAK
MIKU ...
SORRY ...
... BUT I'M GONNA HAVE TO ...
...WALK ON THIS DEAL.

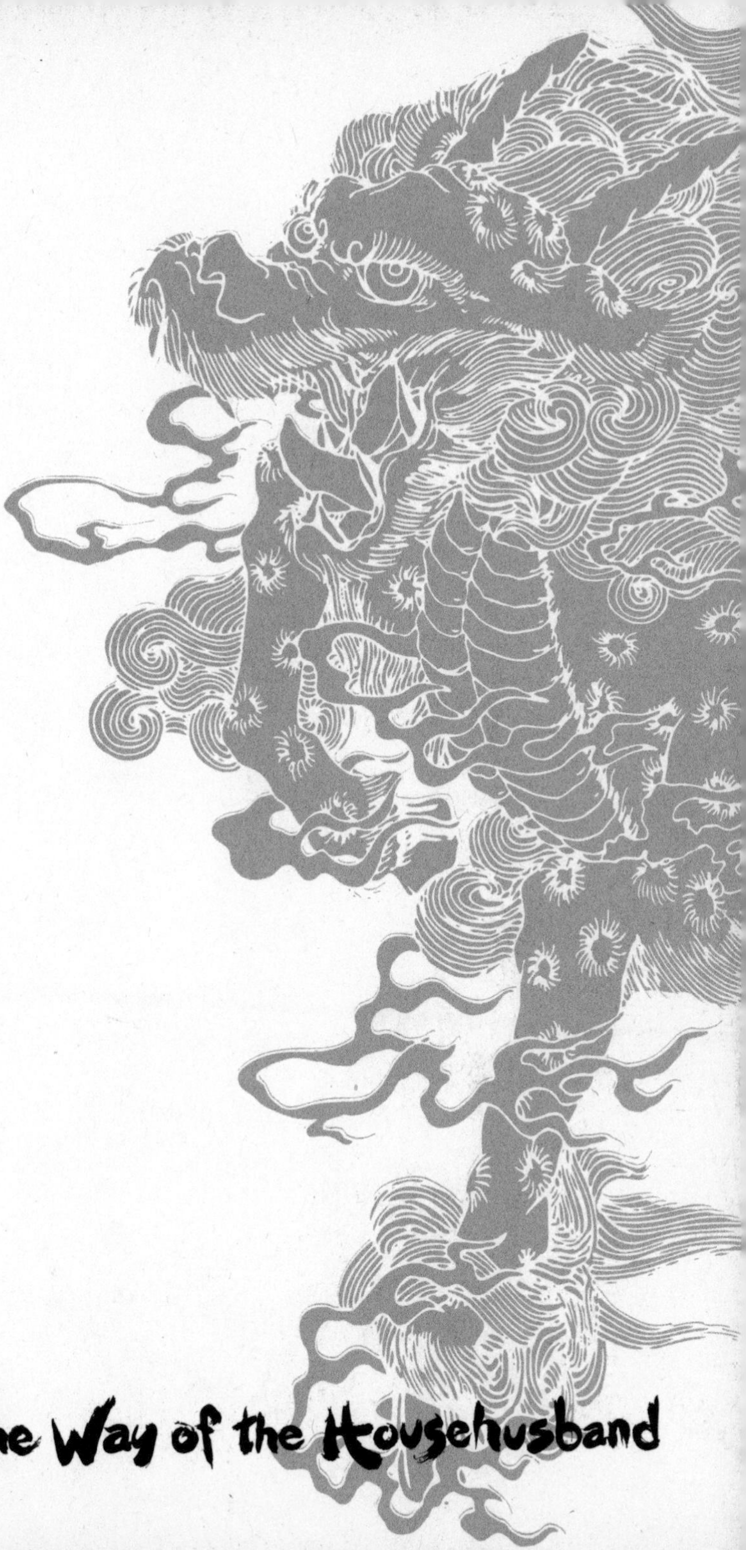

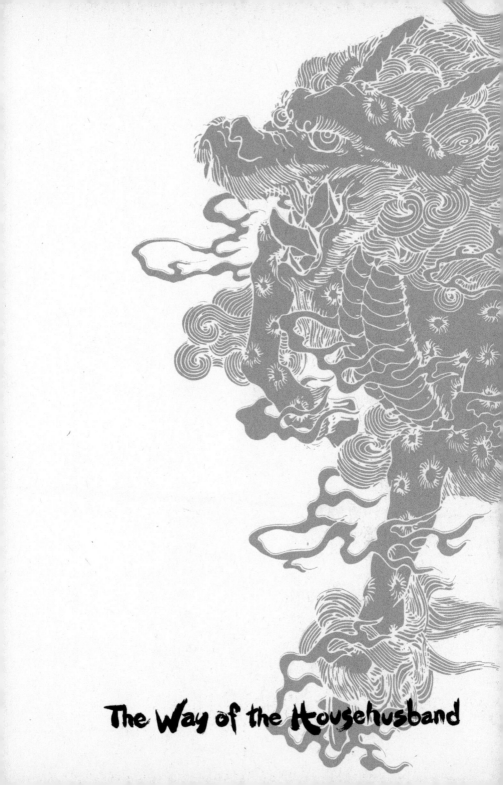

The Way of the Househusband

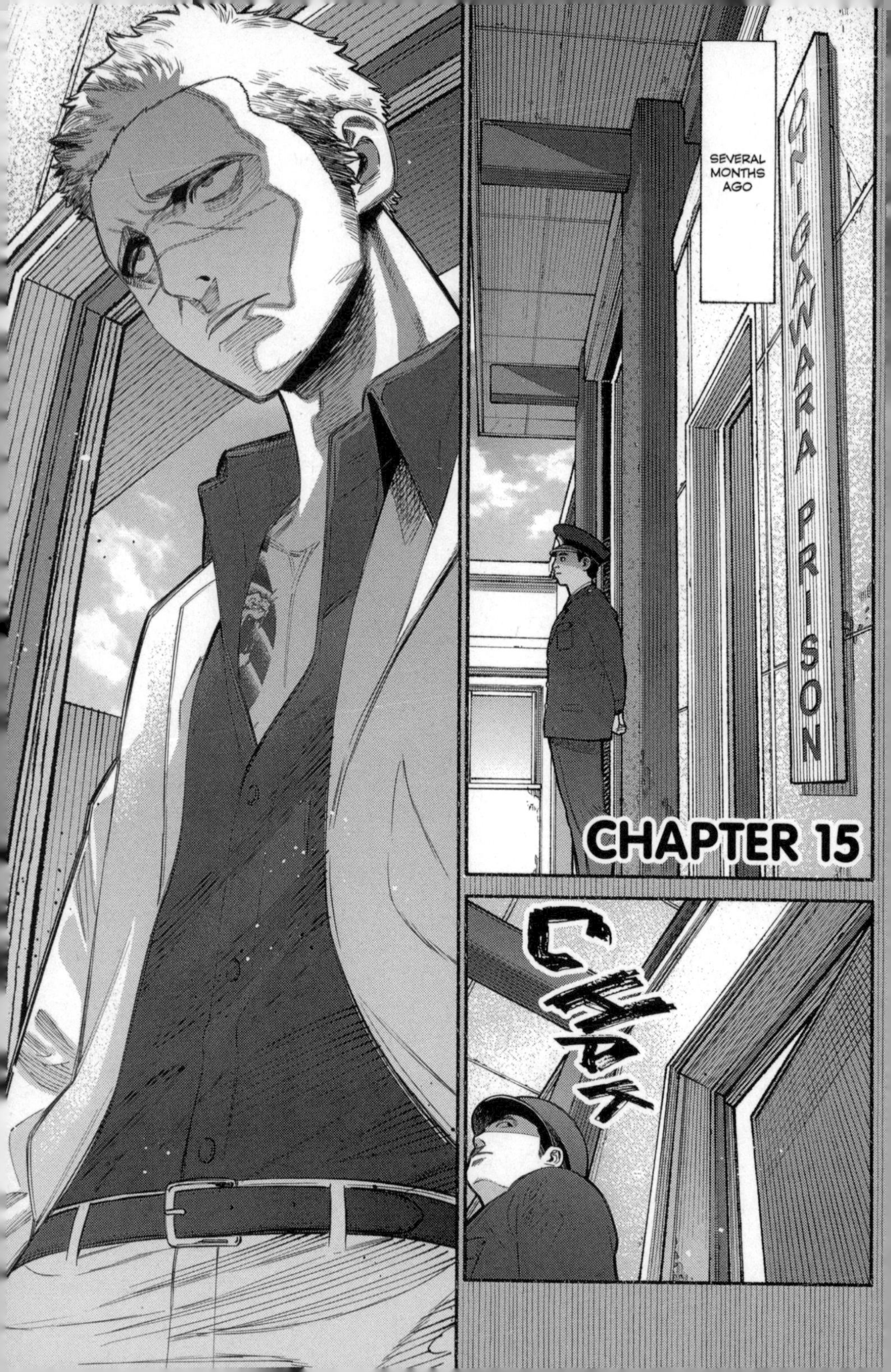

SEVERAL MONTHS AGO
CHIGAWARA PRISON
CHAPTER 15
CHAK

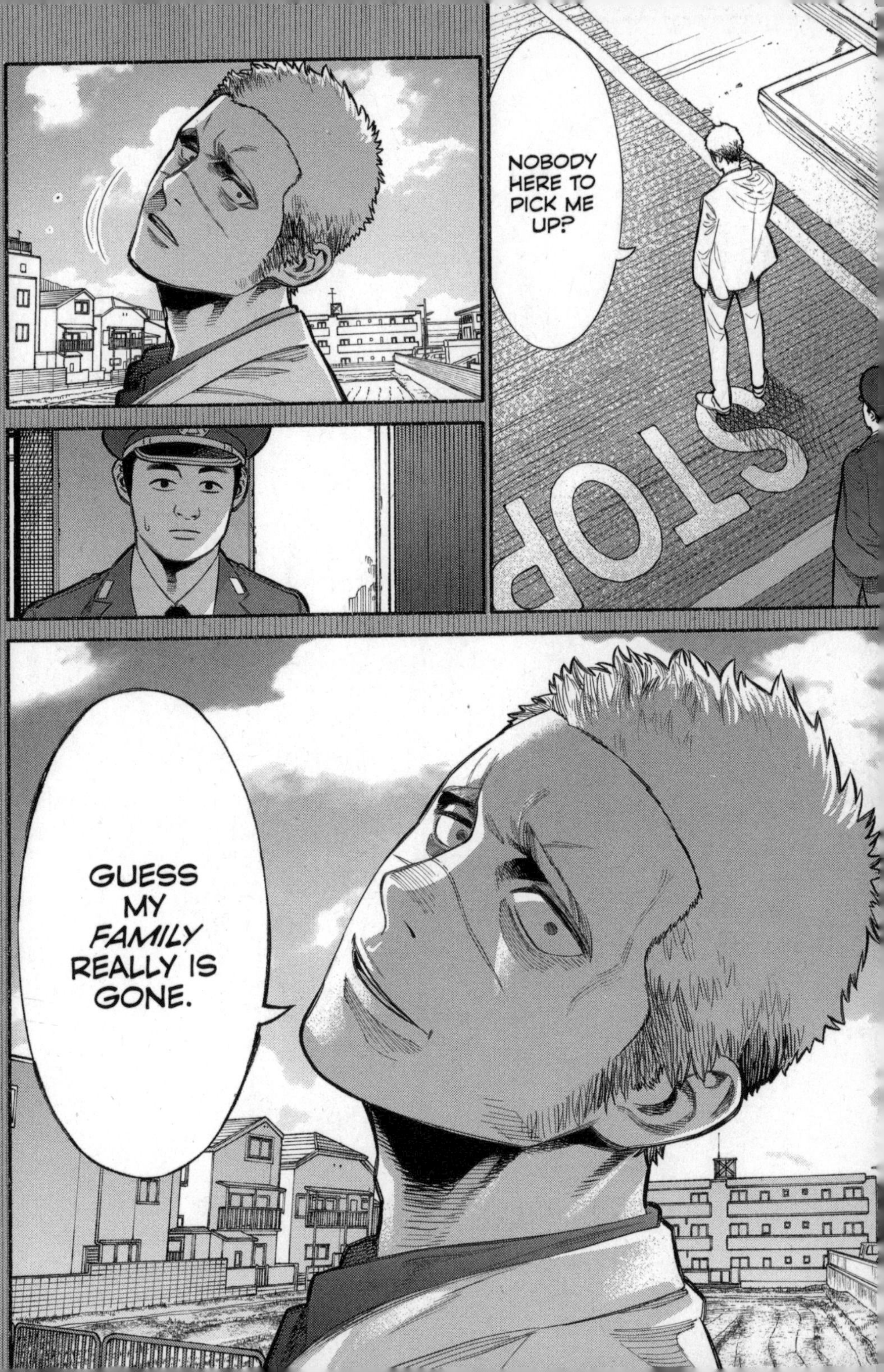
NOBODY HERE TO PICK ME UP?
STOP
GUESS MY *FAMILY* REALLY IS GONE.

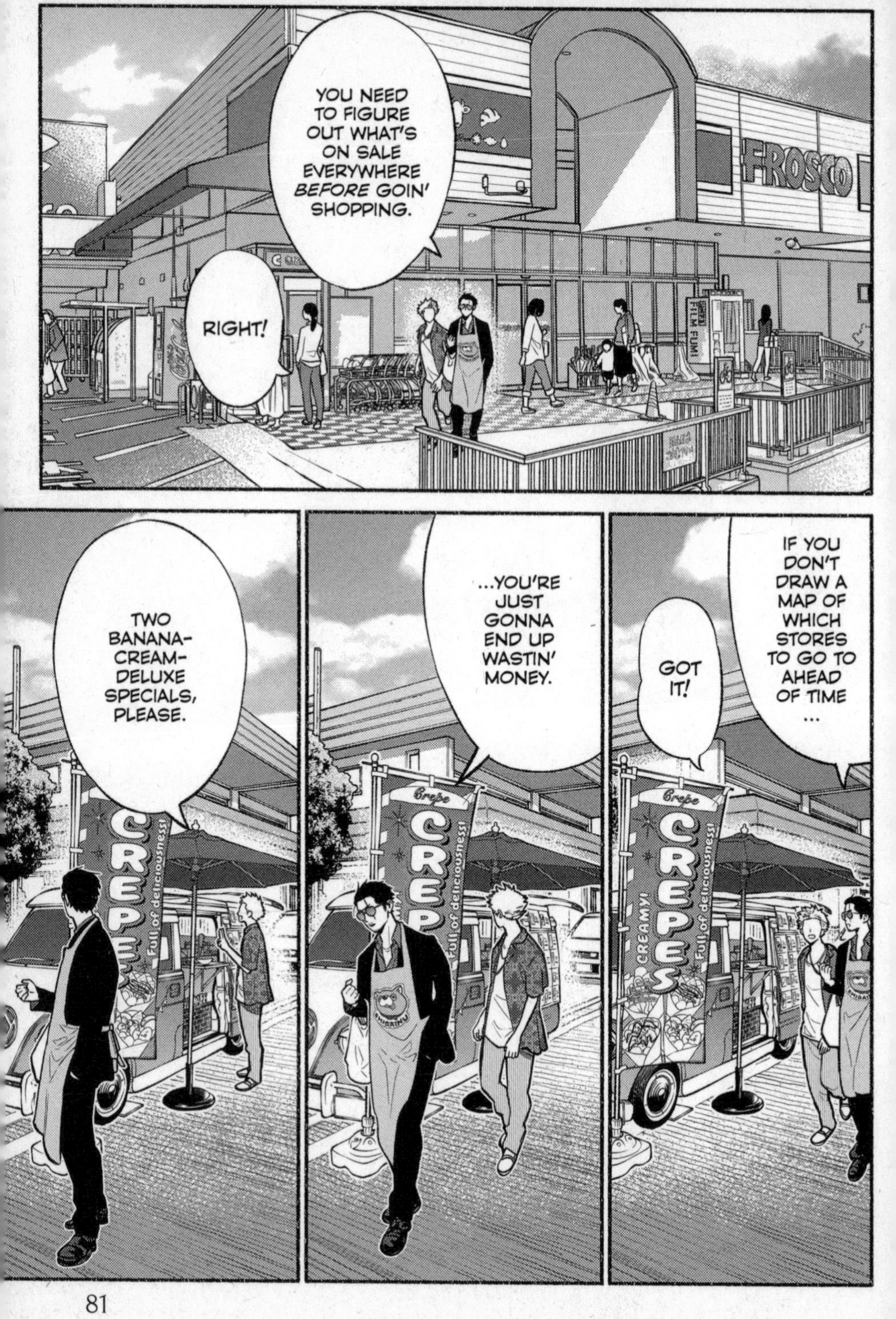
FROSCO
FILM FUMI
YOU NEED TO FIGURE OUT WHAT'S ON SALE EVERYWHERE *BEFORE* GOIN' SHOPPING.
RIGHT!
IF YOU DON'T DRAW A MAP OF WHICH STORES TO GO TO AHEAD OF TIME ...
GOT IT!
Crepe
CREPES
Full of deliciousness!
CREAMY!
...YOU'RE JUST GONNA END UP WASTIN' MONEY.
TWO BANANA-CREAM-DELUXE SPECIALS, PLEASE.

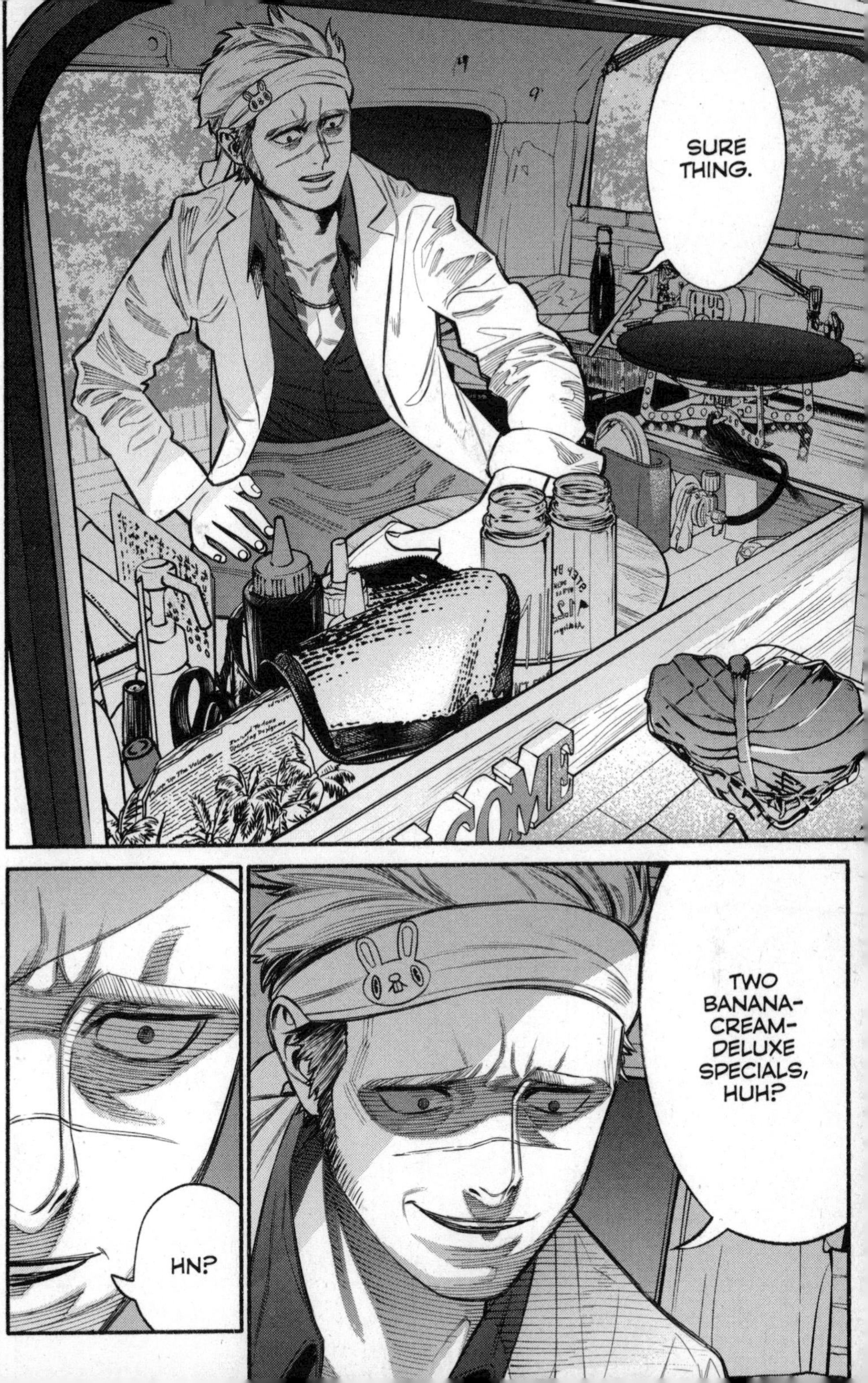
SURE THING.
TWO BANANA-CREAM-DELUXE SPECIALS, HUH?
HN?

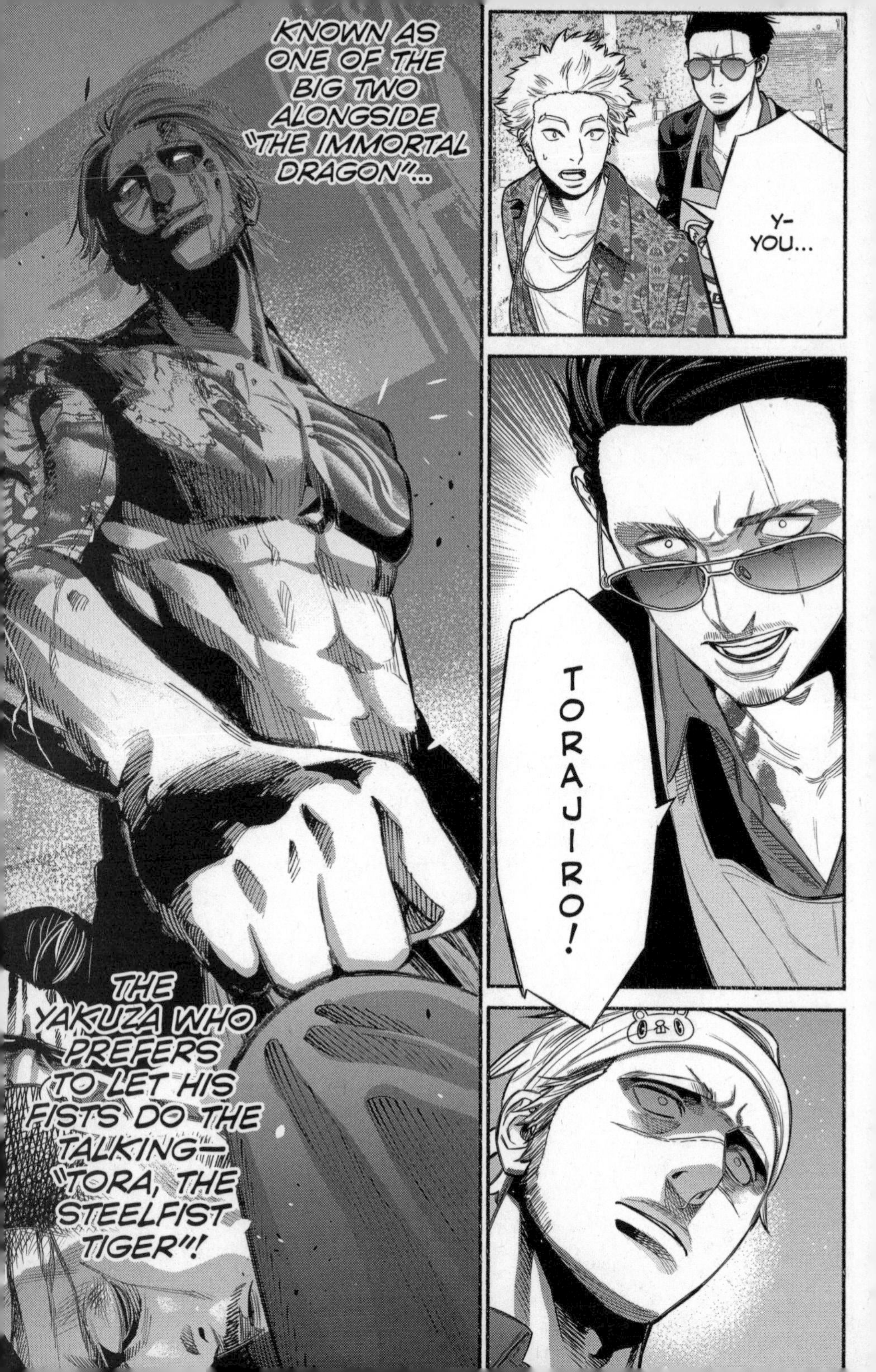
Y-
YOU...
TORAJIRO!
KNOWN AS ONE OF THE BIG TWO ALONGSIDE "THE IMMORTAL DRAGON"...
THE YAKUZA WHO PREFERS TO LET HIS FISTS DO THE TALKING— "TORA, THE STEELFIST TIGER"!

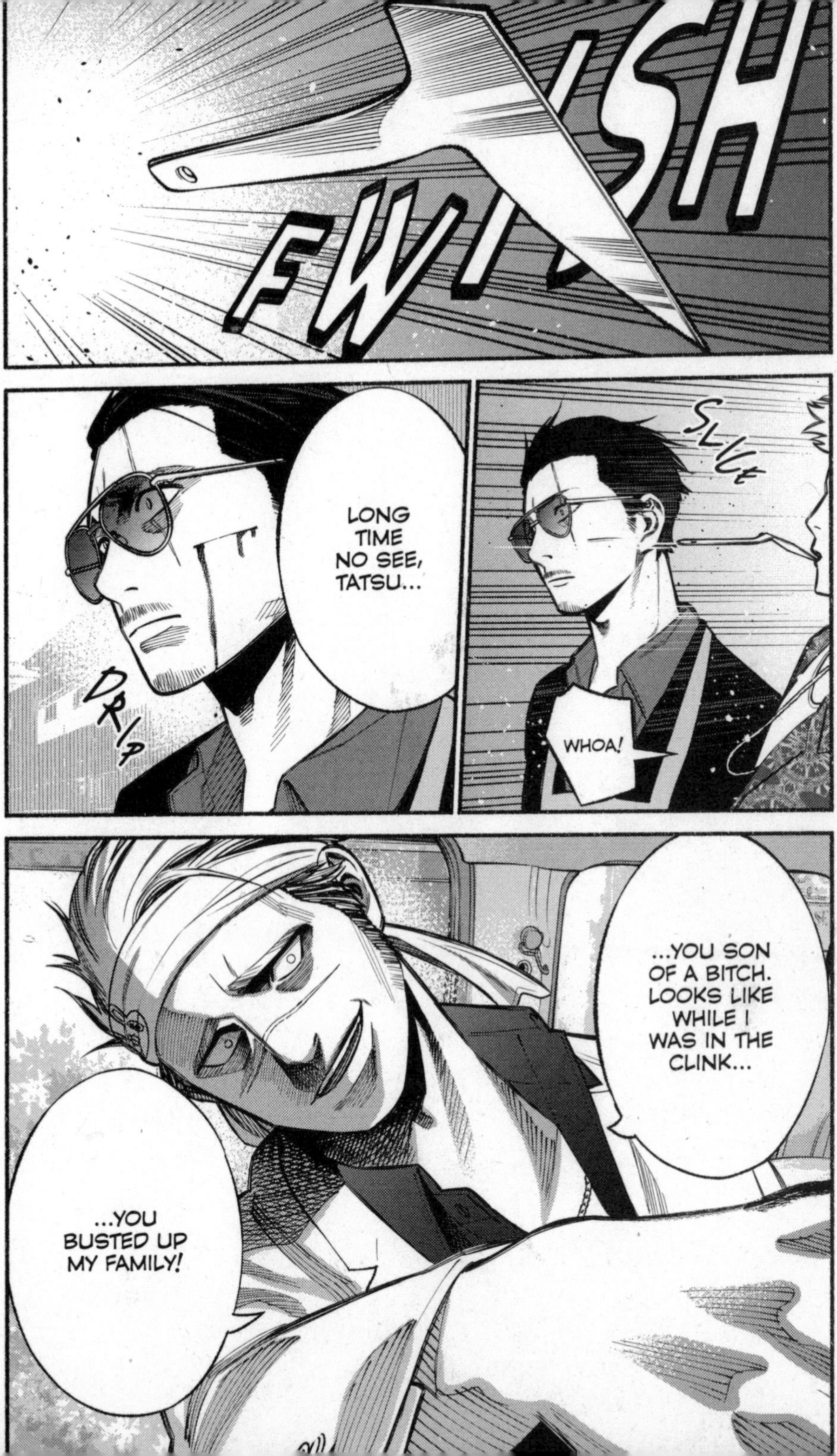
FWISH
SLICE
WHOA!
LONG TIME NO SEE, TATSU...
DRIP
...YOU SON OF A BITCH. LOOKS LIKE WHILE I WAS IN THE CLINK...
...YOU BUSTED UP MY FAMILY!

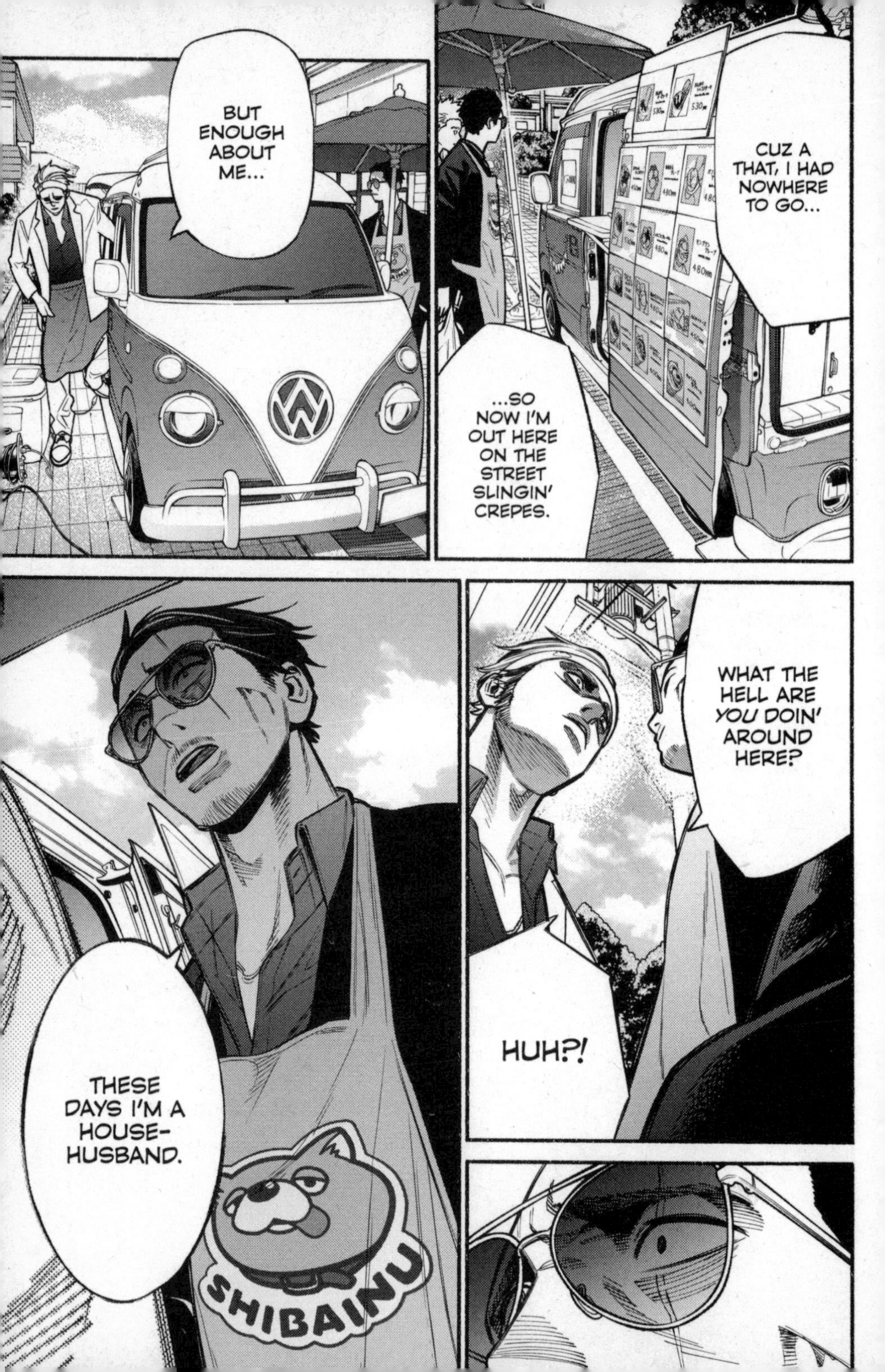
CUZ A THAT, I HAD NOWHERE TO GO...
...SO NOW I'M OUT HERE ON THE STREET SLINGIN' CREPES.
BUT ENOUGH ABOUT ME...
WHAT THE HELL ARE *YOU* DOIN' AROUND HERE?
HUH?!
THESE DAYS I'M A HOUSE-HUSBAND.
SHIBAINU

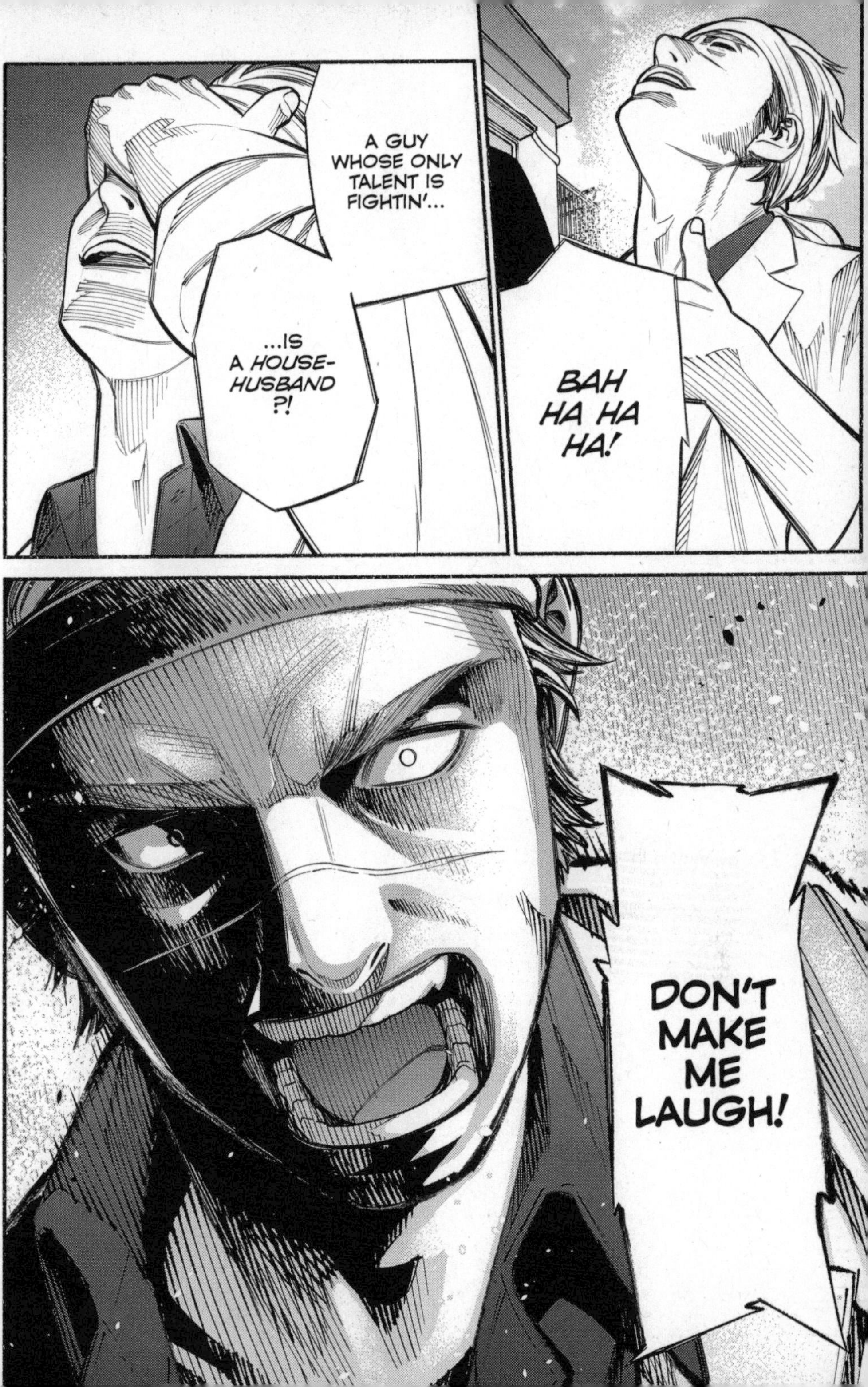
BAH HA HA HA!
A GUY WHOSE ONLY TALENT IS FIGHTIN'...
...IS A *HOUSE-HUSBAND*?!
DON'T MAKE ME LAUGH!

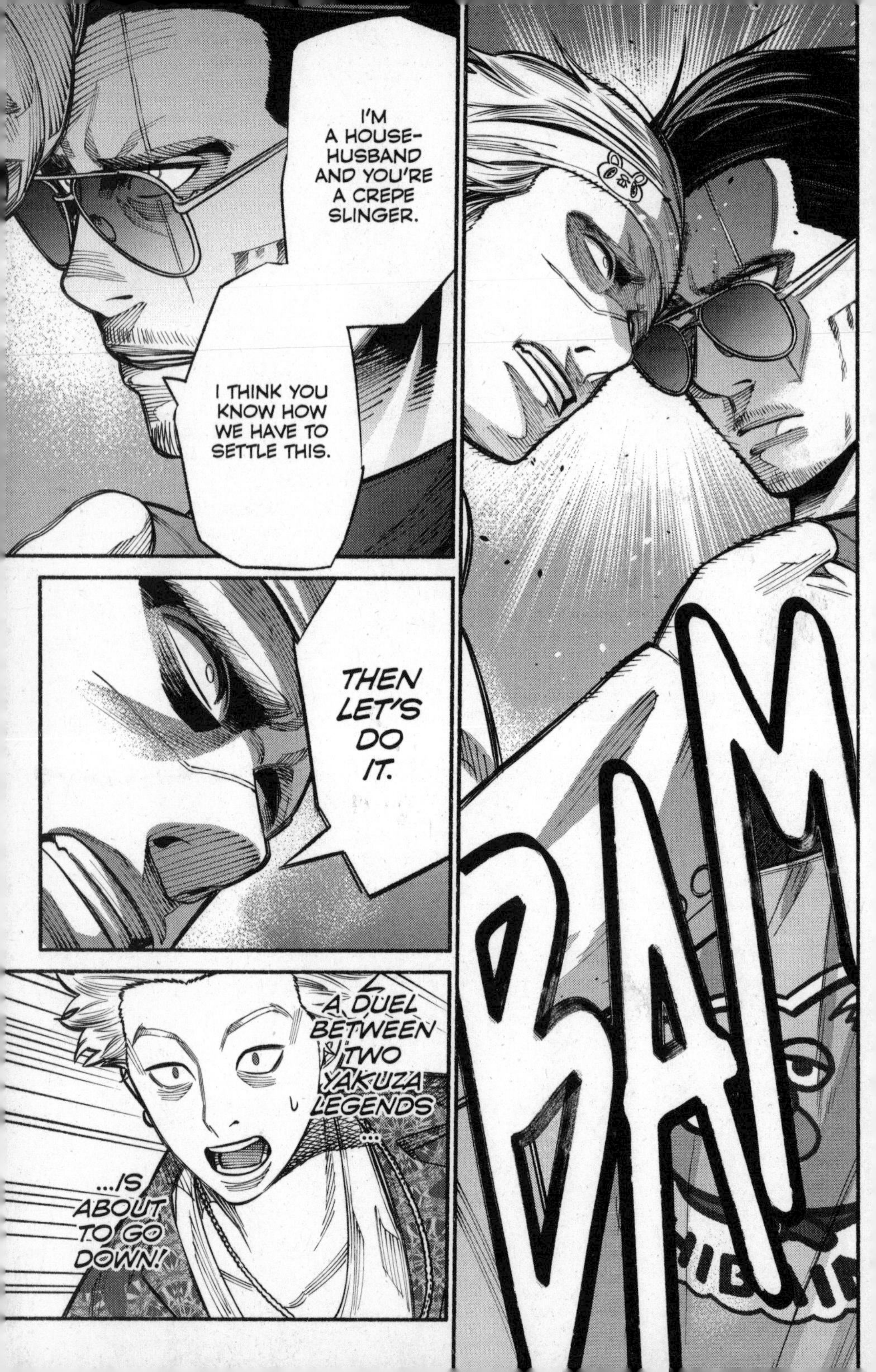
BAM
I'M A HOUSE-HUSBAND AND YOU'RE A CREPE SLINGER.
I THINK YOU KNOW HOW WE HAVE TO SETTLE THIS.
THEN LET'S DO IT.
A DUEL BETWEEN TWO YAKUZA LEGENDS...
...IS ABOUT TO GO DOWN!

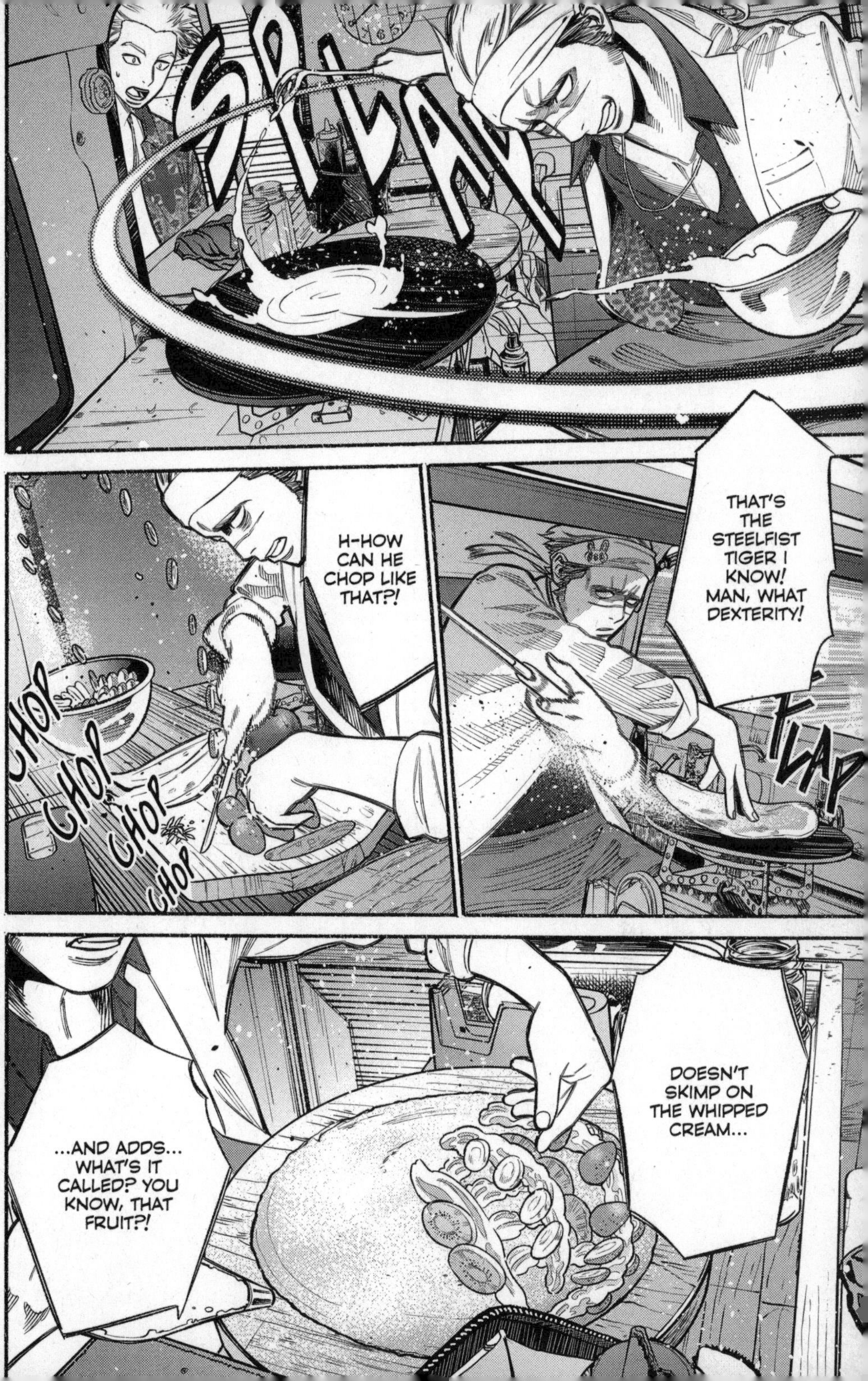
THAT'S THE STEELFIST TIGER I KNOW! MAN, WHAT DEXTERITY!
FLAP
H-HOW CAN HE CHOP LIKE THAT?!
CHOP CHOP CHOP CHOP
DOESN'T SKIMP ON THE WHIPPED CREAM...
...AND ADDS... WHAT'S IT CALLED? YOU KNOW, THAT FRUIT?!

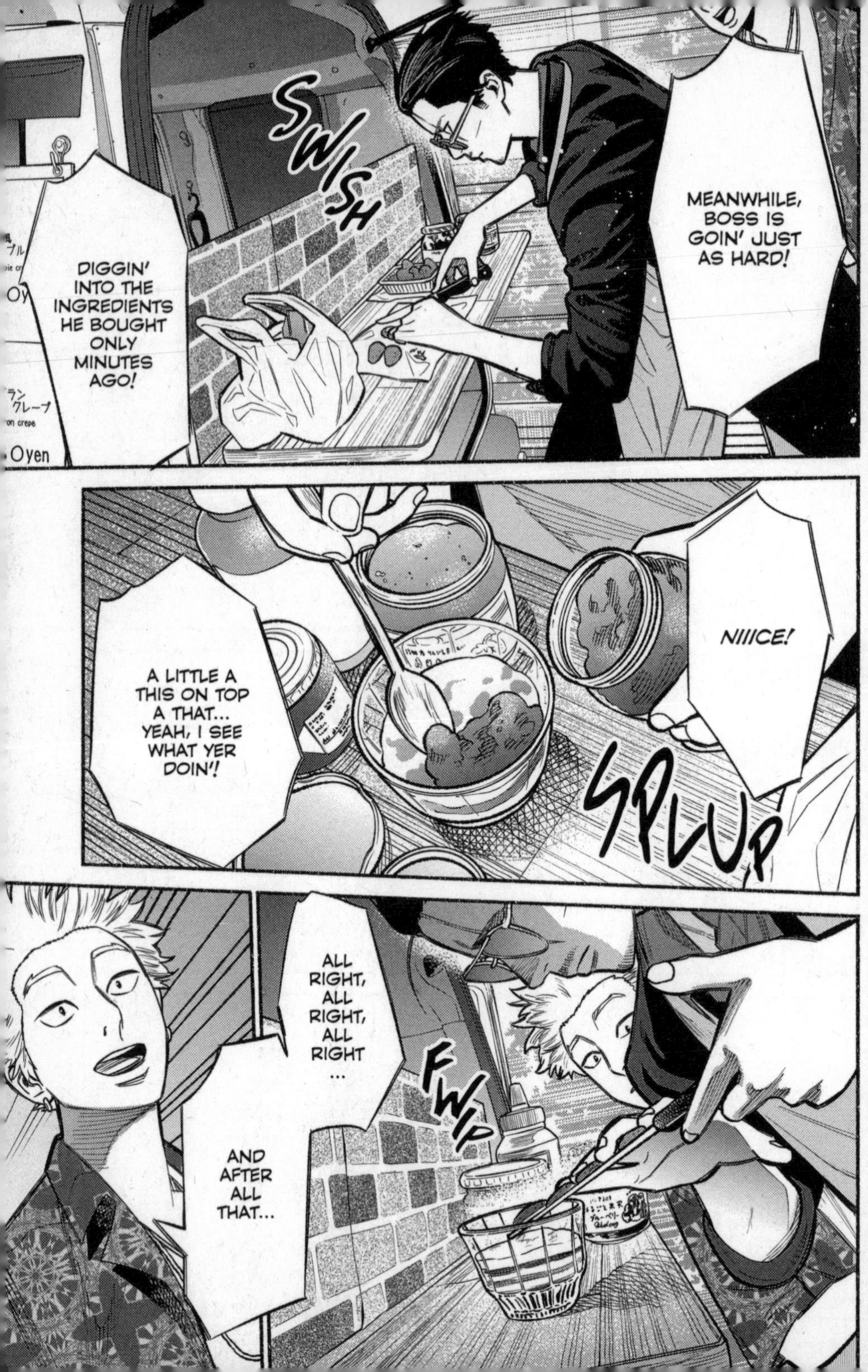
MEANWHILE, BOSS IS GOIN' JUST AS HARD!
SWISH
DIGGIN' INTO THE INGREDIENTS HE BOUGHT ONLY MINUTES AGO!
NIIICE!
SPLUP
A LITTLE A THIS ON TOP A THAT... YEAH, I SEE WHAT YER DOIN'!
ALL RIGHT, ALL RIGHT, ALL RIGHT...
FWIP
AND AFTER ALL THAT...

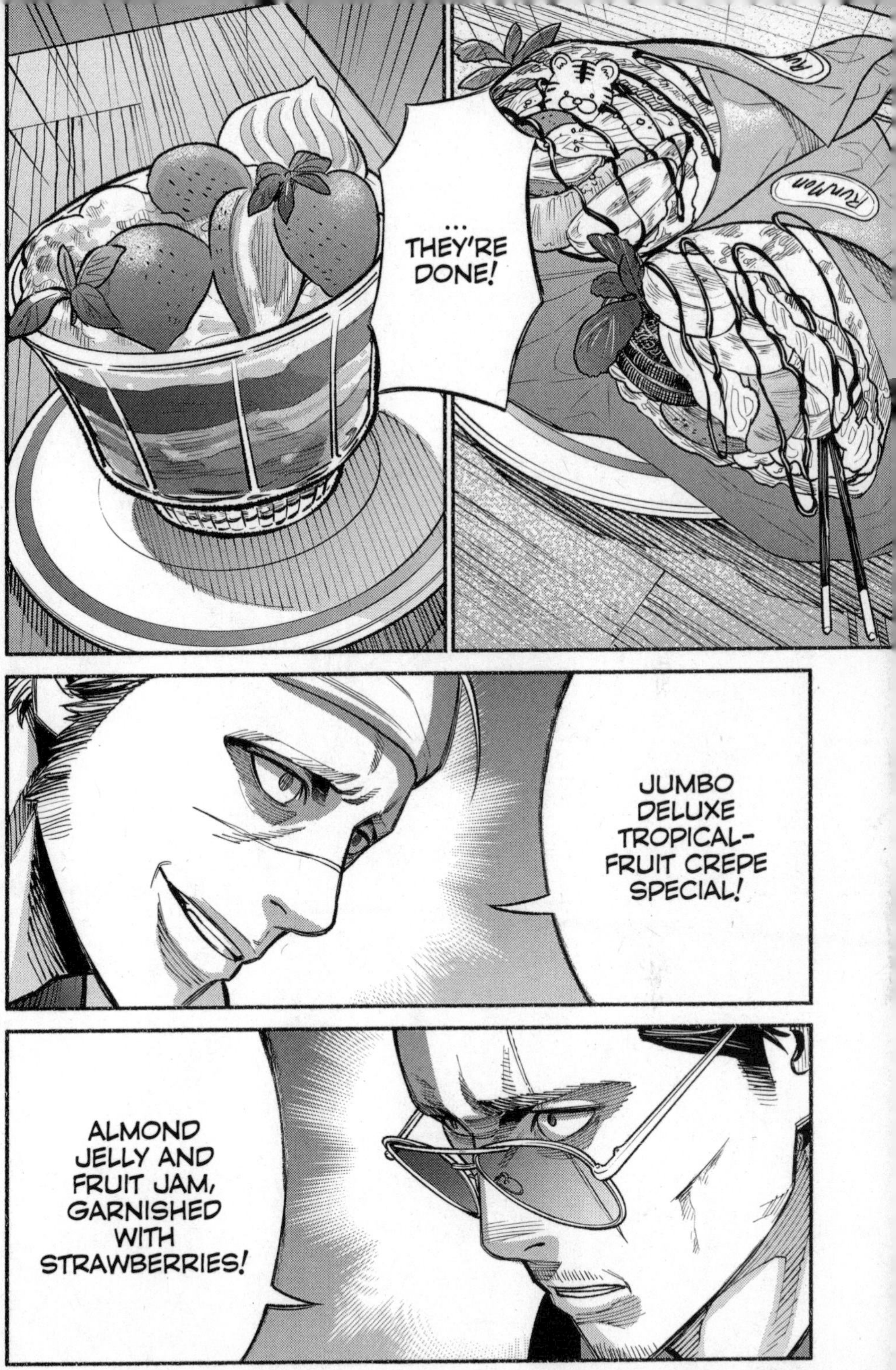
... THEY'RE DONE!
JUMBO DELUXE TROPICAL-FRUIT CREPE SPECIAL!
ALMOND JELLY AND FRUIT JAM, GARNISHED WITH STRAWBERRIES!

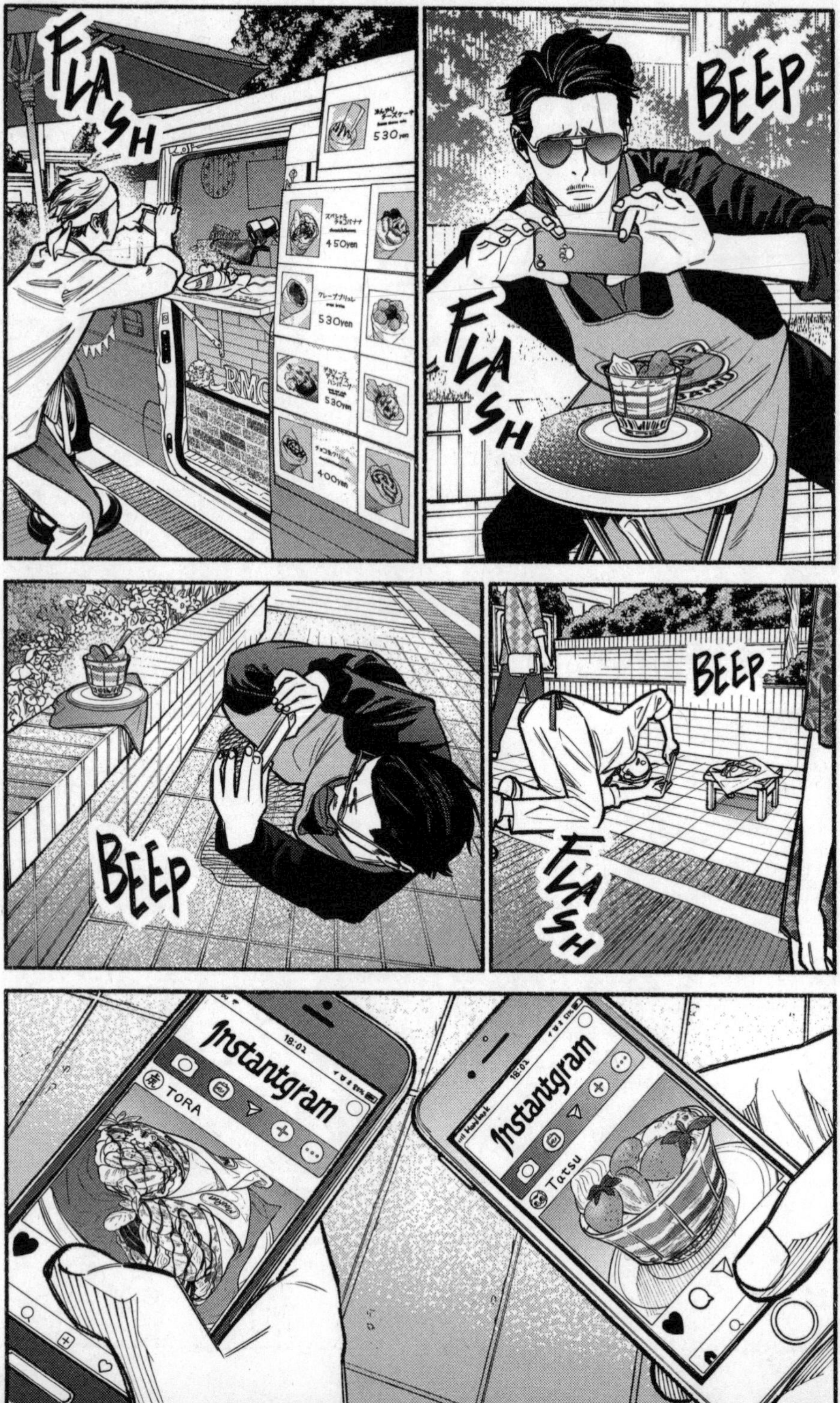
BEEP
FLASH
FLASH
530yen
450yen
530yen
530yen
400yen
RMC
BEEP
FLASH
BEEP
18:01
Instantgram
Tatsu
18:02
Instantgram
TORA

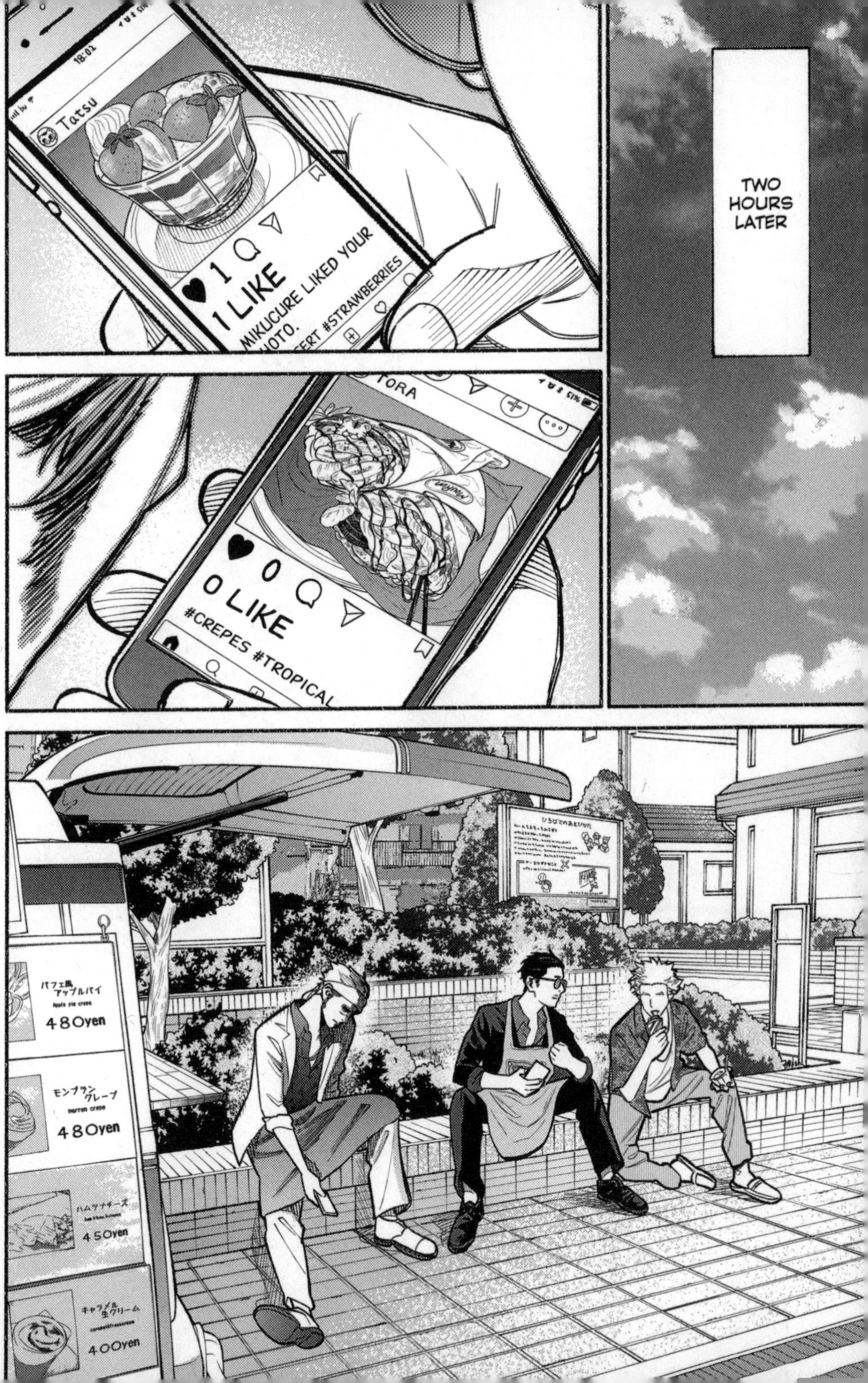
TWO HOURS LATER
Tatsu
1
1 LIKE
MIKUCURE LIKED YOUR
HOTO.
ERT #STRAWBERRIES
TORA
0
0 LIKE
#CREPES #TROPICAL
パフェ風 アップルパイ
Apple pie crepe
480yen
モンブラン クレープ
marron crepe
480yen
ハムツナチーズ
450yen
キャラメル 生クリーム
400yen

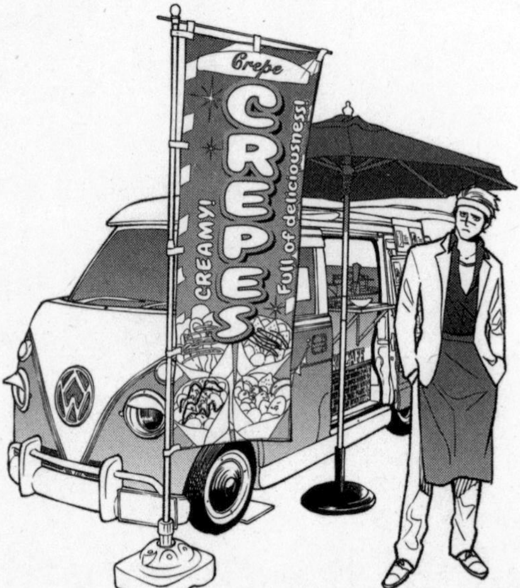

Crepe
CREPES
CREAMY!
Full of deliciousness!

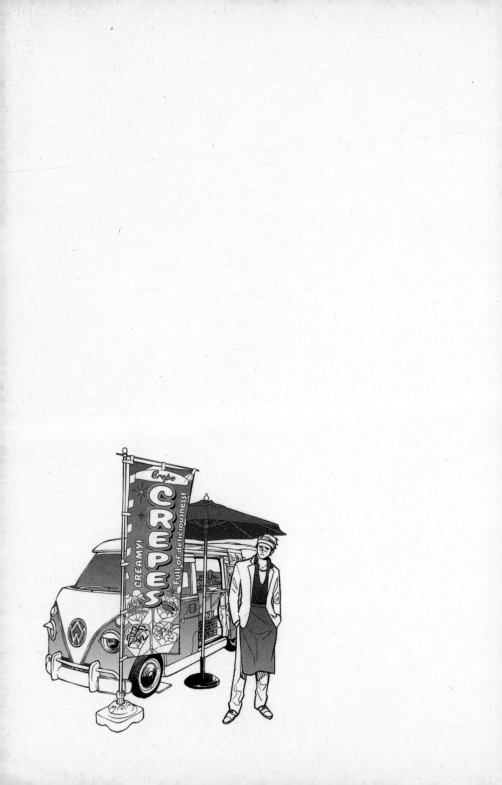

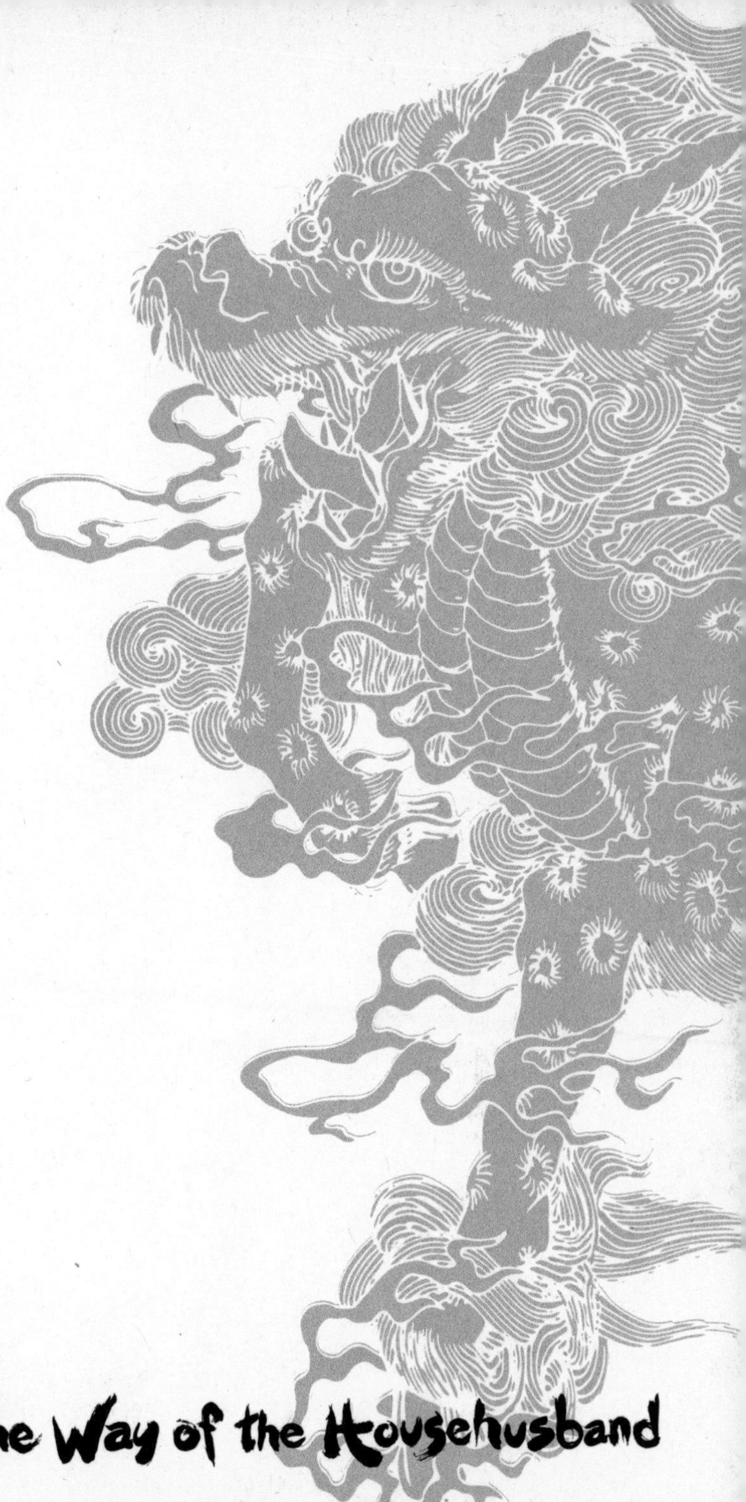

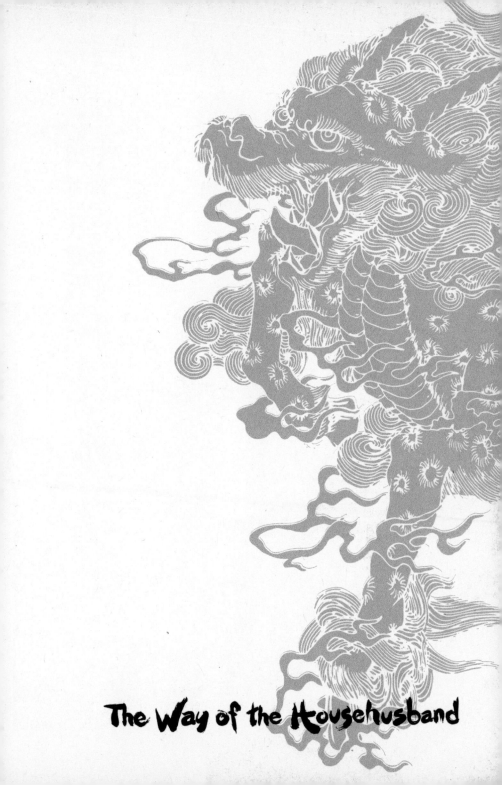

The Way of the Househusband

CHAPTER 16

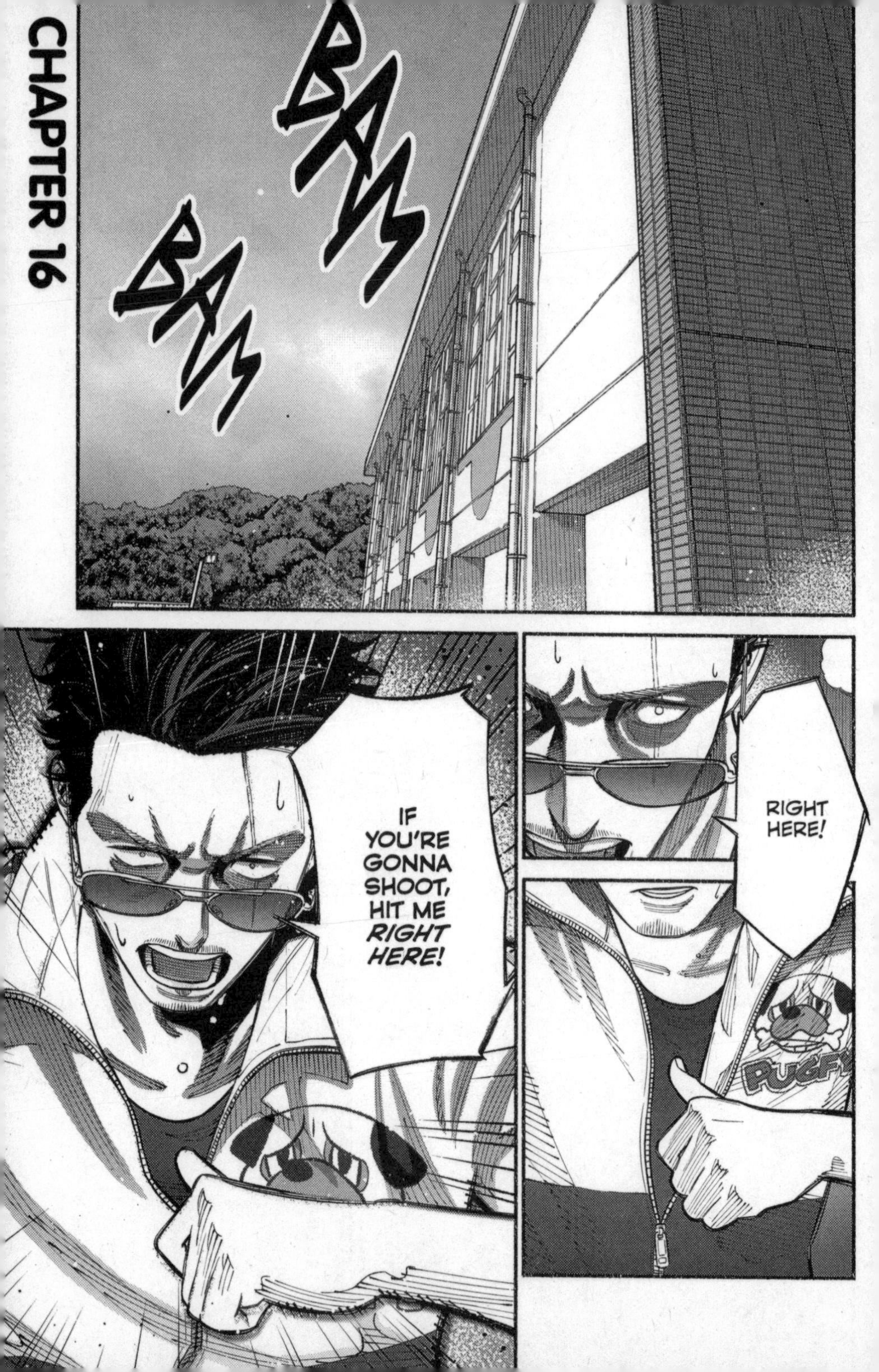
BAM
BAM
RIGHT HERE!
IF YOU'RE GONNA SHOOT, HIT ME *RIGHT HERE!*

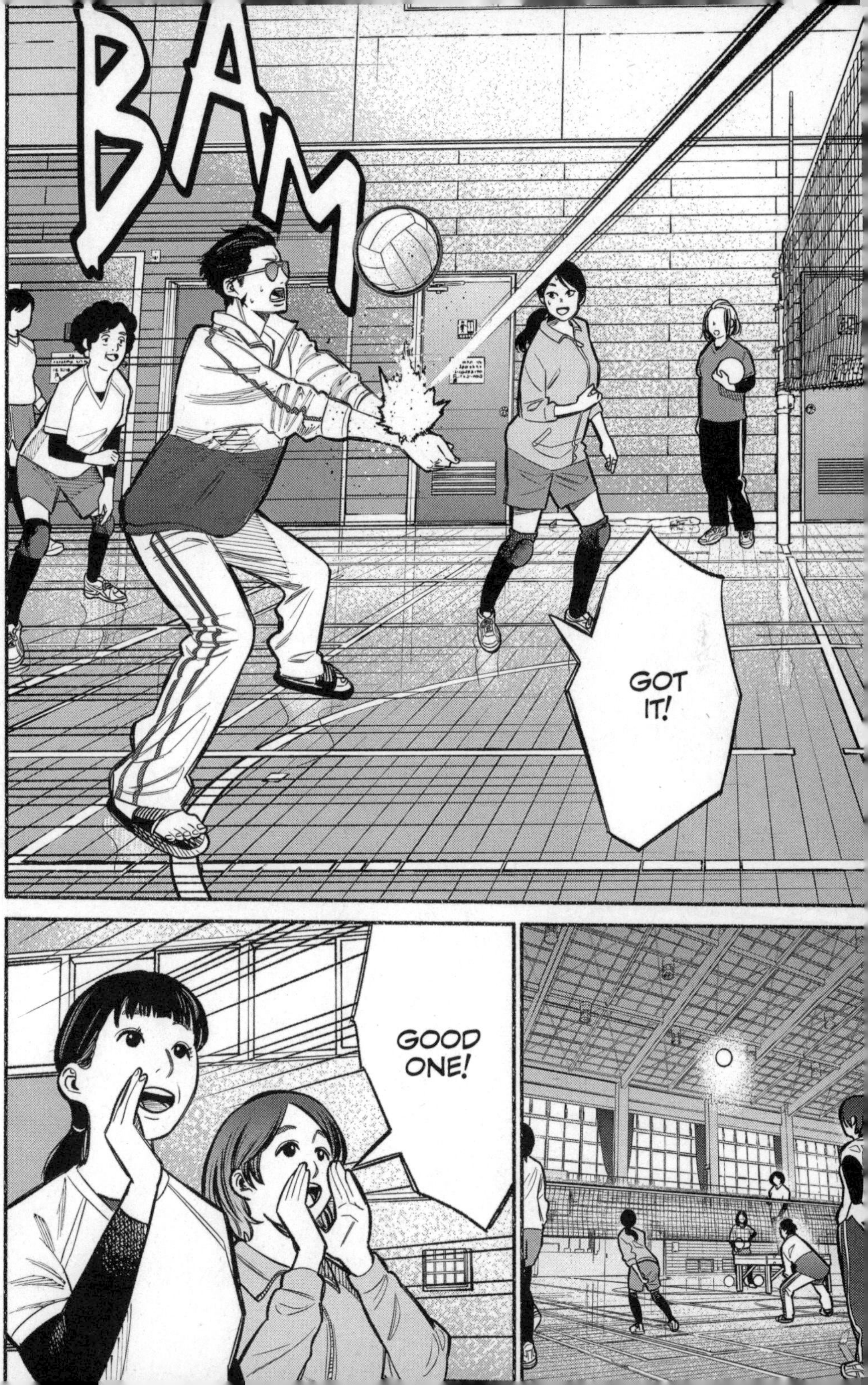
BAM
GOT IT!
GOOD ONE!

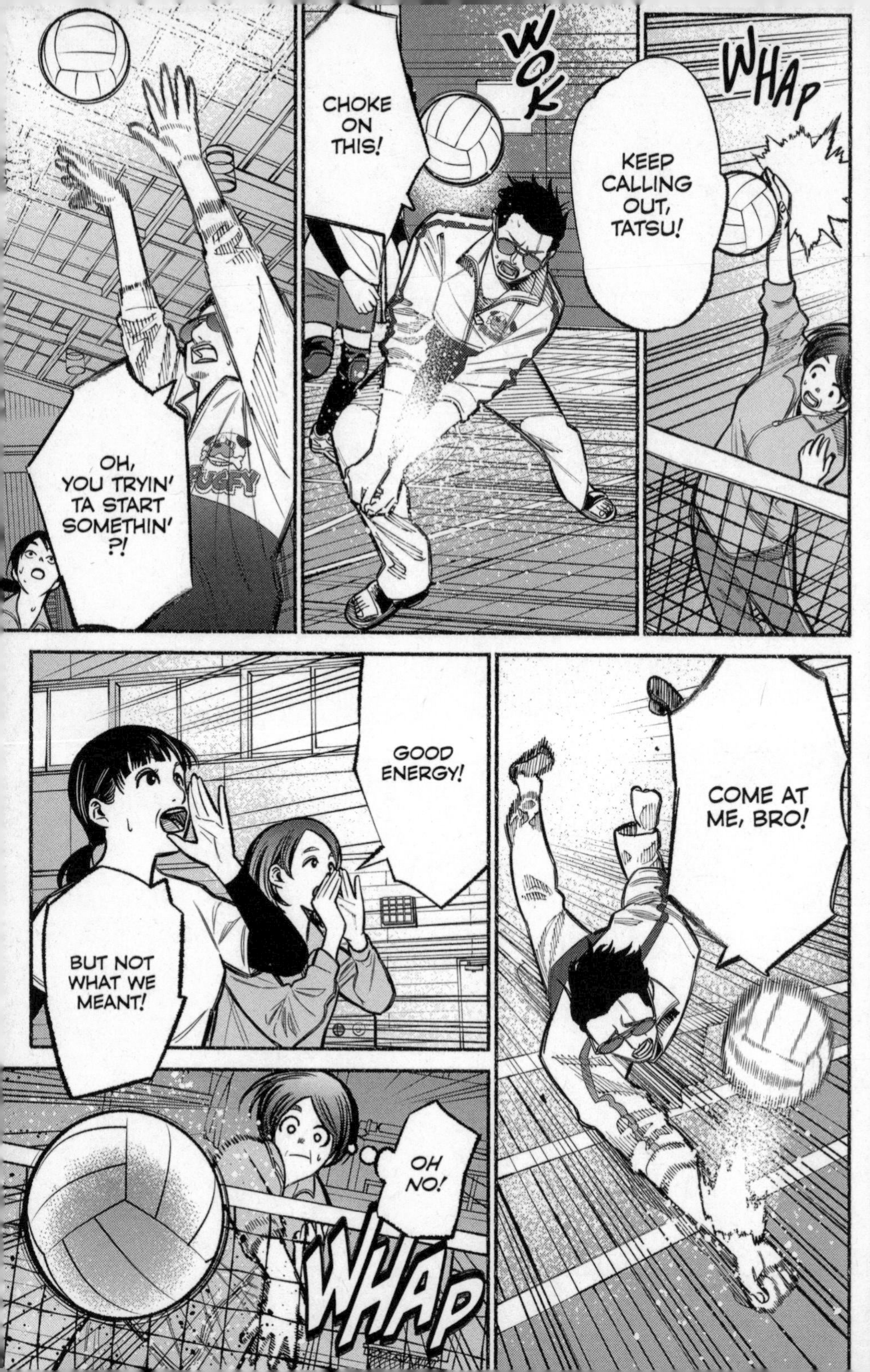
WHAP
KEEP CALLING OUT, TATSU!
WOK
CHOKE ON THIS!
OH, YOU TRYIN' TA START SOMETHIN' ?!
COME AT ME, BRO!
GOOD ENERGY!
BUT NOT WHAT WE MEANT!
OH NO!
WHAP

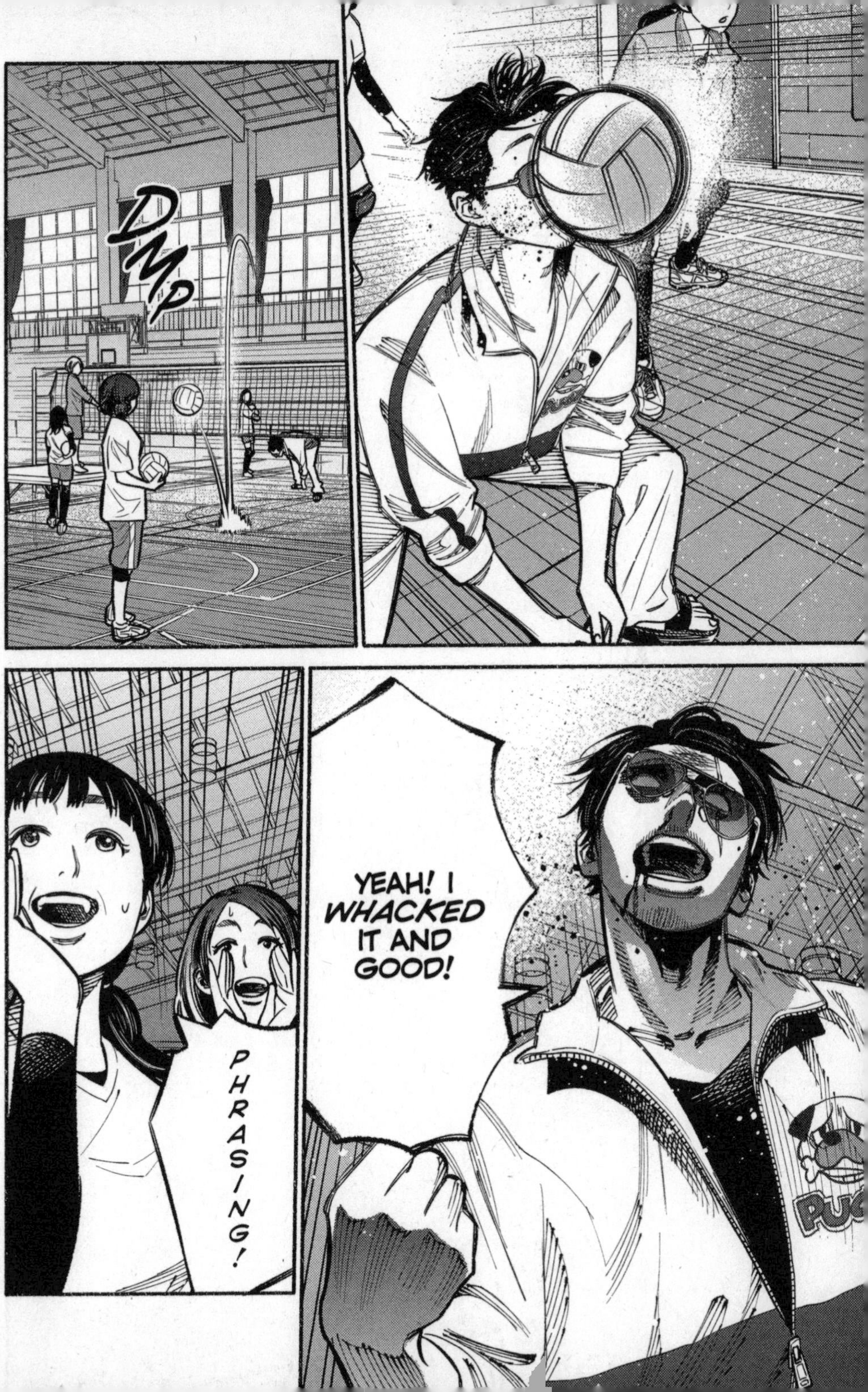
DMP
YEAH! I WHACKED IT AND GOOD!
PHRASING!

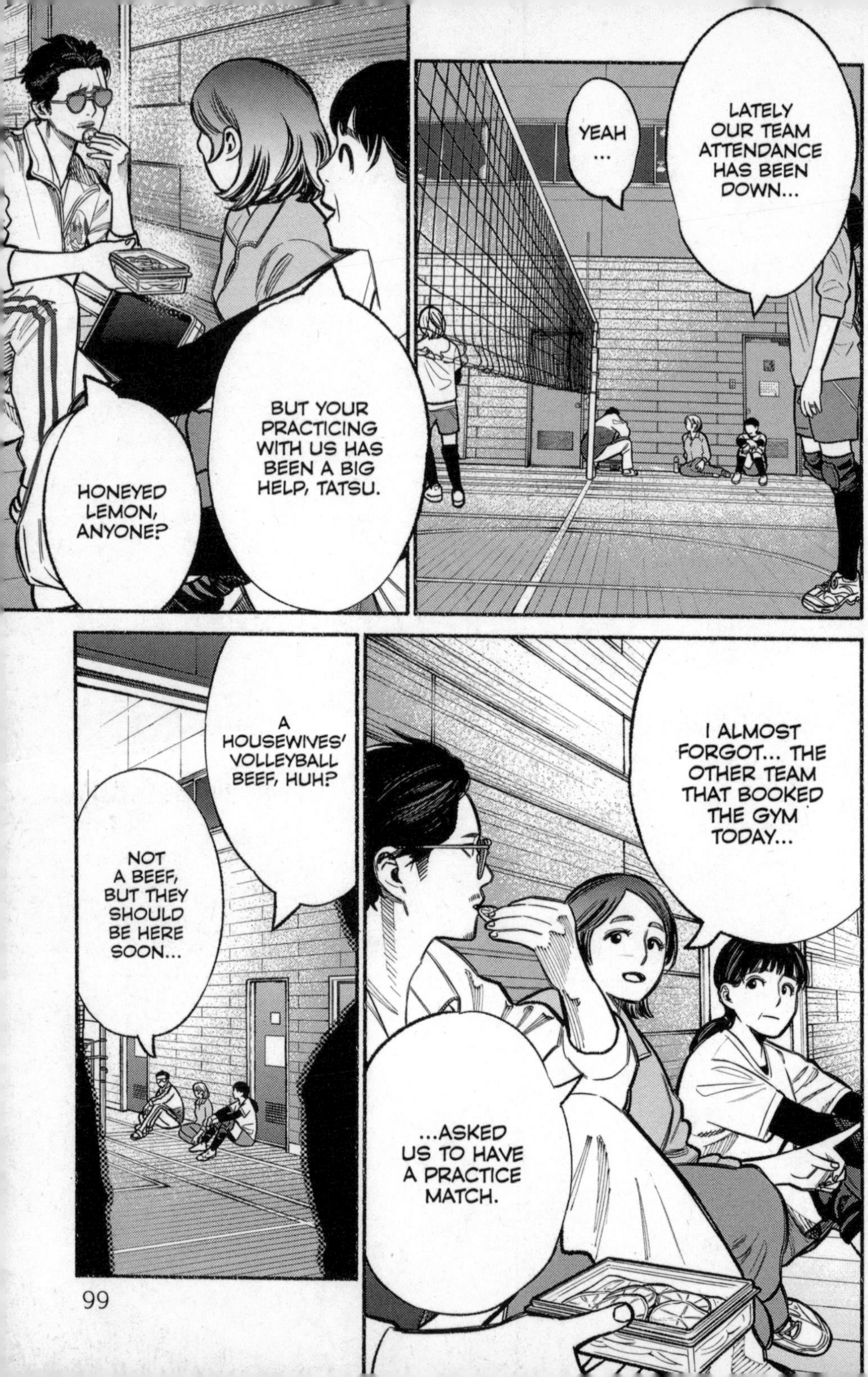
LATELY OUR TEAM ATTENDANCE HAS BEEN DOWN...
YEAH ...
BUT YOUR PRACTICING WITH US HAS BEEN A BIG HELP, TATSU.
HONEYED LEMON, ANYONE?
I ALMOST FORGOT... THE OTHER TEAM THAT BOOKED THE GYM TODAY...
...ASKED US TO HAVE A PRACTICE MATCH.
A HOUSEWIVES' VOLLEYBALL BEEF, HUH?
NOT A BEEF, BUT THEY SHOULD BE HERE SOON...

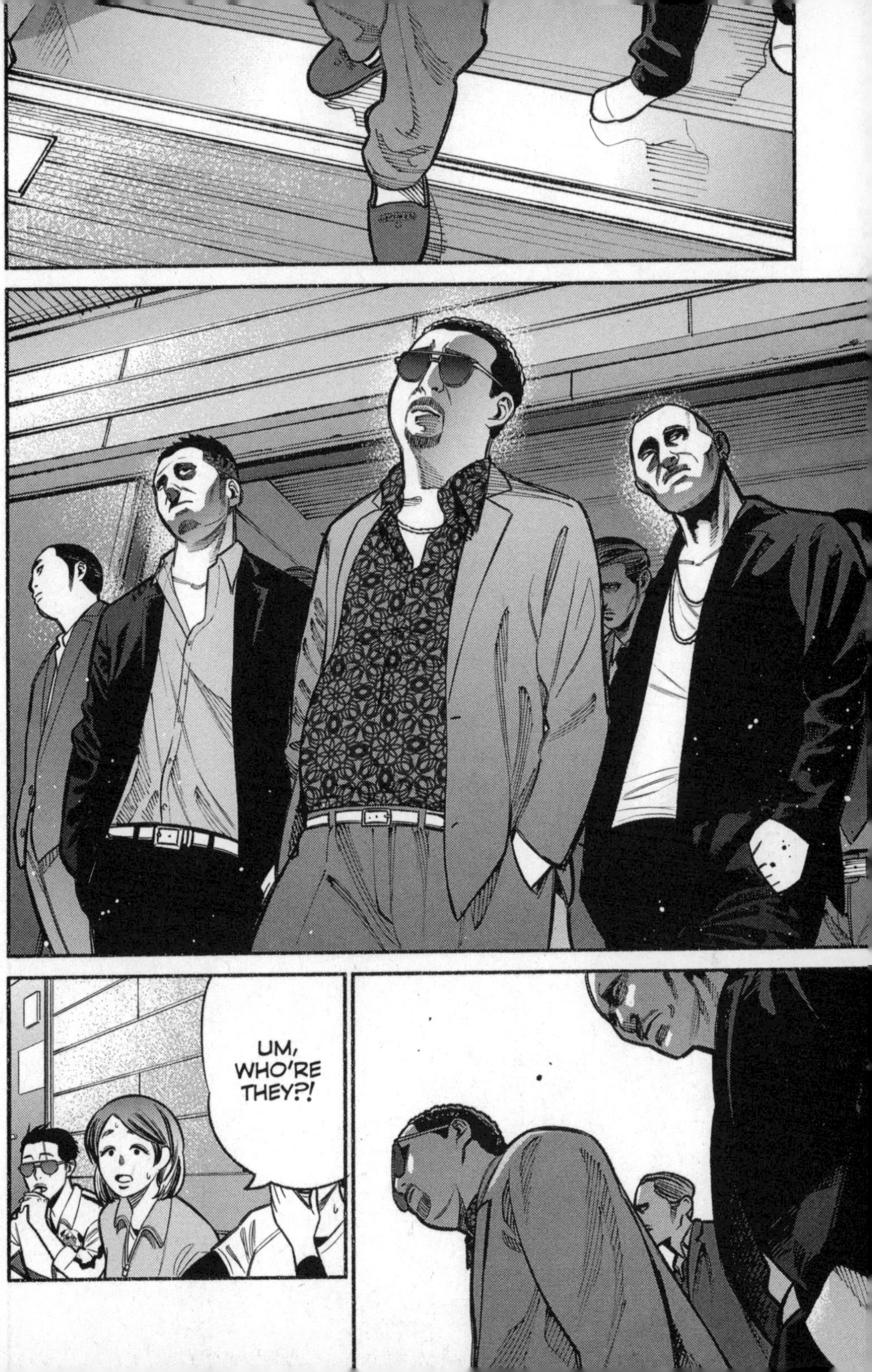
UM, WHO'RE THEY?!

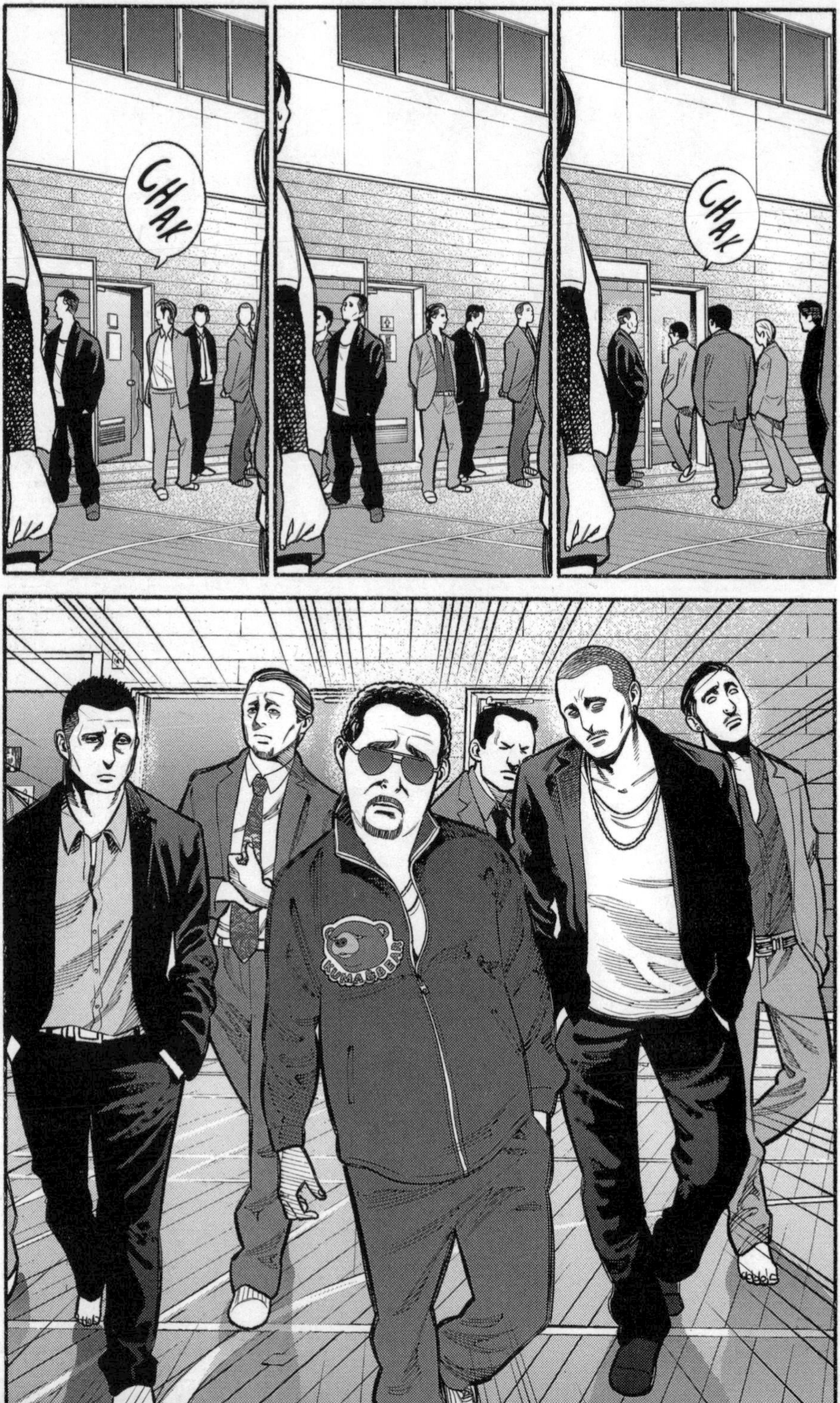
CHAK
CHAK

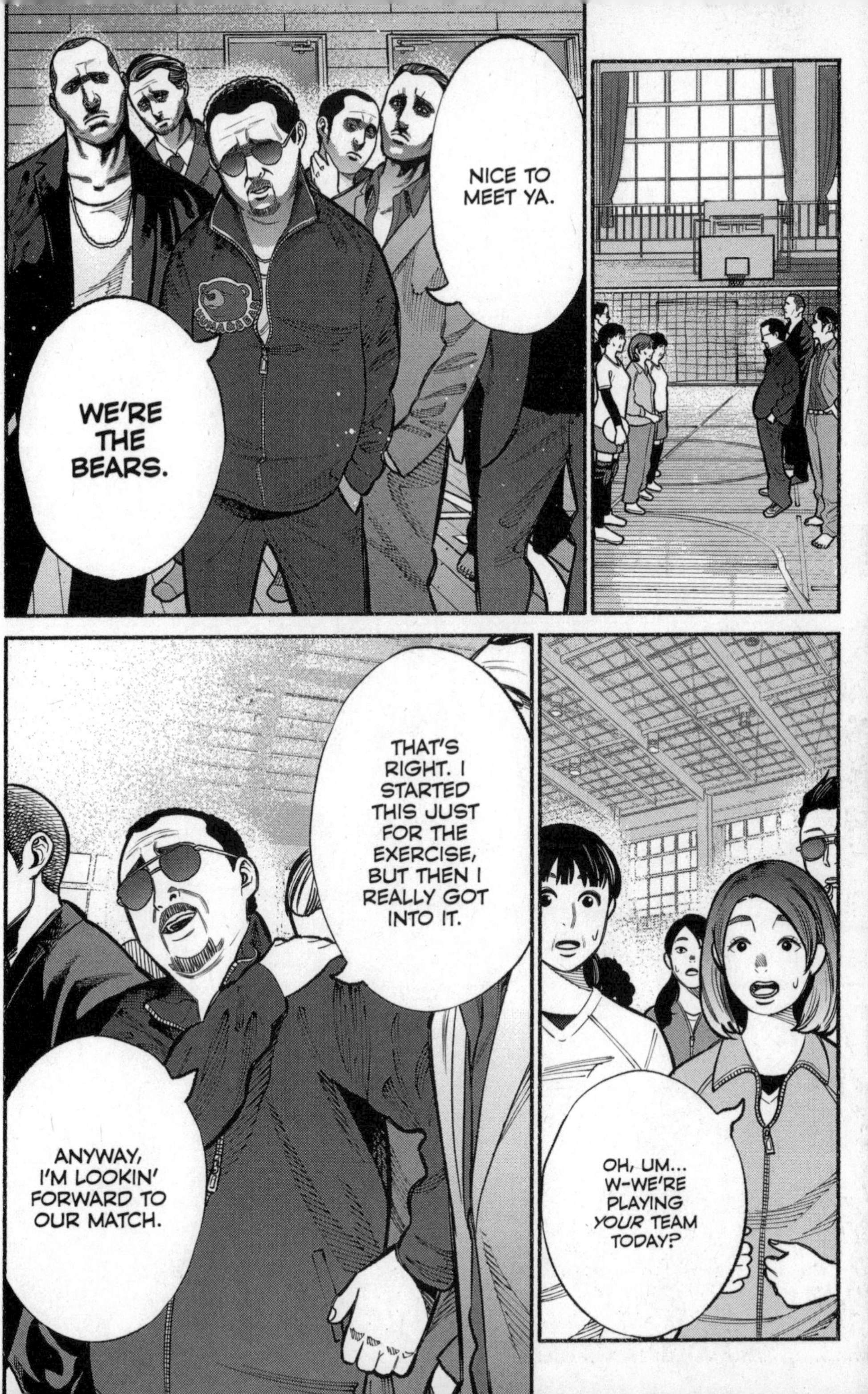
NICE TO MEET YA.
WE'RE THE BEARS.
OH, UM... W-WE'RE PLAYING *YOUR* TEAM TODAY?
THAT'S RIGHT. I STARTED THIS JUST FOR THE EXERCISE, BUT THEN I REALLY GOT INTO IT.
ANYWAY, I'M LOOKIN' FORWARD TO OUR MATCH.

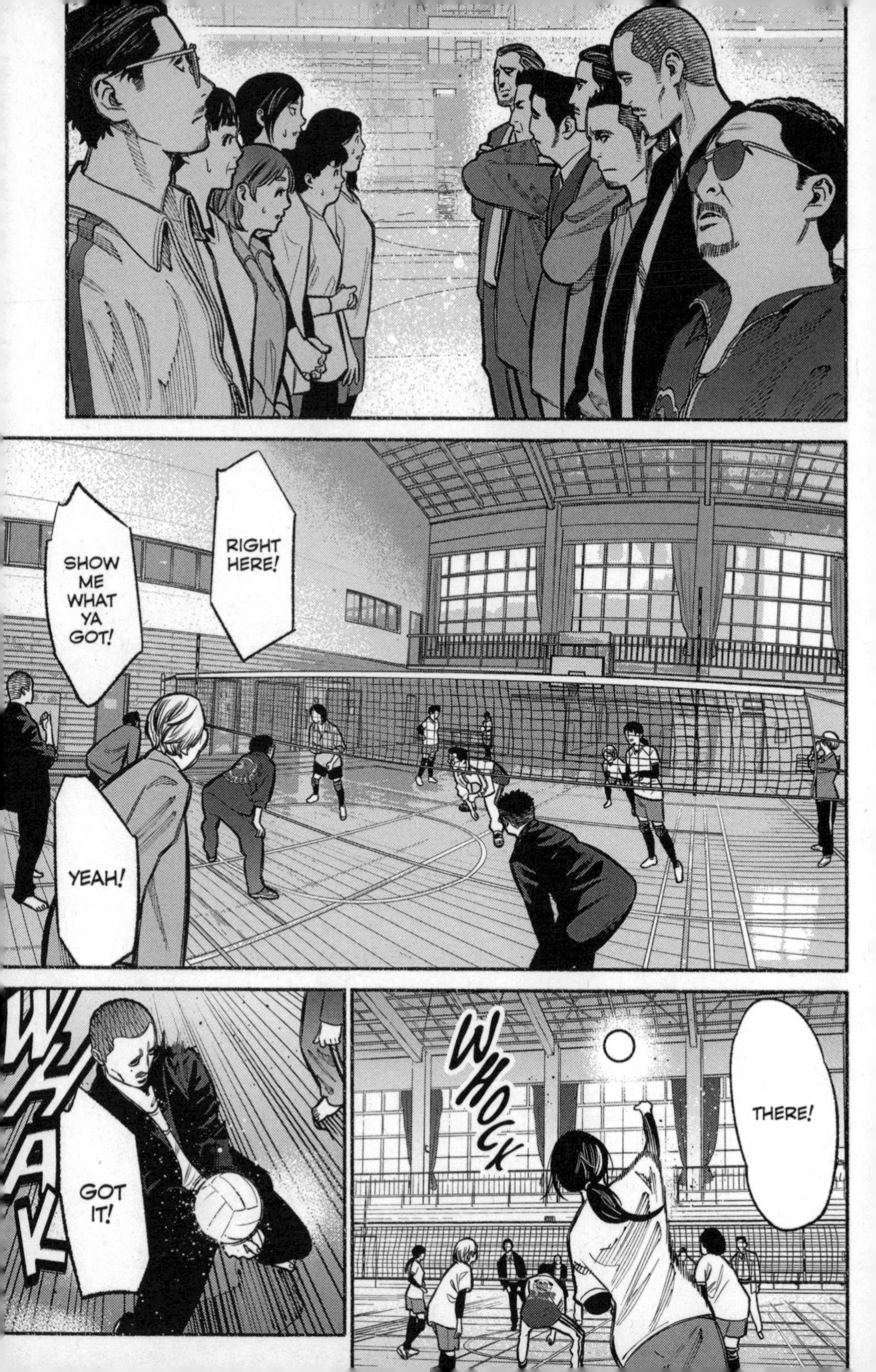
RIGHT HERE!
SHOW ME WHAT YA GOT!
YEAH!
WHOCK
THERE!
WHAK
GOT IT!

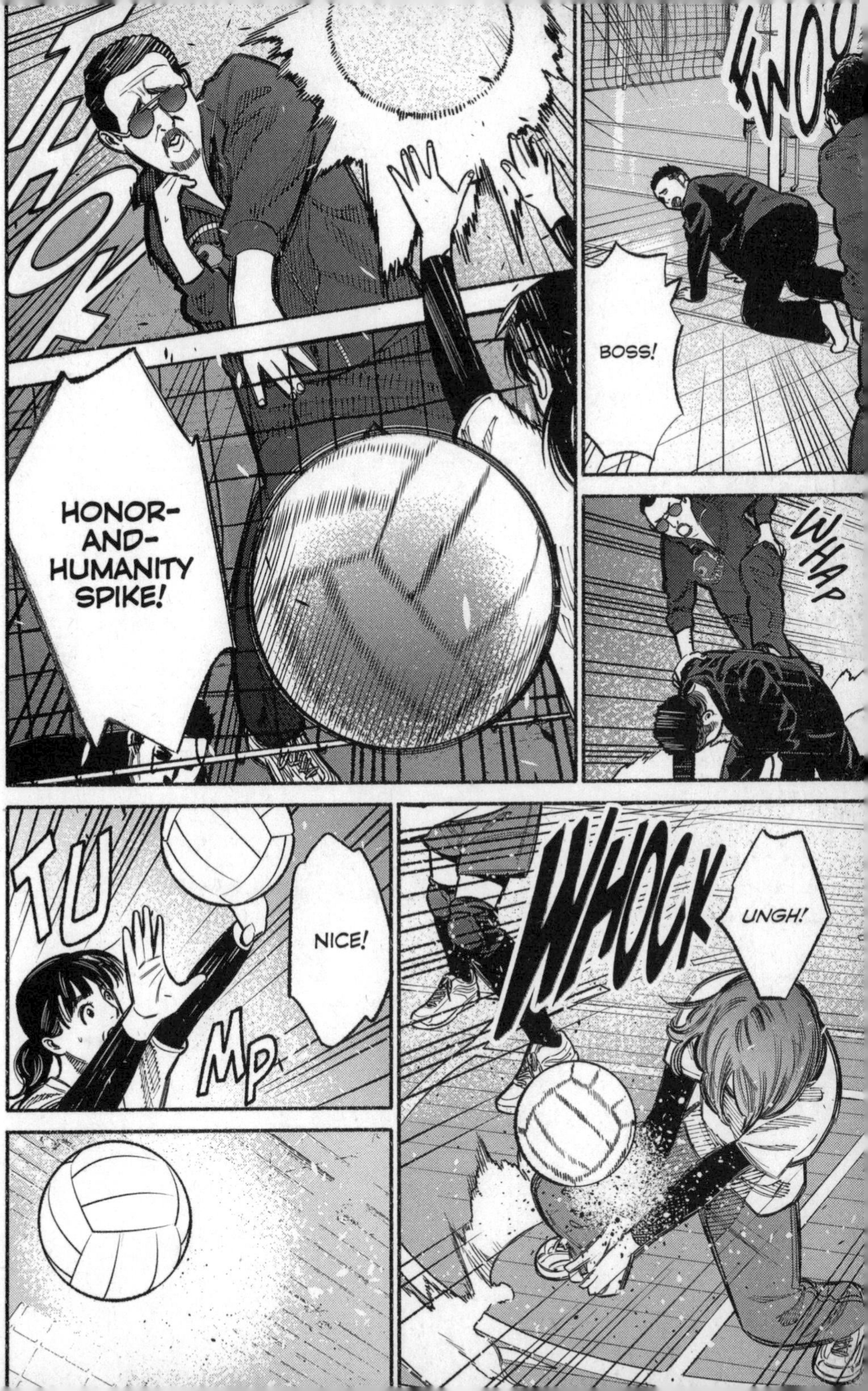
BOSS!
WHAP
HONOR-AND-HUMANITY SPIKE!
WHOCK
UNGH!
NICE!
TU
Mp

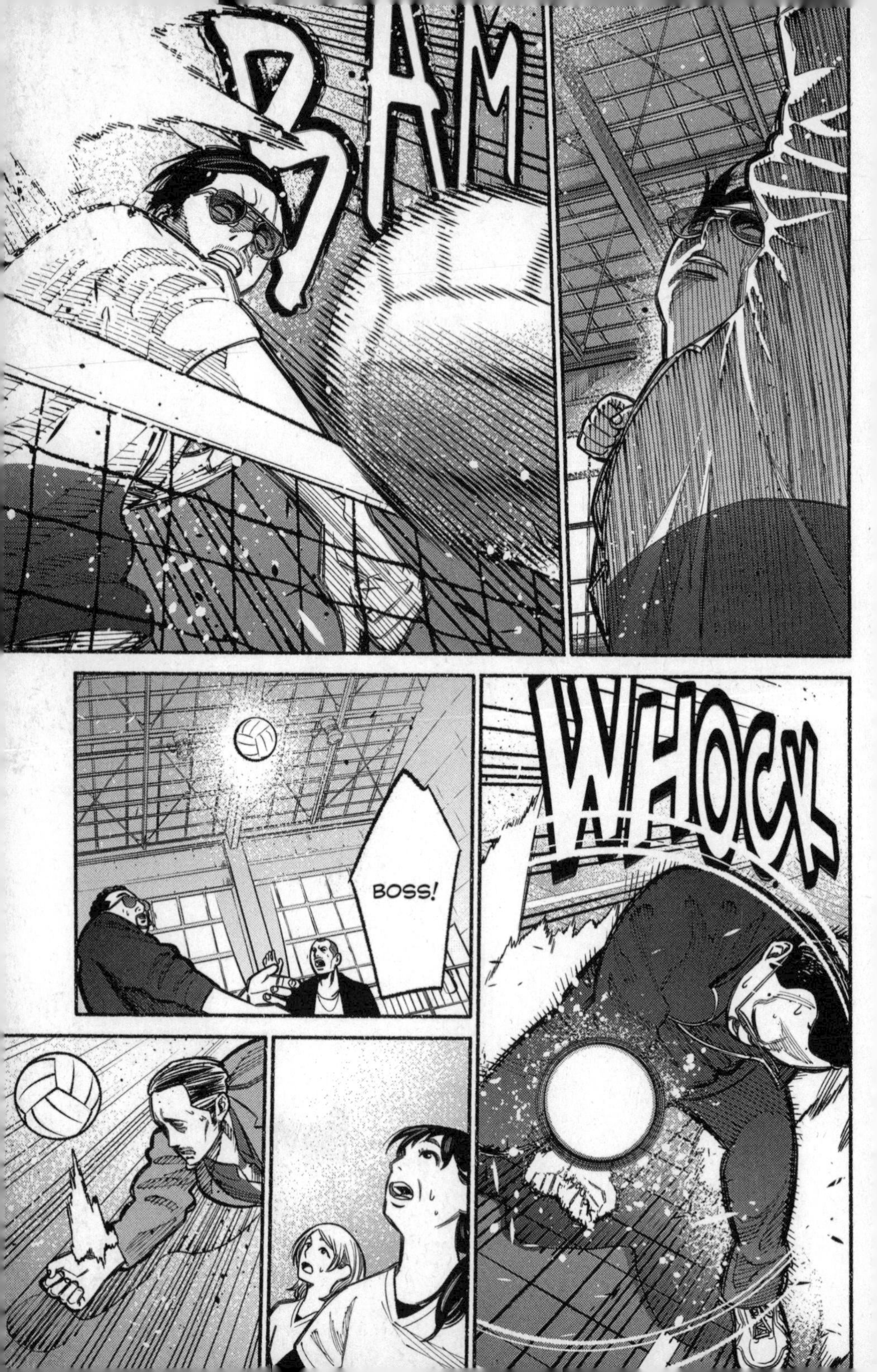
BAM
WHOCK
BOSS!

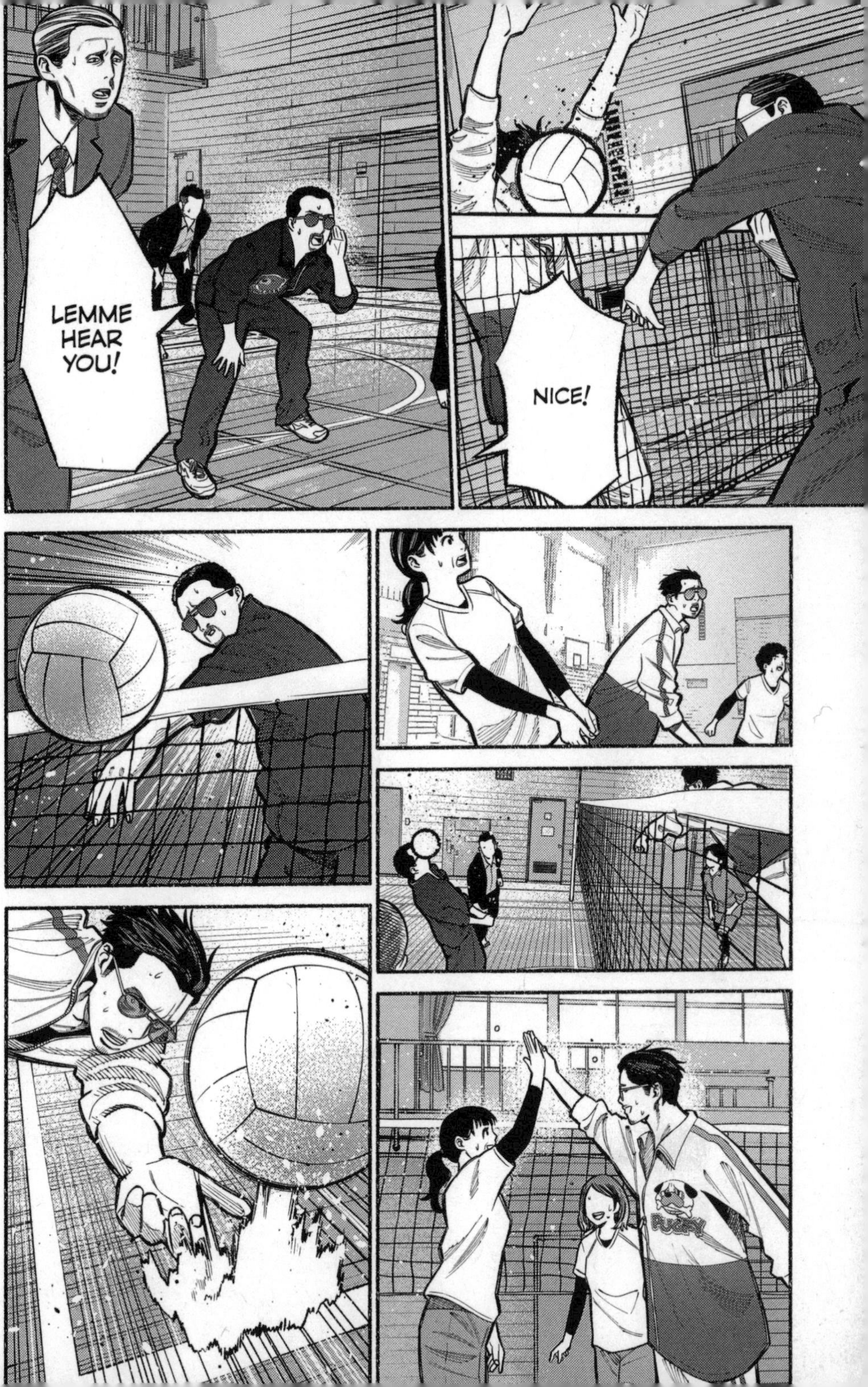
NICE!
LEMME HEAR YOU!

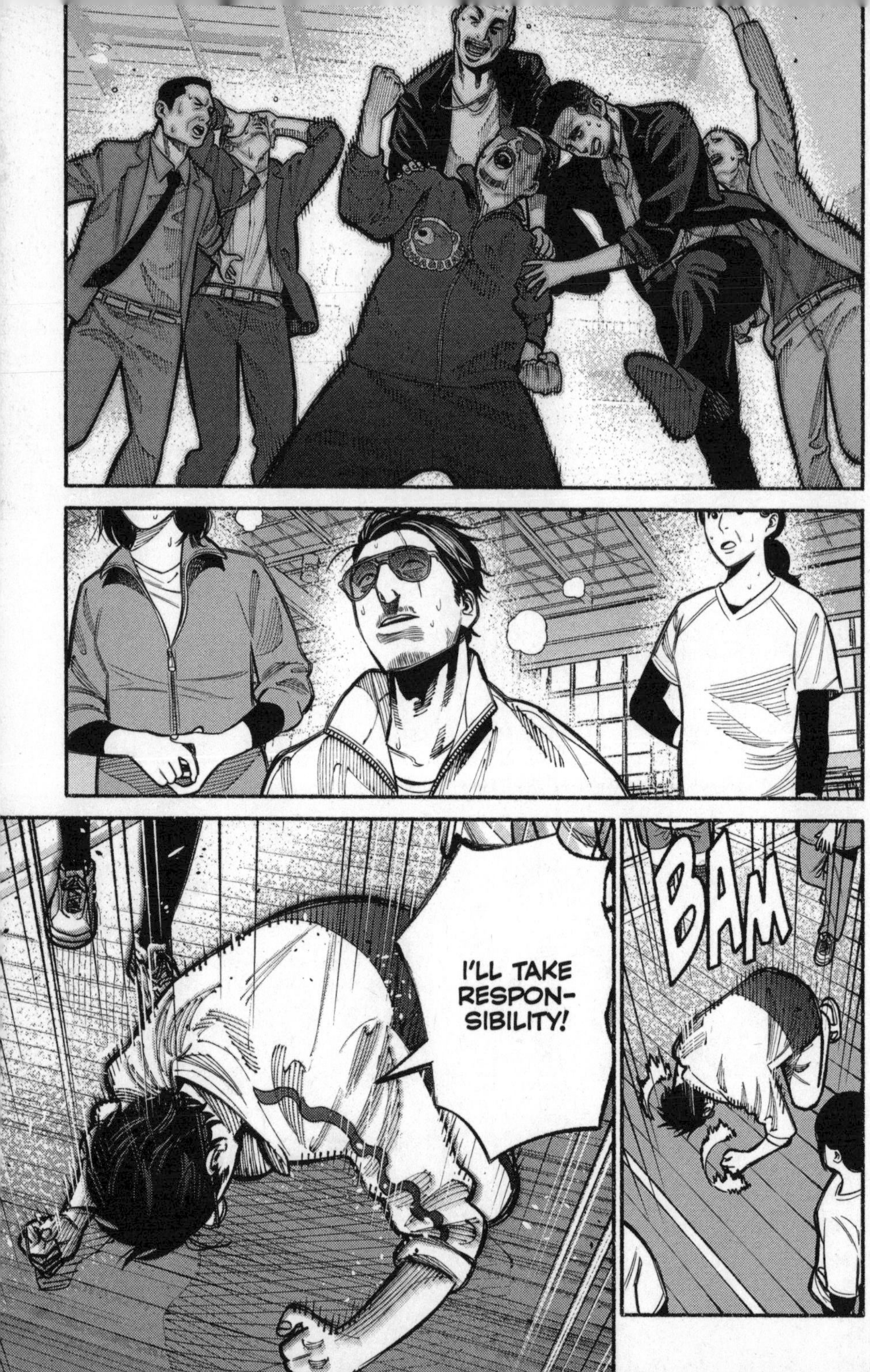
BAM
I'LL TAKE RESPON-SIBILITY!

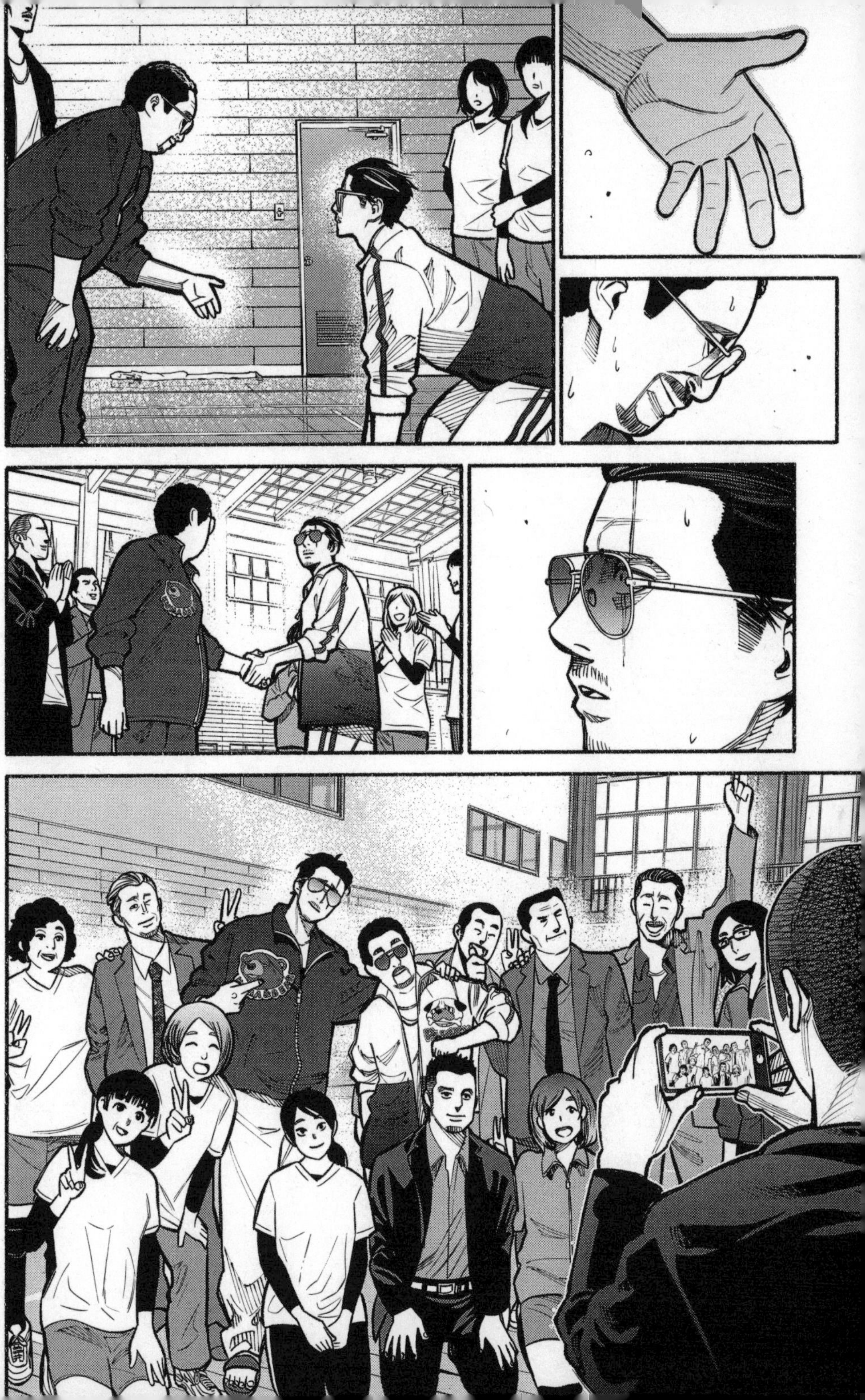

KUMA & BEAR

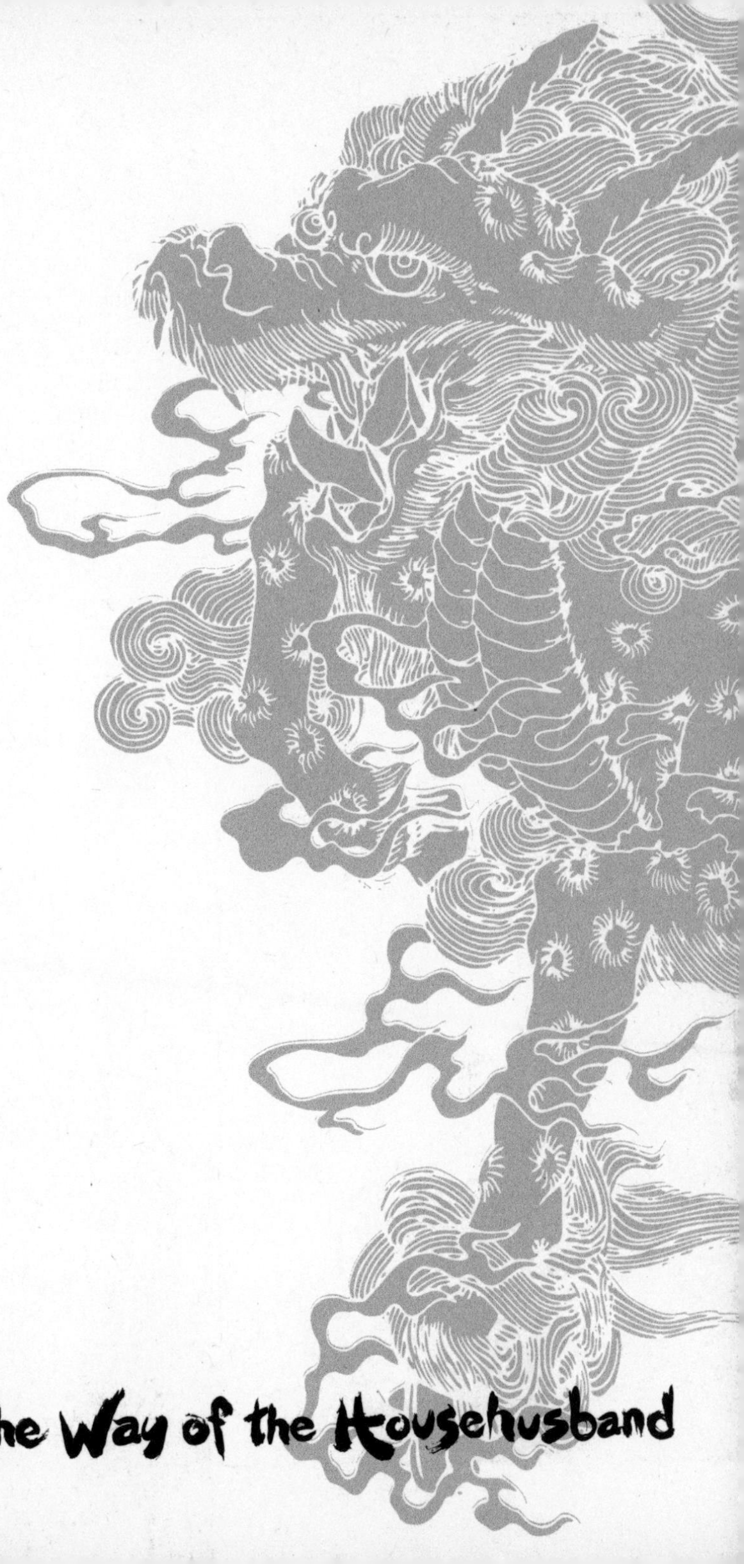

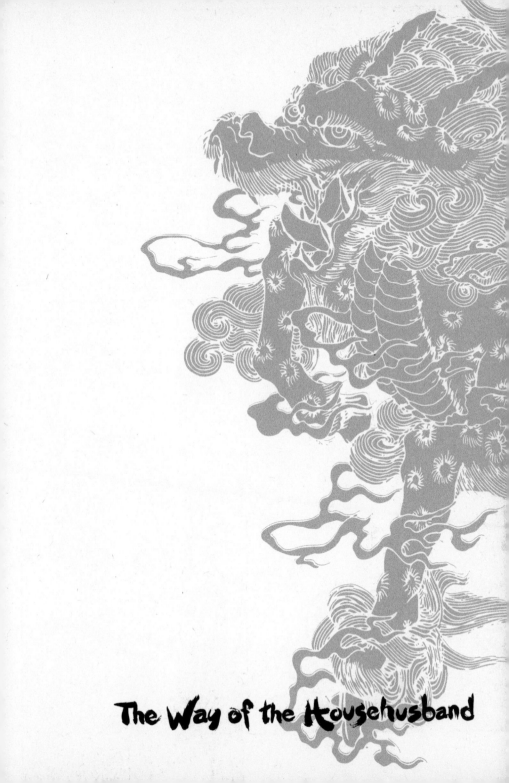

The Way of the Househusband

CHAPTER 17

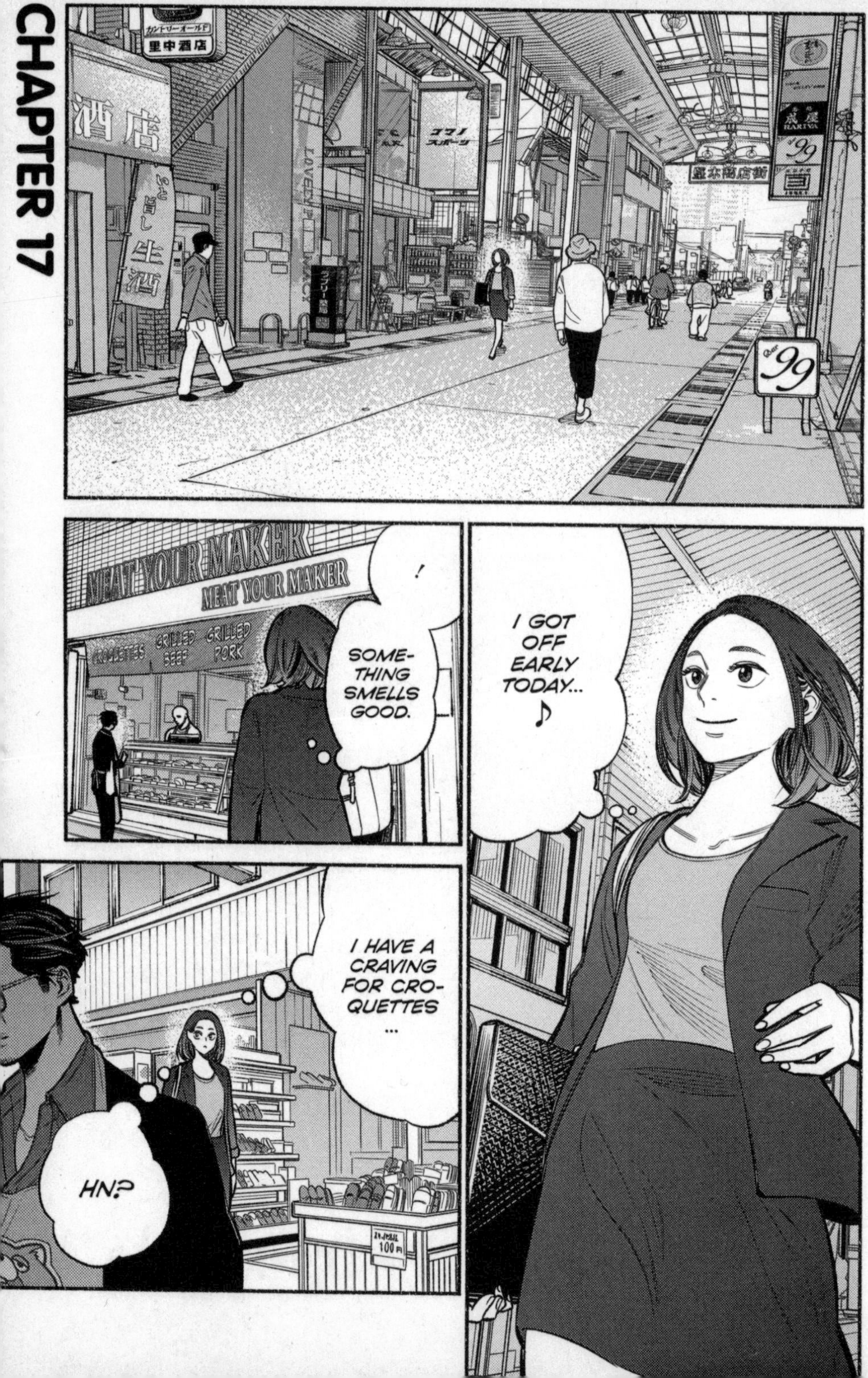
I GOT OFF EARLY TODAY... ♪
MEAT YOUR MAKER
MEAT YOUR MAKER
CROQUETTES
GRILLED BEEF
GRILLED PORK
!
SOME-THING SMELLS GOOD.
I HAVE A CRAVING FOR CRO-QUETTES ...
HN?

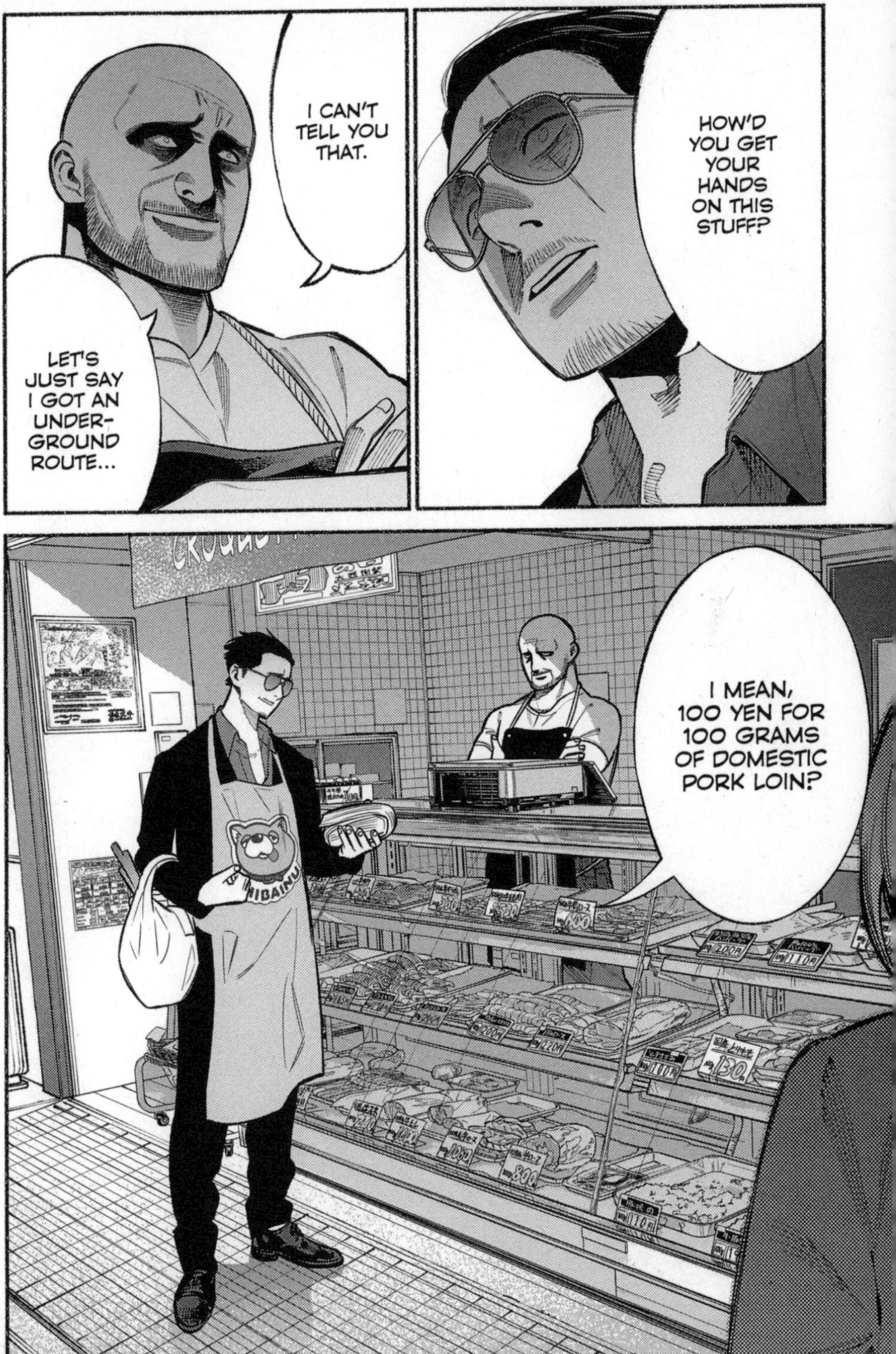
HOW'D YOU GET YOUR HANDS ON THIS STUFF?
I CAN'T TELL YOU THAT.
LET'S JUST SAY I GOT AN UNDER-GROUND ROUTE...
I MEAN, 100 YEN FOR 100 GRAMS OF DOMESTIC PORK LOIN?

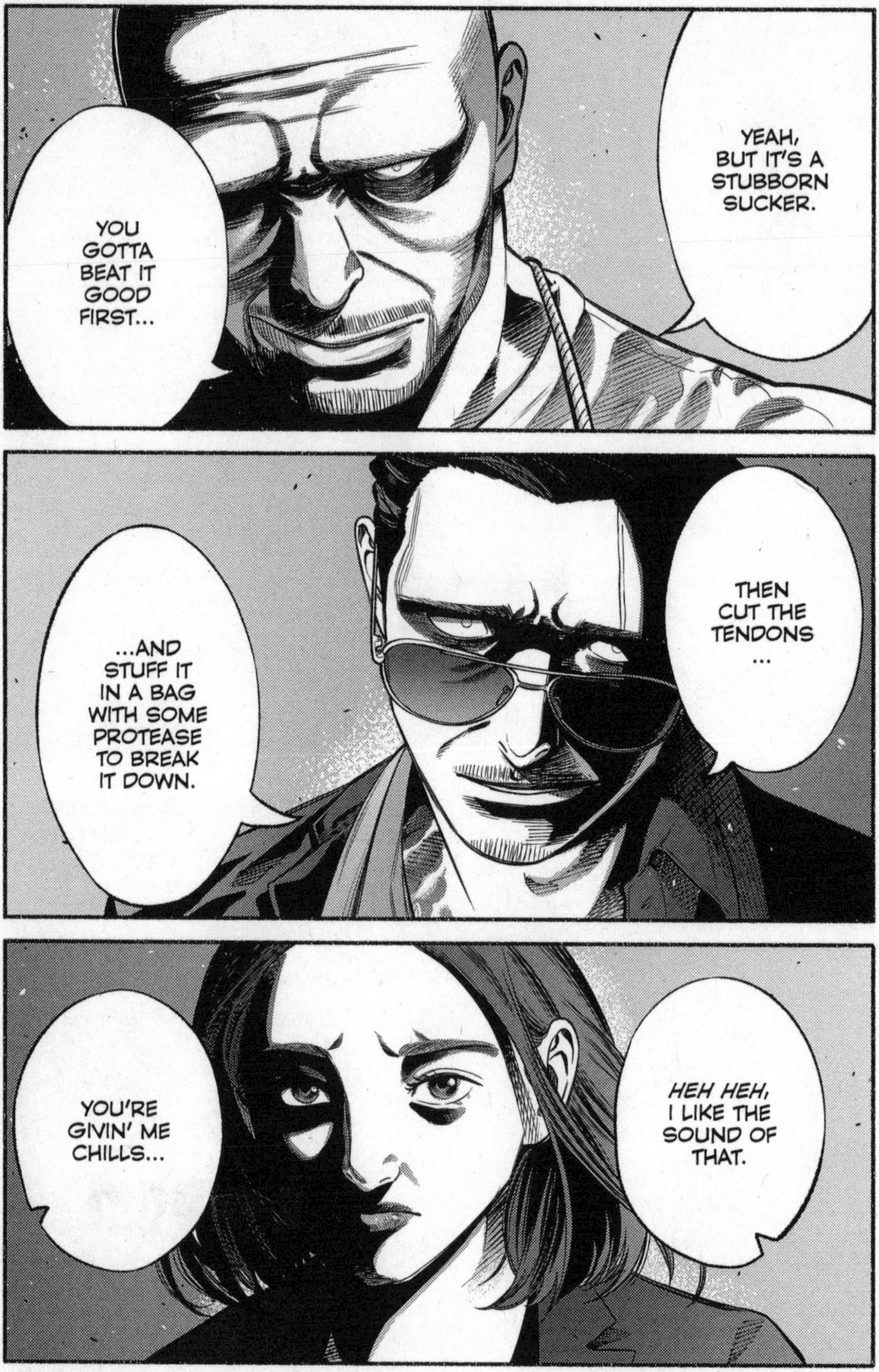
YEAH, BUT IT'S A STUBBORN SUCKER.
YOU GOTTA BEAT IT GOOD FIRST...
THEN CUT THE TENDONS ...
...AND STUFF IT IN A BAG WITH SOME PROTEASE TO BREAK IT DOWN.
HEH HEH, I LIKE THE SOUND OF THAT.
YOU'RE GIVIN' ME CHILLS...

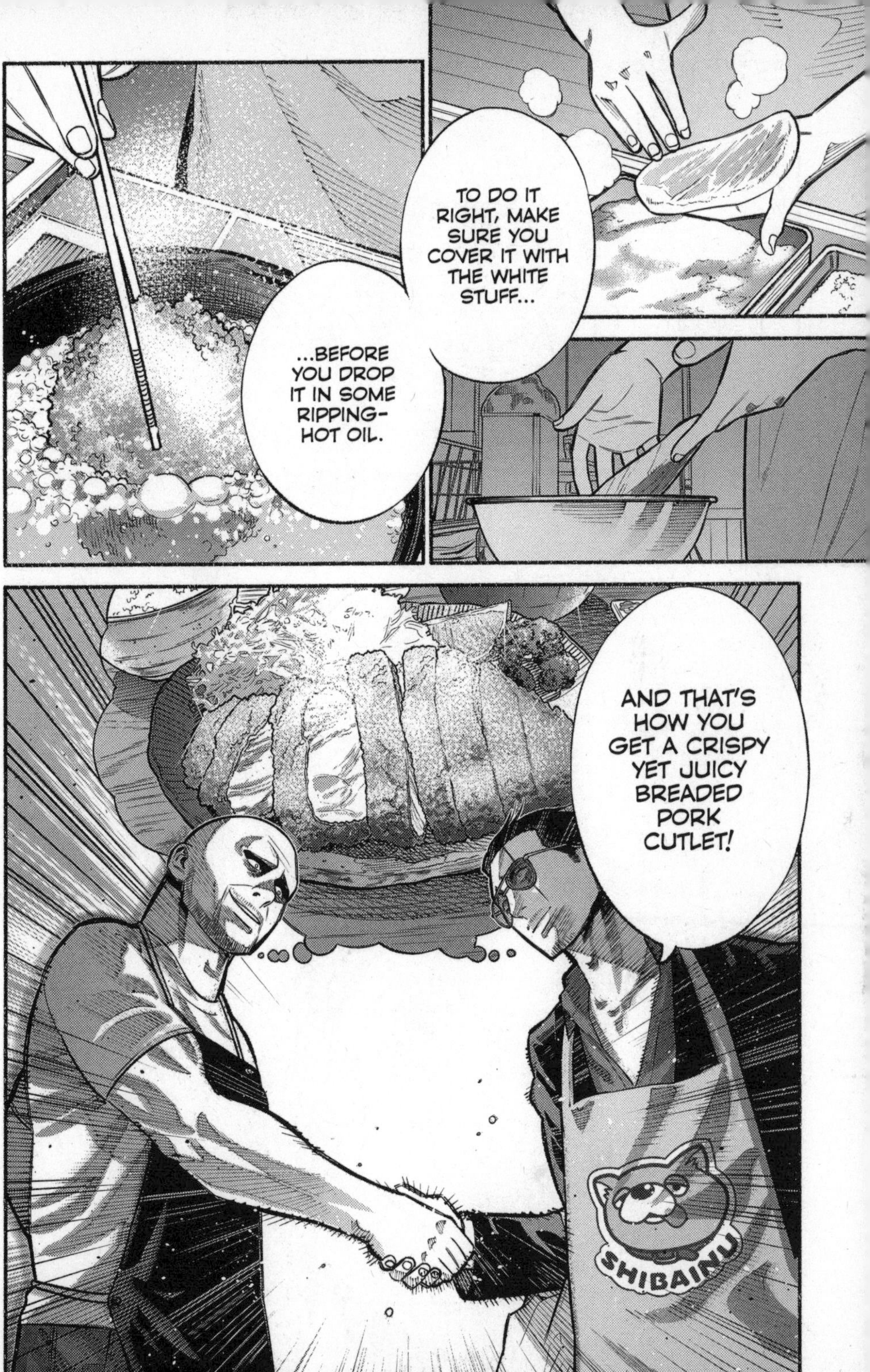
TO DO IT RIGHT, MAKE SURE YOU COVER IT WITH THE WHITE STUFF...
...BEFORE YOU DROP IT IN SOME RIPPING-HOT OIL.
AND THAT'S HOW YOU GET A CRISPY YET JUICY BREADED PORK CUTLET!
SHIBAINU

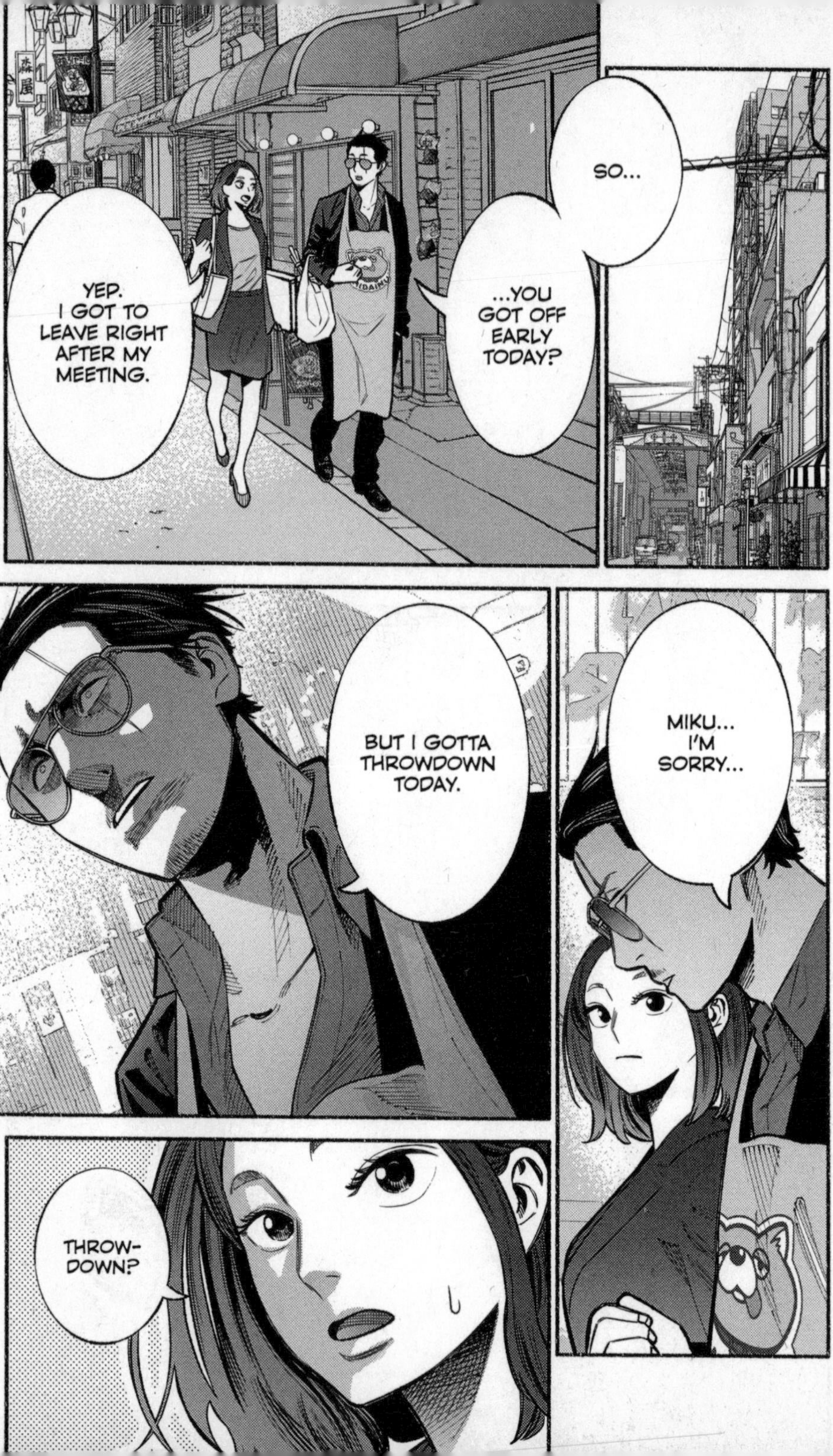
SO...
...YOU GOT OFF EARLY TODAY?
YEP. I GOT TO LEAVE RIGHT AFTER MY MEETING.
MIKU... I'M SORRY...
BUT I GOTTA THROWDOWN TODAY.
THROW-DOWN?

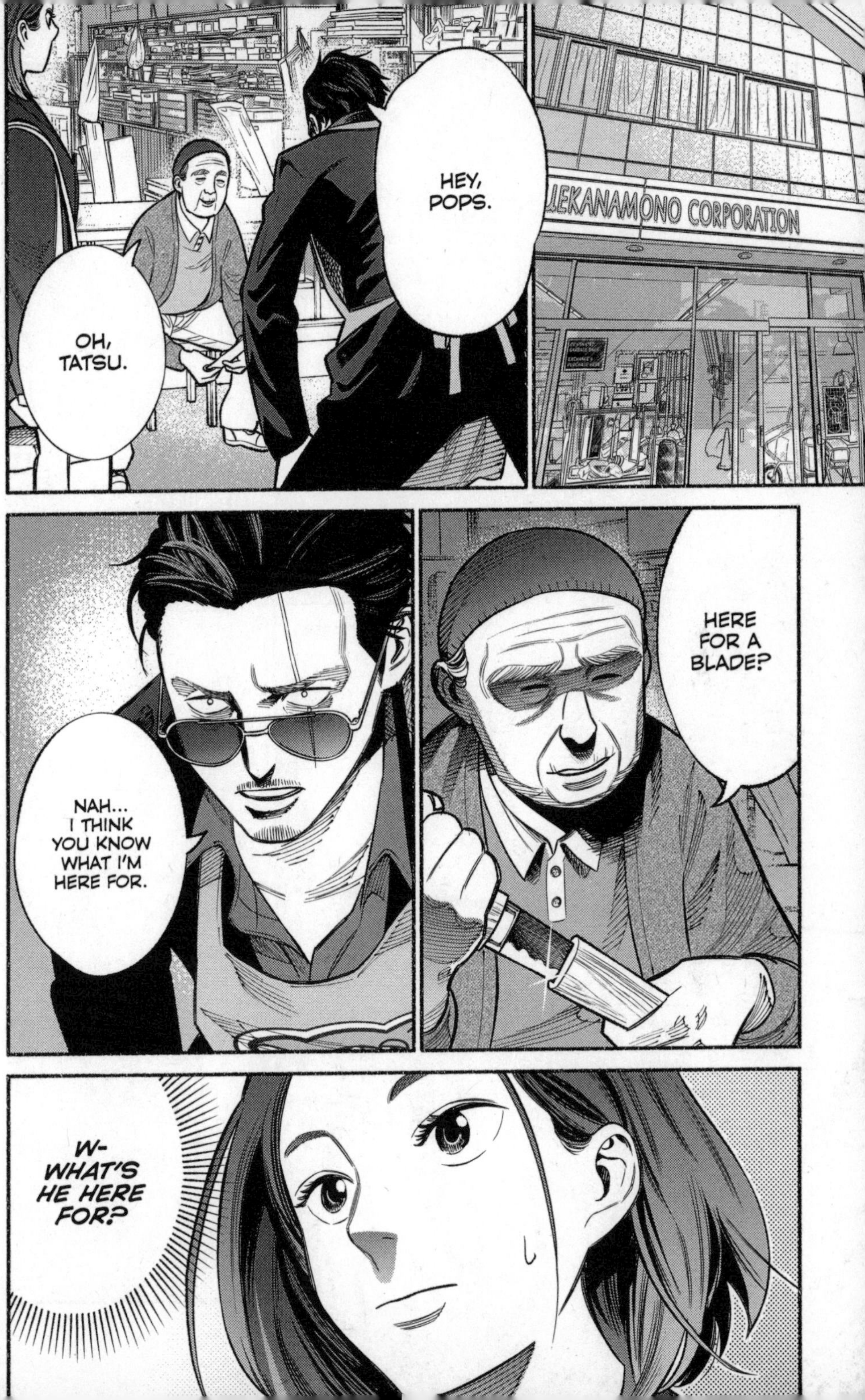
EKANAMONO CORPORATION
HEY, POPS.
OH, TATSU.
HERE FOR A BLADE?
NAH... I THINK YOU KNOW WHAT I'M HERE FOR.
W- WHAT'S HE HERE FOR?

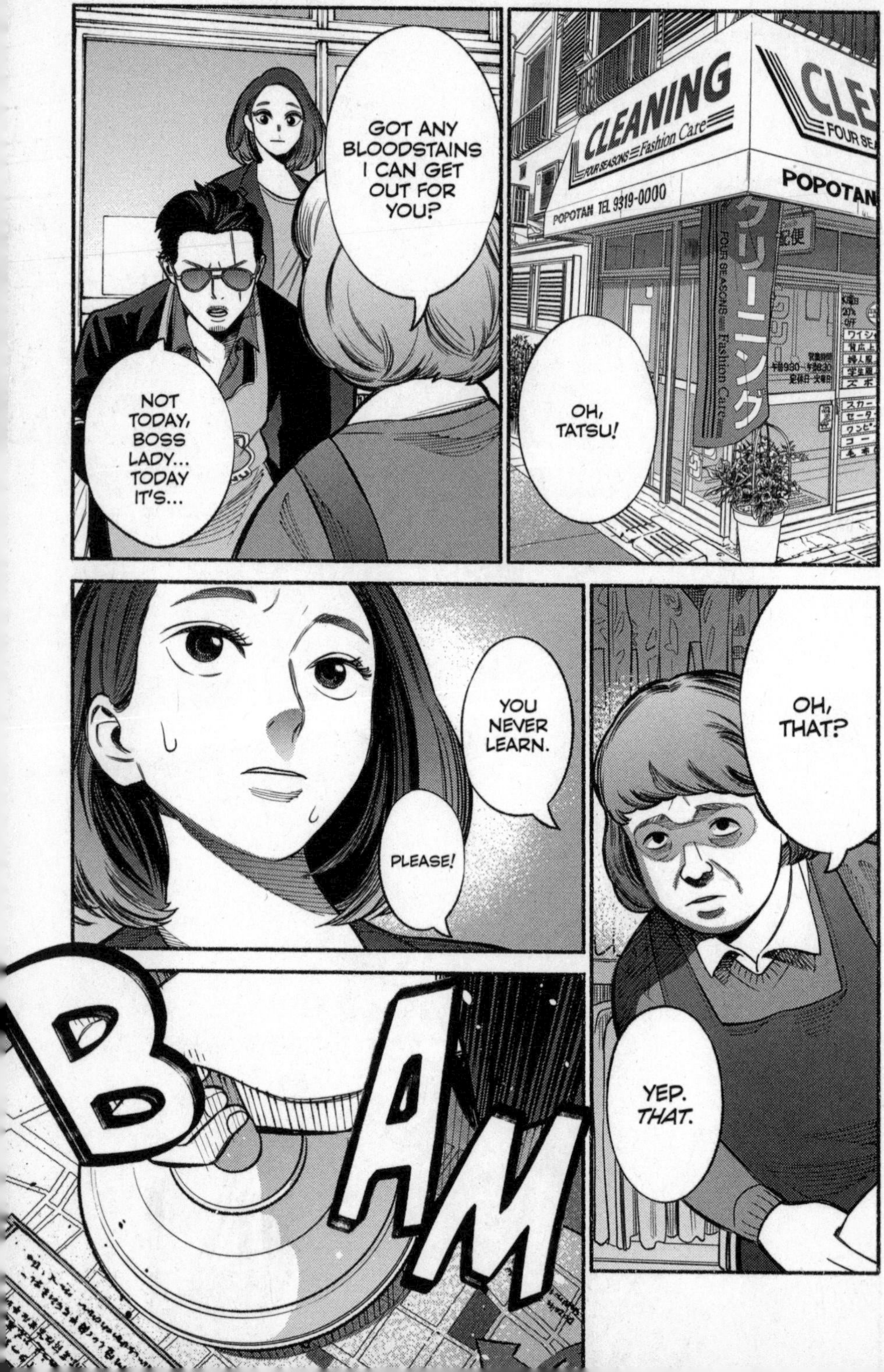
CLEANING
FOUR SEASONS Fashion Care
POPOTAN TEL 9319-0000
POPOTAN
FOUR SEASONS Fashion Care
OH, TATSU!
GOT ANY BLOODSTAINS I CAN GET OUT FOR YOU?
NOT TODAY, BOSS LADY... TODAY IT'S...
OH, THAT?
YEP. *THAT.*
YOU NEVER LEARN.
PLEASE!
BAM

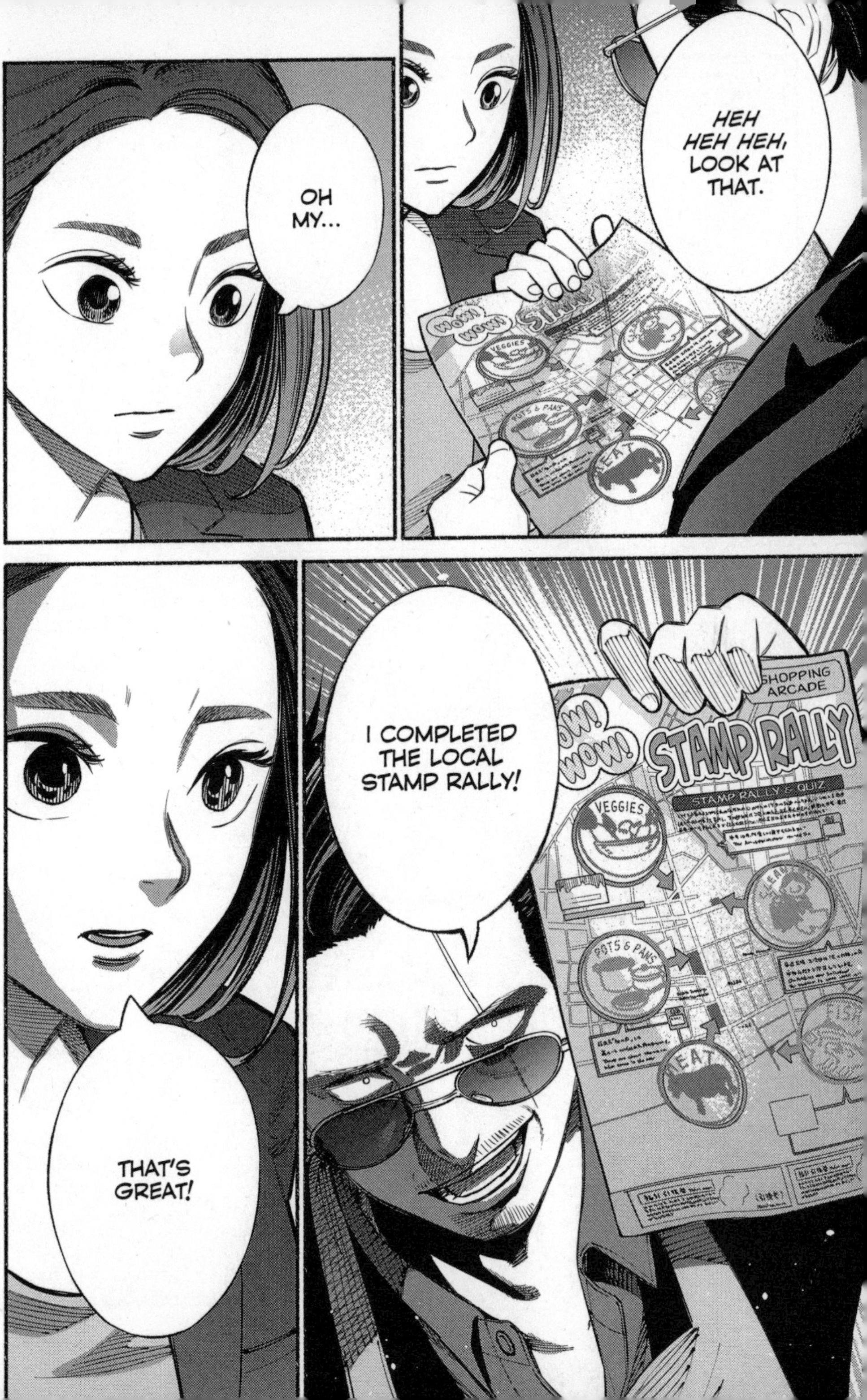
HEH HEH HEH, LOOK AT THAT.
VEGGIES
POTS & PANS
MEAT
OH MY...
I COMPLETED THE LOCAL STAMP RALLY!
SHOPPING ARCADE
WOW!
STAMP RALLY
STAMP RALLY & QUIZ
VEGGIES
POTS & PANS
MEAT
THAT'S GREAT!

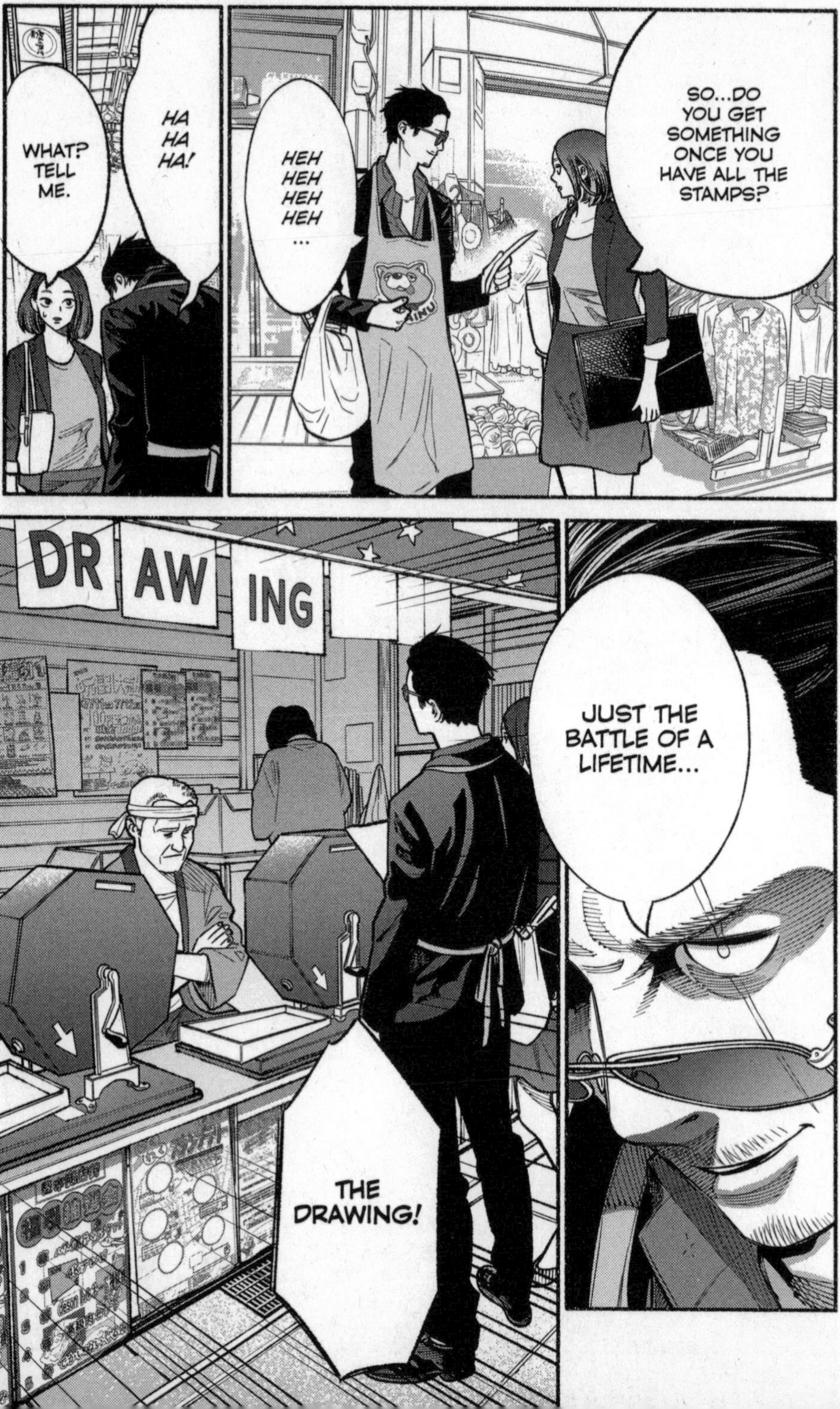
SO...DO YOU GET SOMETHING ONCE YOU HAVE ALL THE STAMPS?
HEH HEH HEH HEH ...
HA HA HA!
WHAT? TELL ME.
JUST THE BATTLE OF A LIFETIME...
DR AW ING
THE DRAWING!

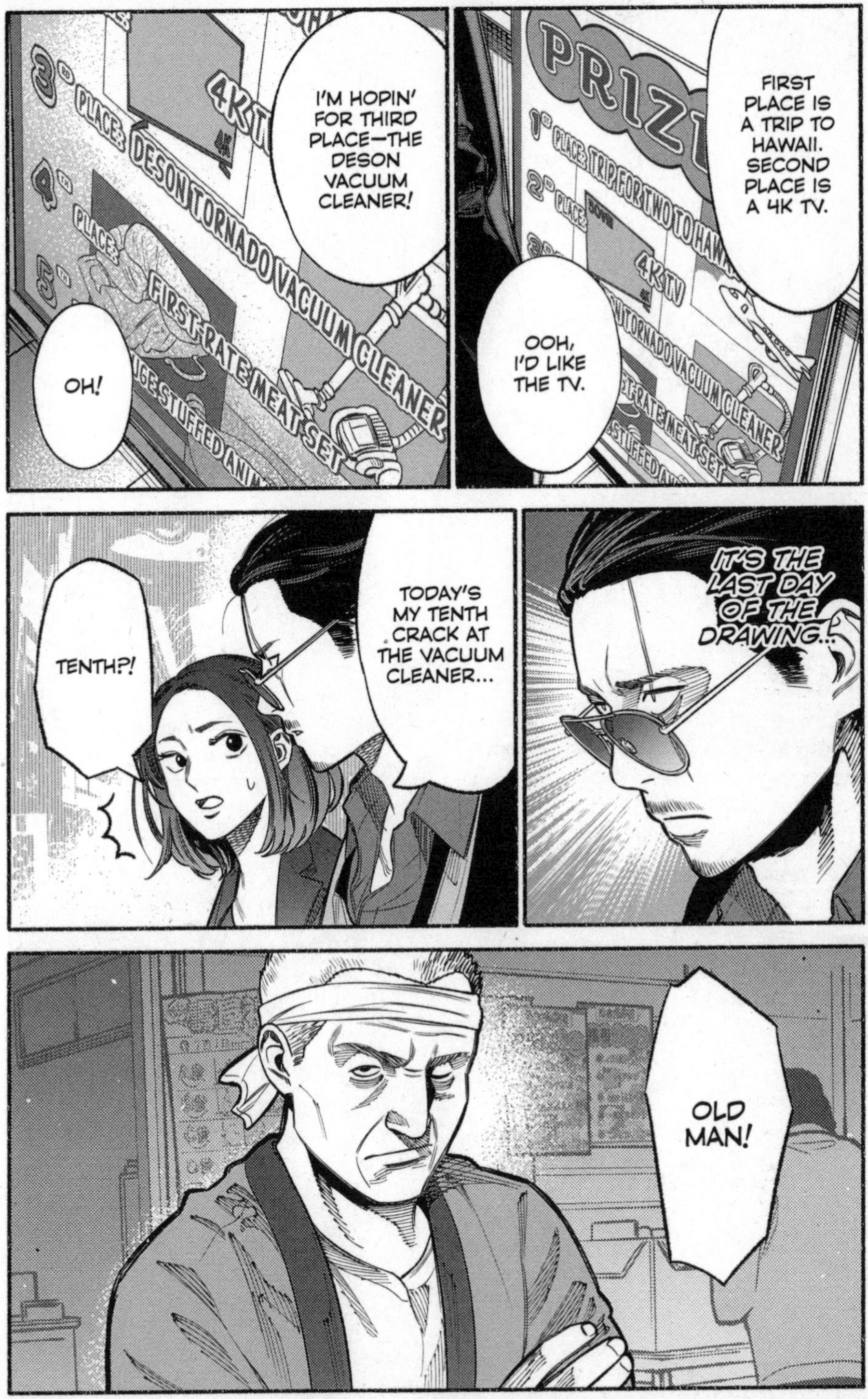
FIRST PLACE IS A TRIP TO HAWAII. SECOND PLACE IS A 4K TV.
4K TV
OOH, I'D LIKE THE TV.
I'M HOPIN' FOR THIRD PLACE—THE DESON VACUUM CLEANER!
DESON TORNADO VACUUM CLEANER
FIRST-RATE MEAT SET
OH!
IT'S THE LAST DAY OF THE DRAWING...
TODAY'S MY TENTH CRACK AT THE VACUUM CLEANER...
TENTH?!
OLD MAN!

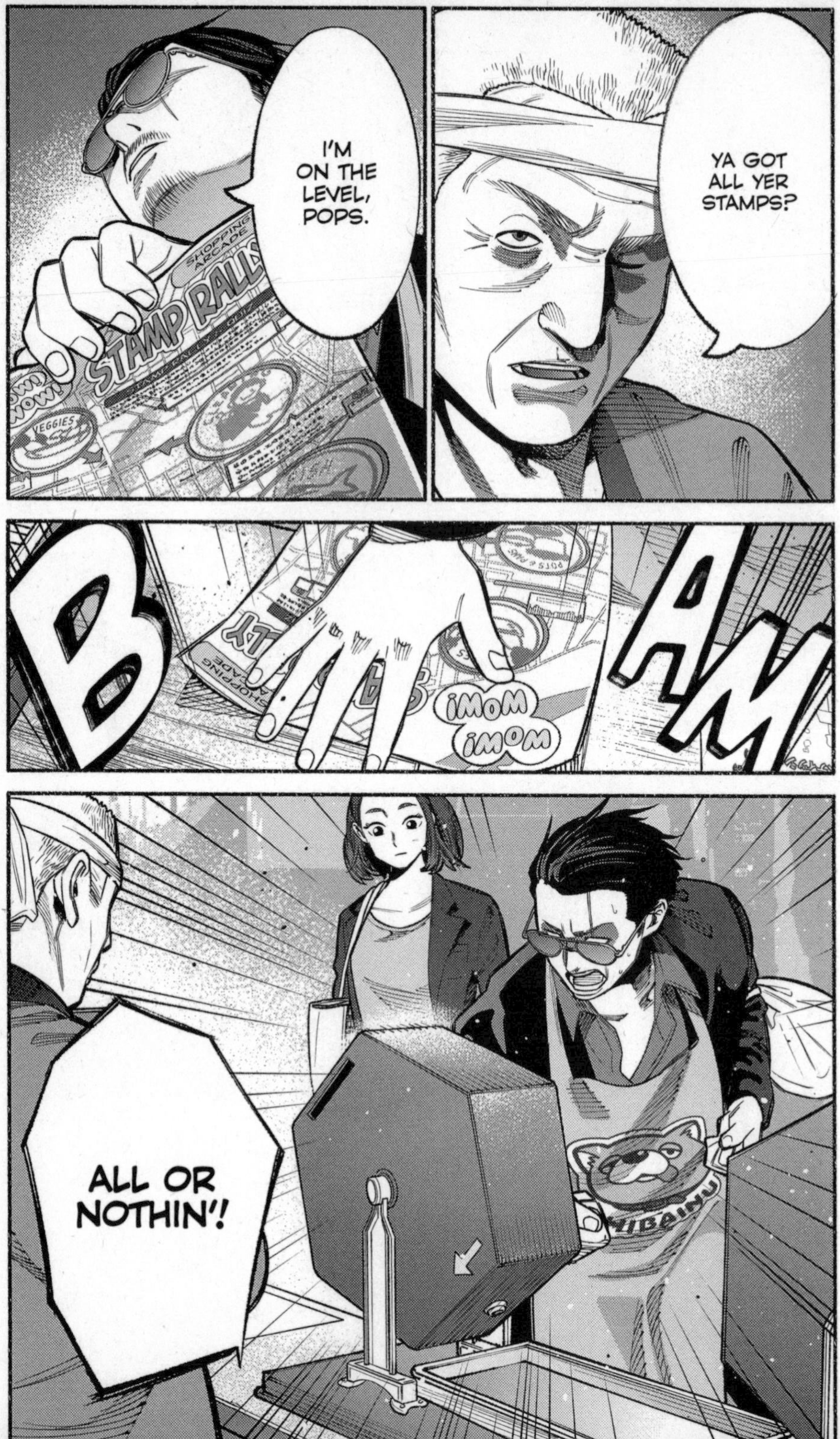
YA GOT ALL YER STAMPS?
I'M ON THE LEVEL, POPS.
SHOPPING ARCADE
STAMP RALLY
WOW!
VEGGIES
BAM
WOW! WOW!
ALL OR NOTHIN'!

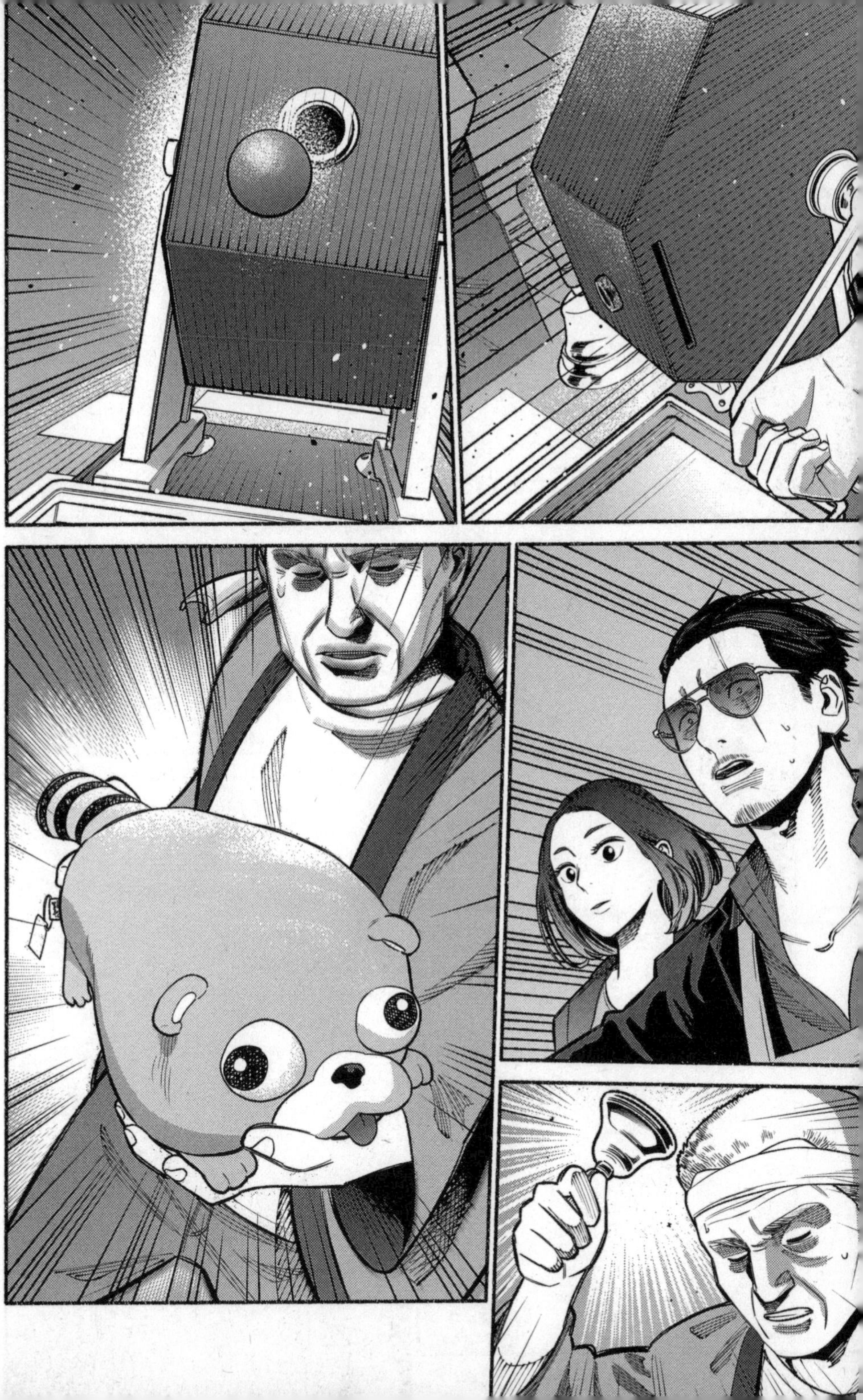

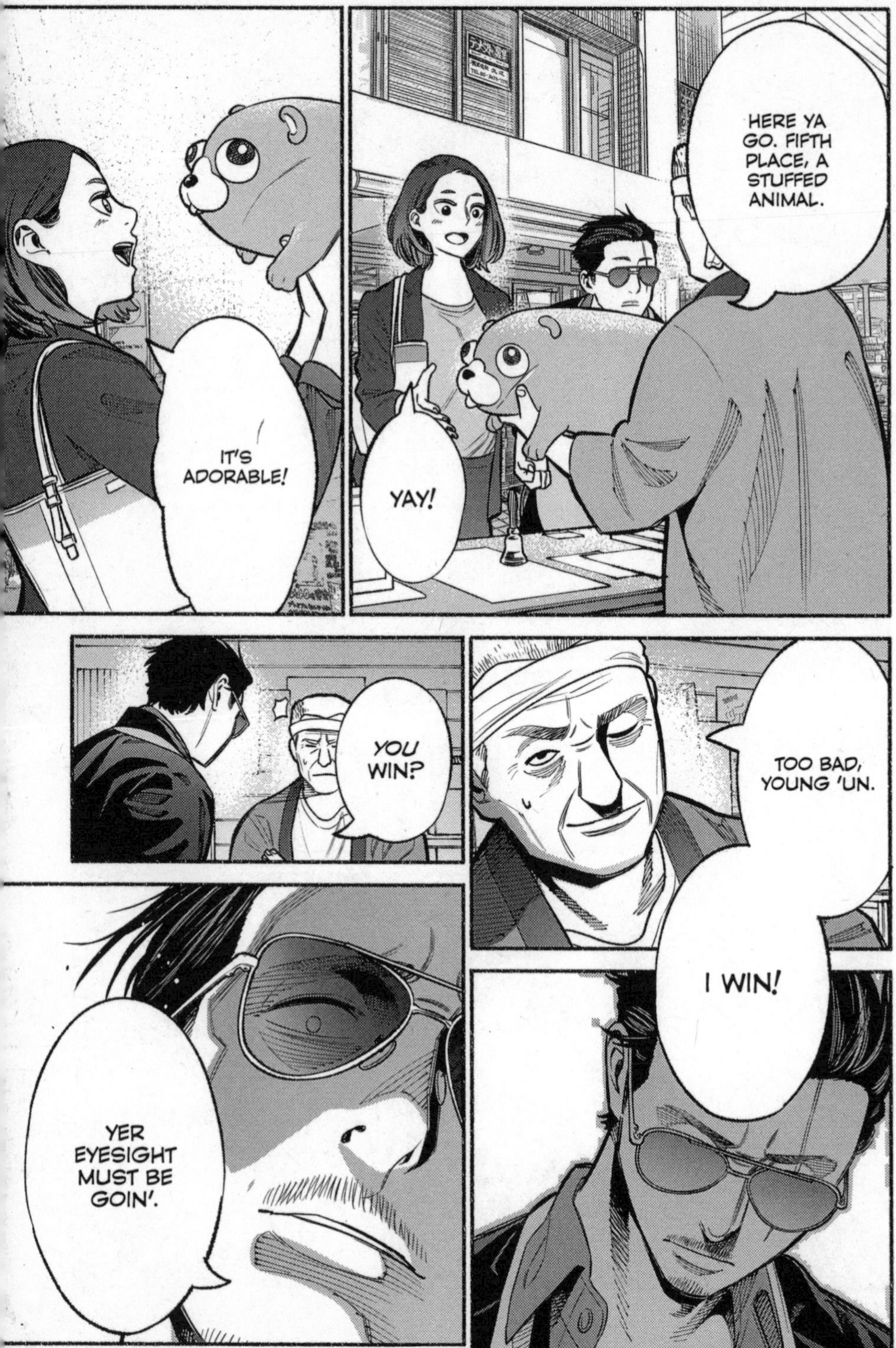
HERE YA GO. FIFTH PLACE, A STUFFED ANIMAL.
YAY!
IT'S ADORABLE!
TOO BAD, YOUNG 'UN.
I WIN!
YOU WIN?
YER EYESIGHT MUST BE GOIN'.

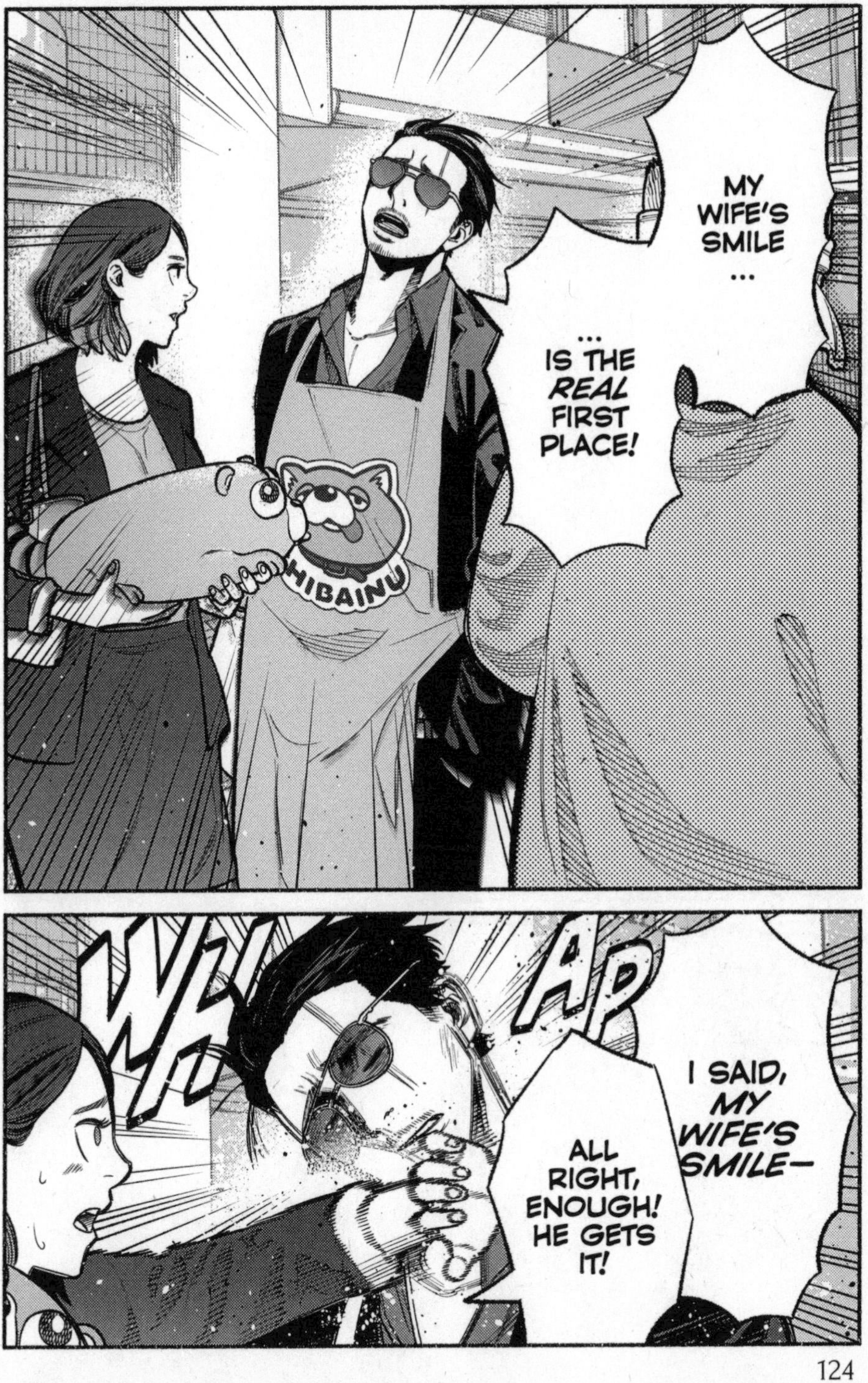
MY WIFE'S SMILE ...
... IS THE *REAL* FIRST PLACE!
HIBAINU
WHAP
I SAID, *MY WIFE'S SMILE*—
ALL RIGHT, ENOUGH! HE GETS IT!

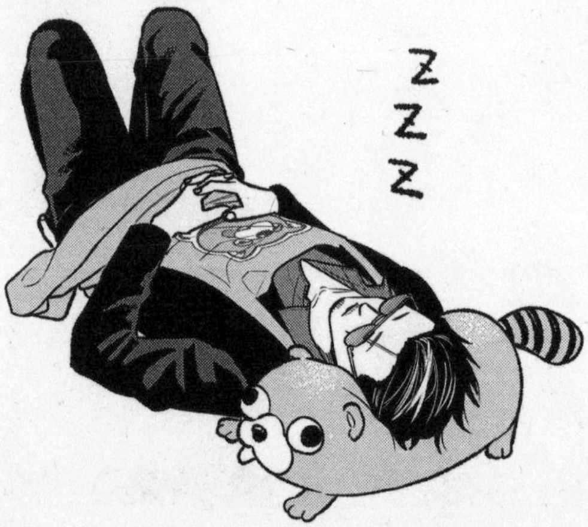
Z
Z
Z

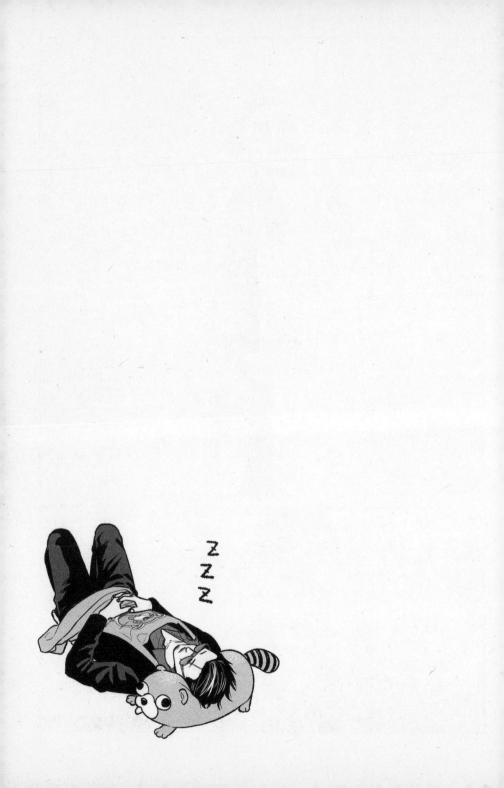

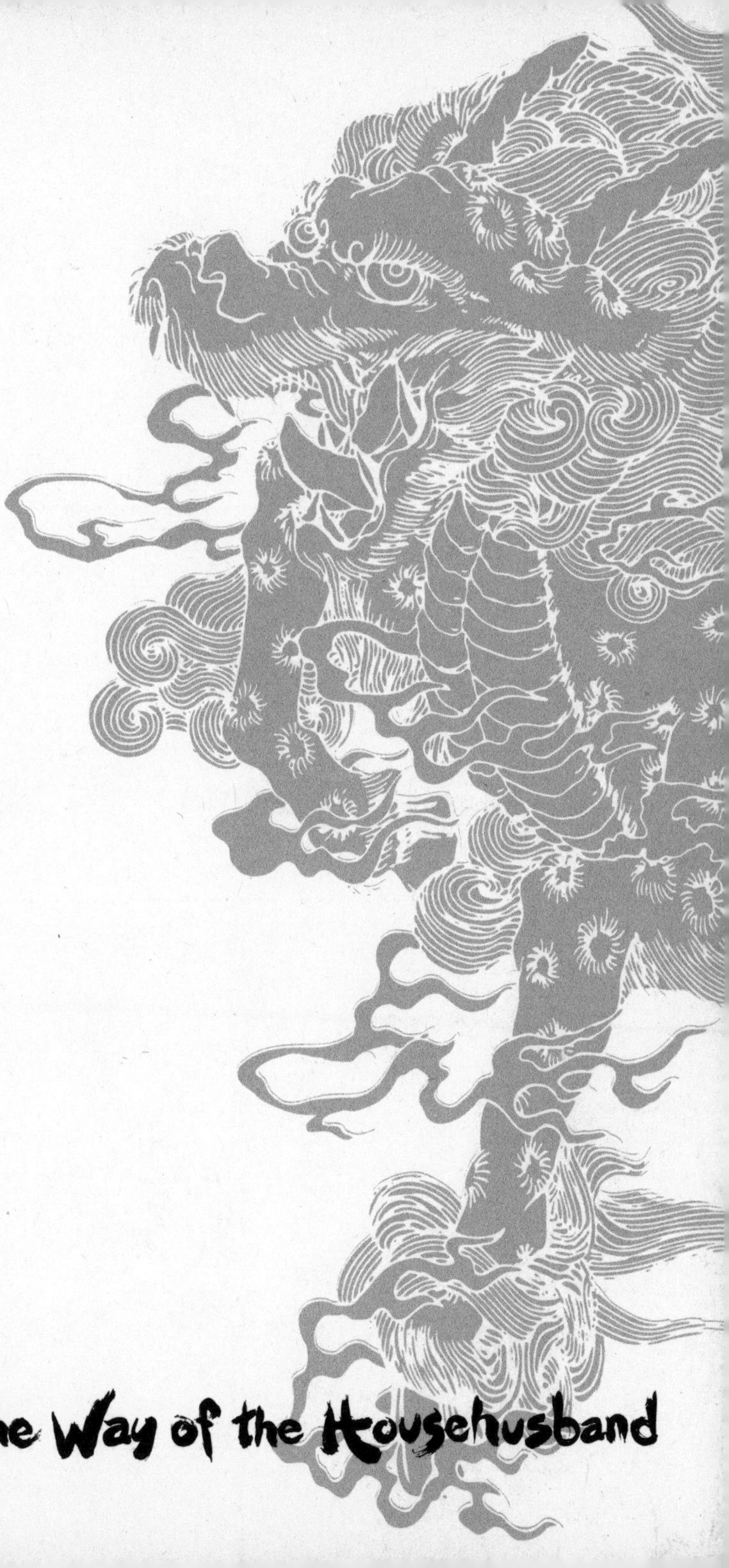

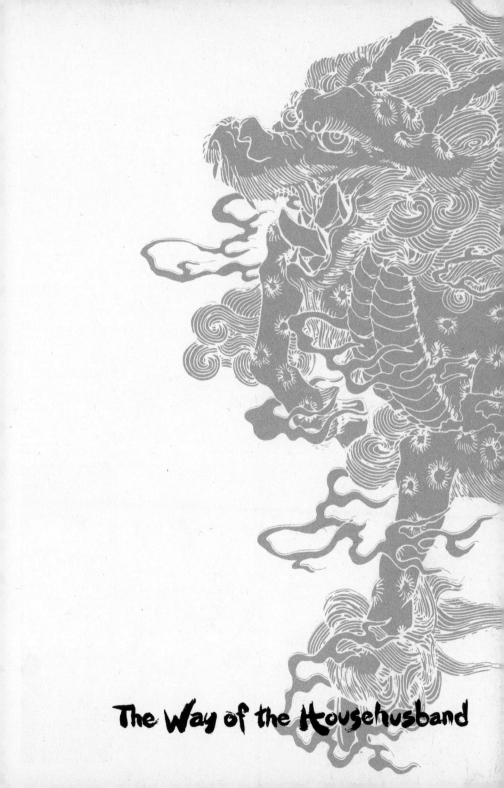

The Way of the Househusband

CHAPTER 18

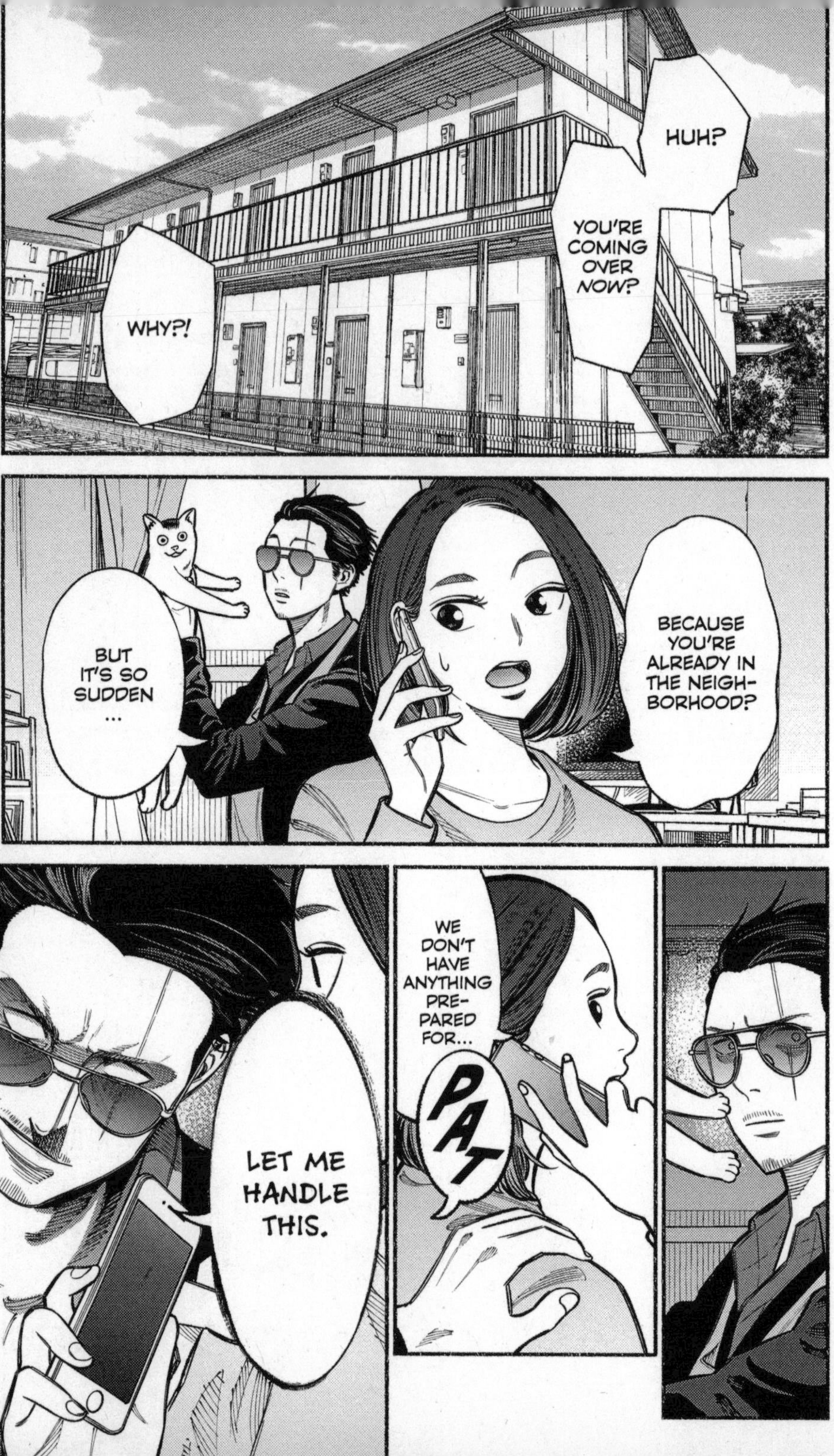
HUH?
YOU'RE COMING OVER NOW?
WHY?!
BECAUSE YOU'RE ALREADY IN THE NEIGH-BORHOOD?
BUT IT'S SO SUDDEN ...
WE DON'T HAVE ANYTHING PRE-PARED FOR...
PAT
LET ME HANDLE THIS.

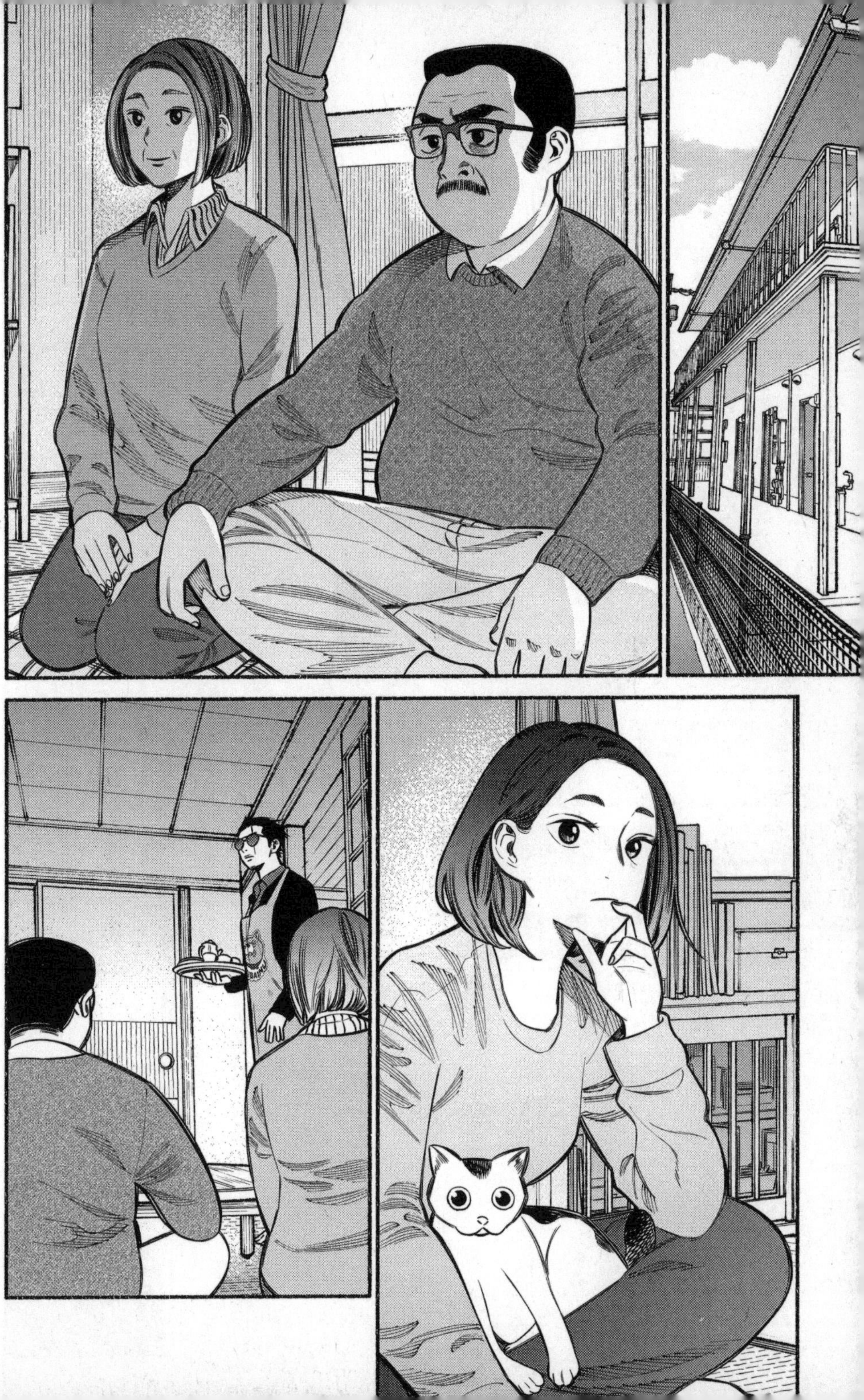

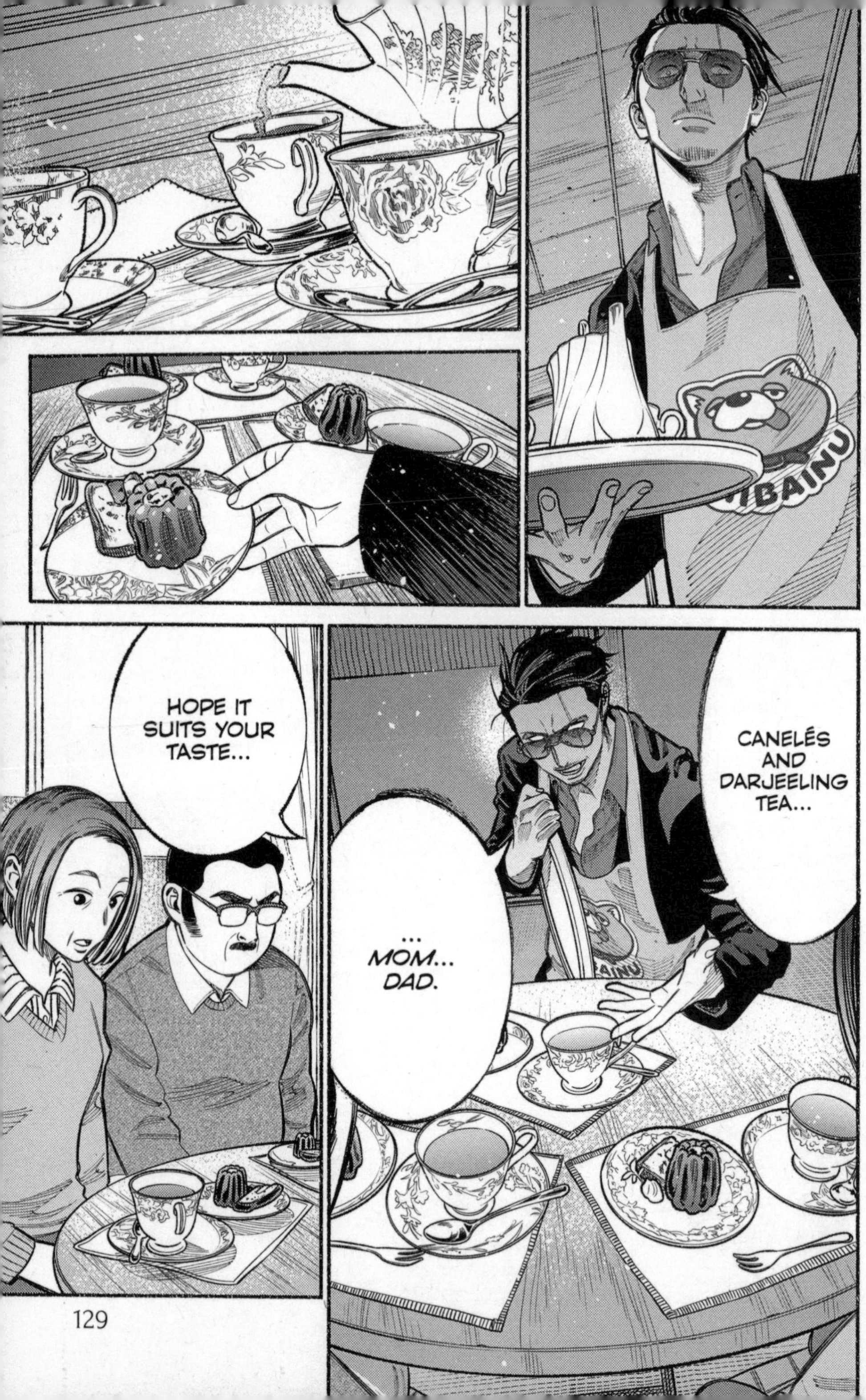
CANELÉS AND DARJEELING TEA...
... MOM... DAD.
HOPE IT SUITS YOUR TASTE...

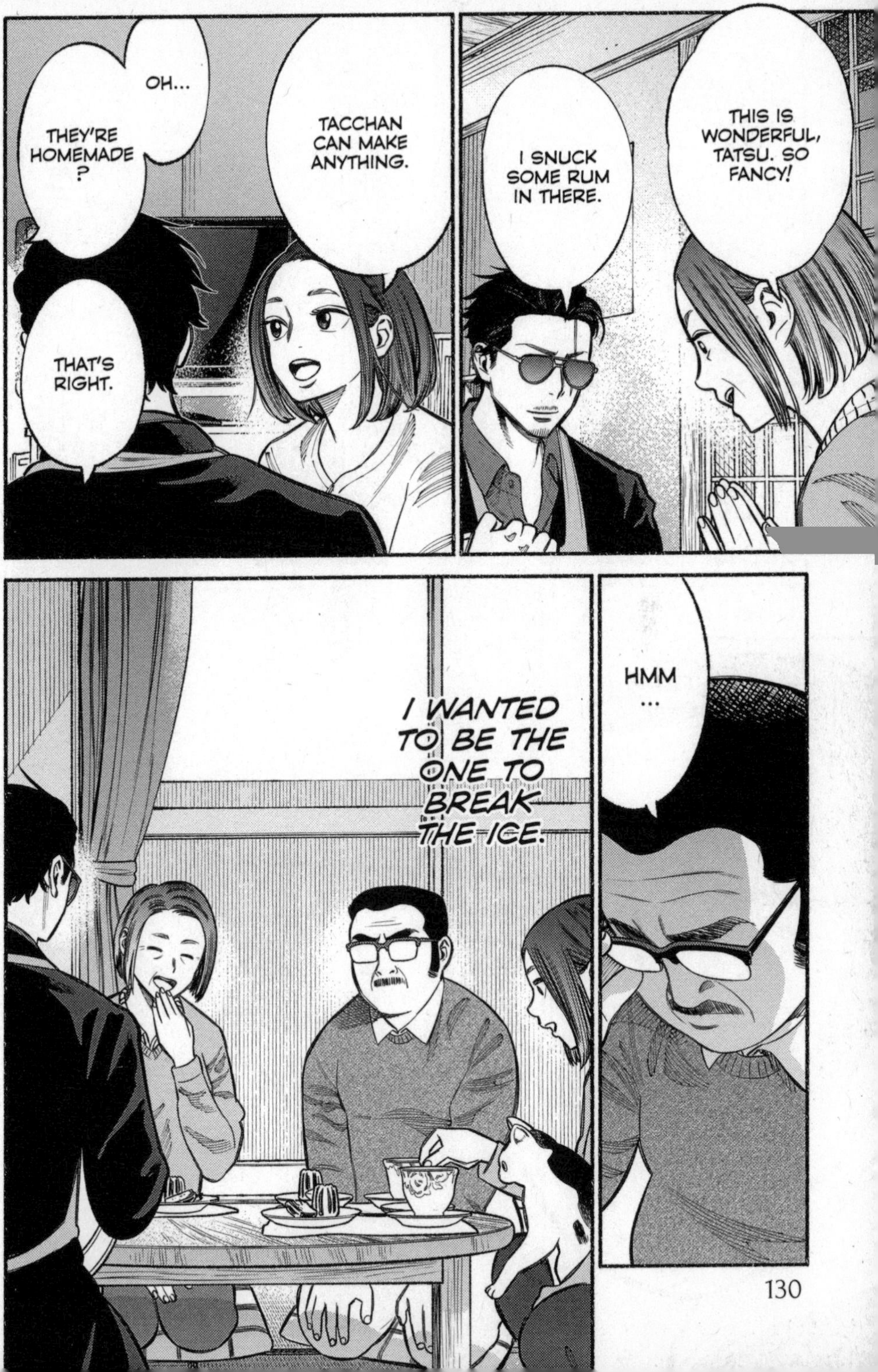
THIS IS WONDERFUL, TATSU. SO FANCY!
I SNUCK SOME RUM IN THERE.
TACCHAN CAN MAKE ANYTHING.
OH...
THEY'RE HOMEMADE?
THAT'S RIGHT.
HMM...
I WANTED TO BE THE ONE TO BREAK THE ICE.

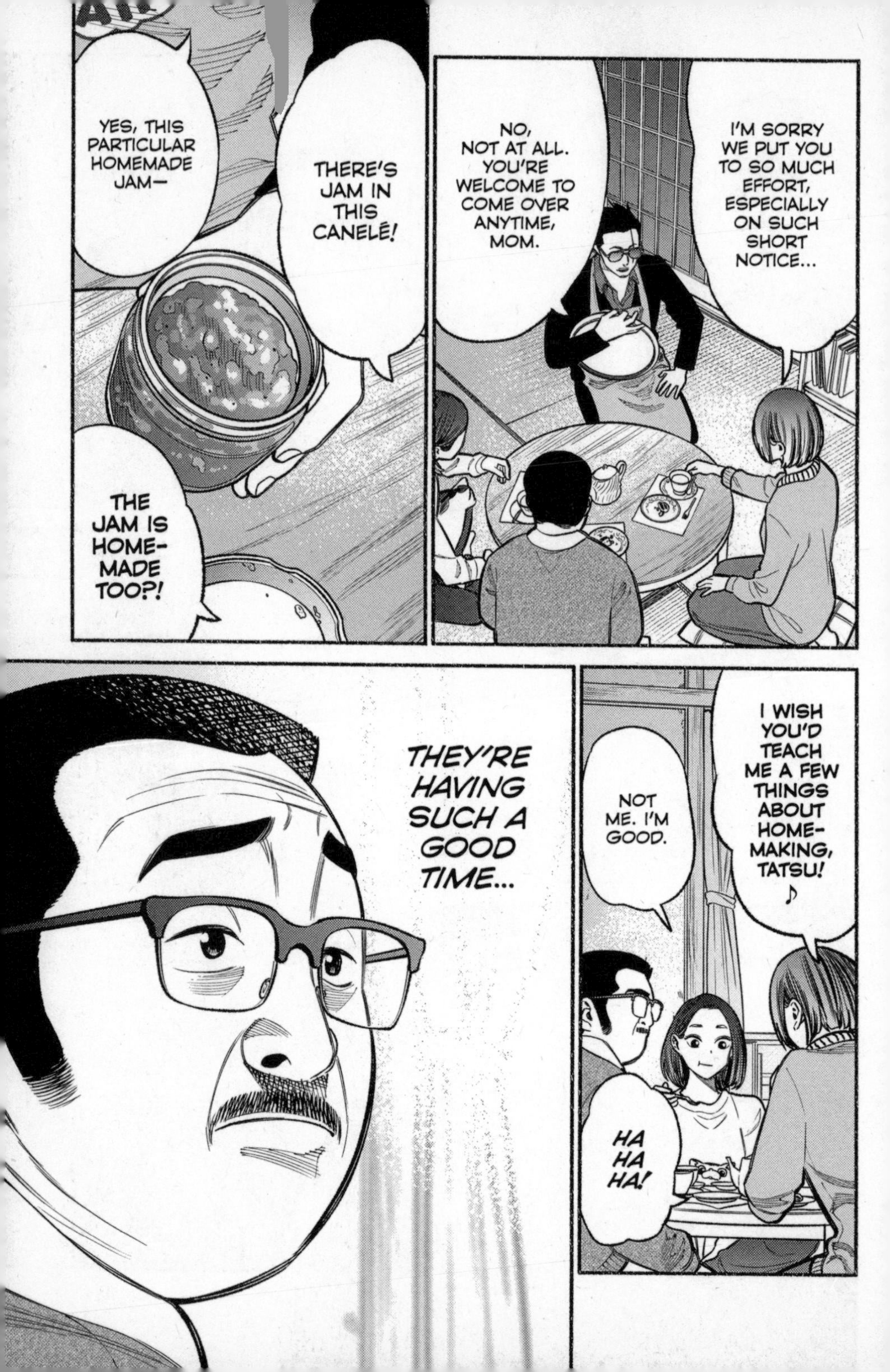
I'M SORRY WE PUT YOU TO SO MUCH EFFORT, ESPECIALLY ON SUCH SHORT NOTICE...
NO, NOT AT ALL. YOU'RE WELCOME TO COME OVER ANYTIME, MOM.
THERE'S JAM IN THIS CANELÉ!
YES, THIS PARTICULAR HOMEMADE JAM—
THE JAM IS HOME-MADE TOO?!
I WISH YOU'D TEACH ME A FEW THINGS ABOUT HOME-MAKING, TATSU! ♪
NOT ME. I'M GOOD.
HA HA HA!
THEY'RE HAVING SUCH A GOOD TIME...

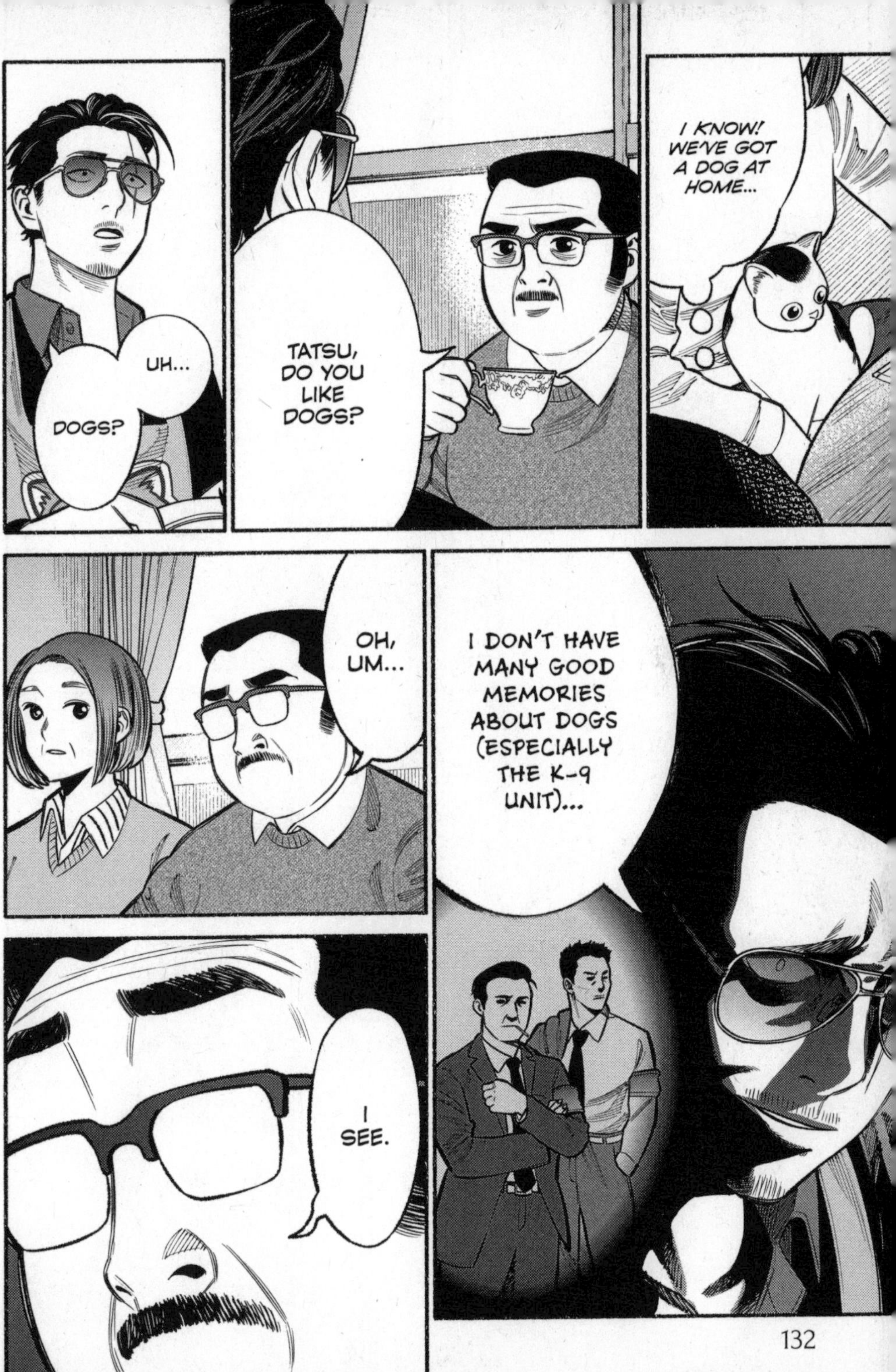
I KNOW! WE'VE GOT A DOG AT HOME...
TATSU, DO YOU LIKE DOGS?
UH...
DOGS?
I DON'T HAVE MANY GOOD MEMORIES ABOUT DOGS (ESPECIALLY THE K-9 UNIT)...
OH, UM...
I SEE.

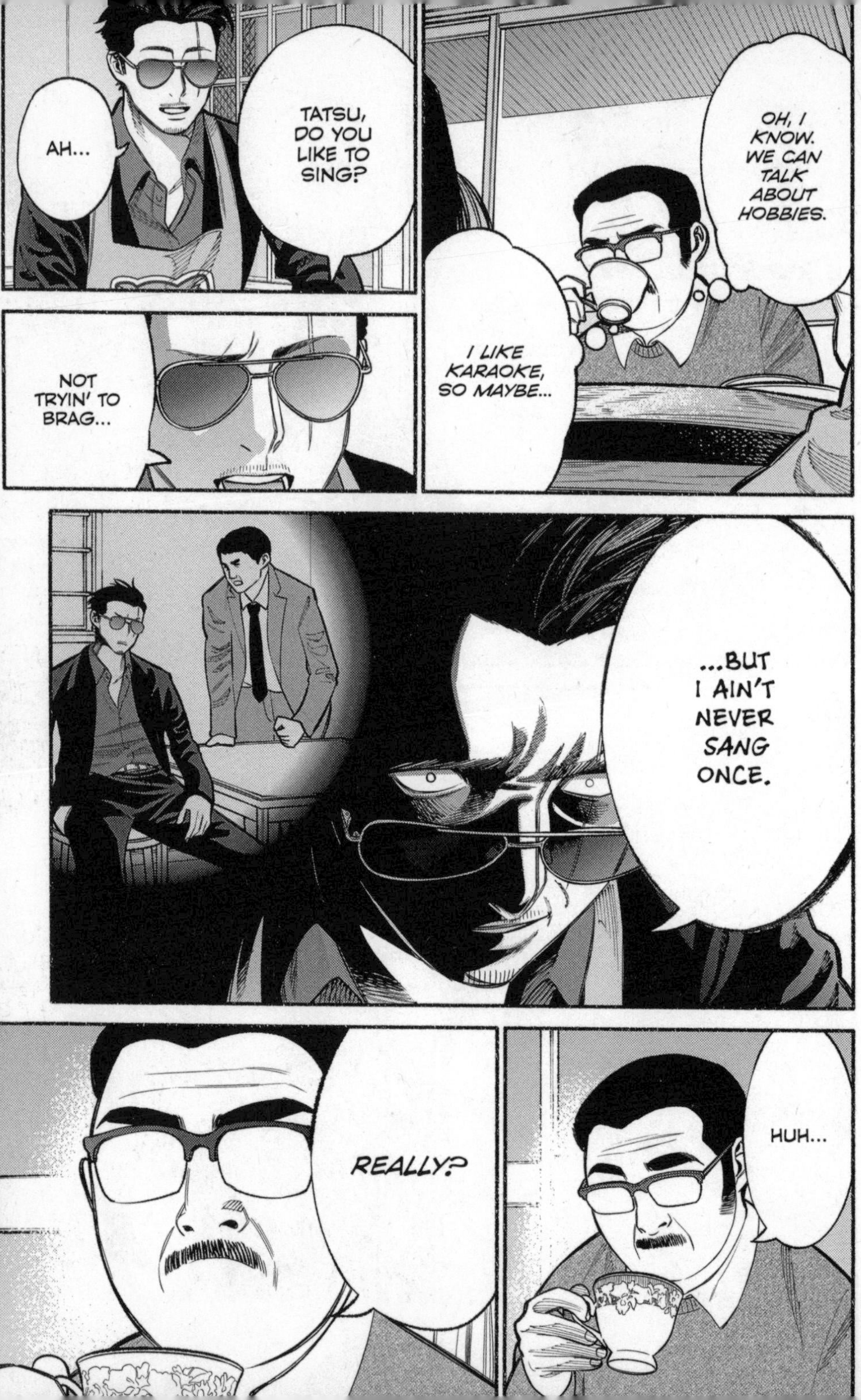
OH, I KNOW. WE CAN TALK ABOUT HOBBIES.
I LIKE KARAOKE, SO MAYBE...
TATSU, DO YOU LIKE TO SING?
AH...
NOT TRYIN' TO BRAG...
...BUT I AIN'T NEVER SANG ONCE.
HUH...
REALLY?

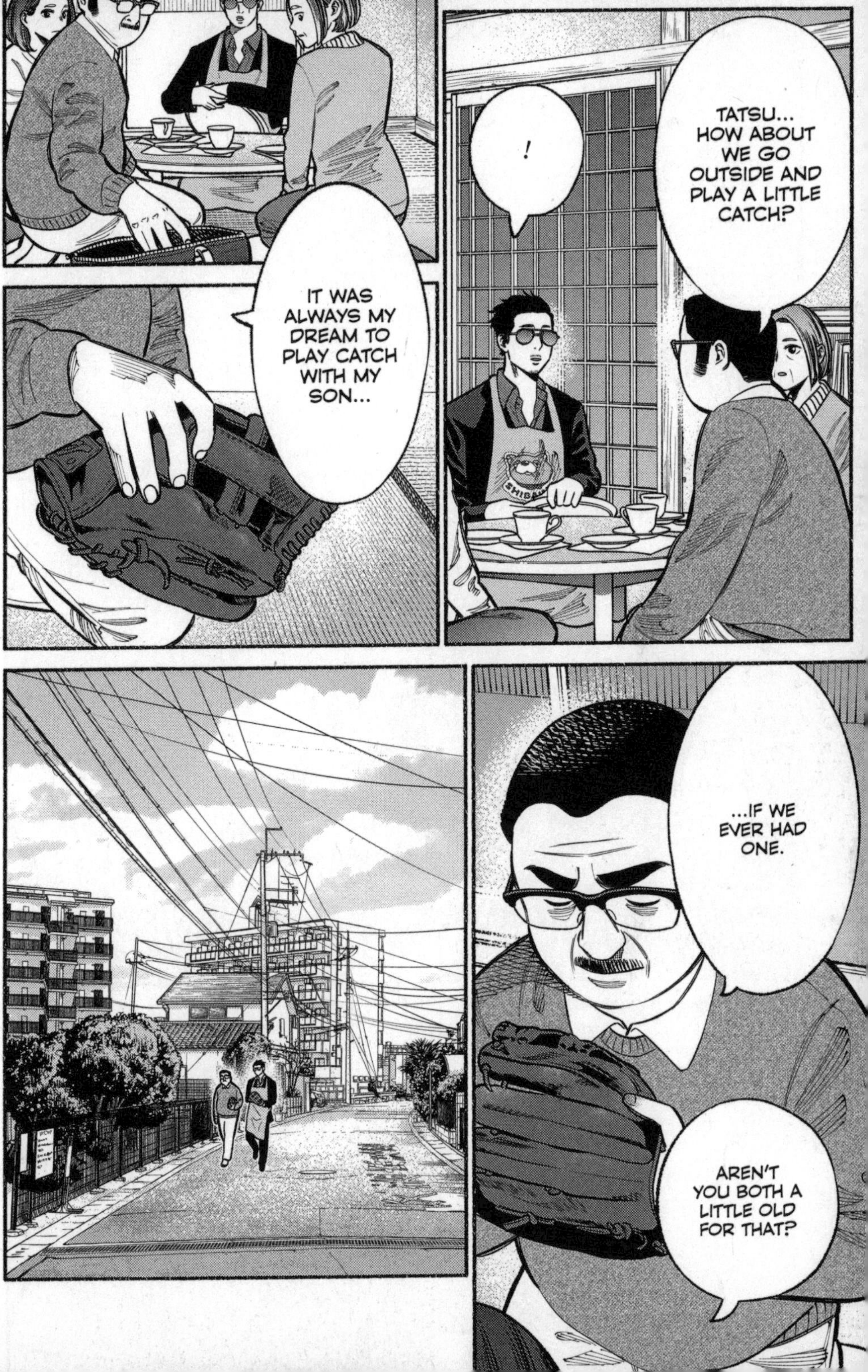
TATSU... HOW ABOUT WE GO OUTSIDE AND PLAY A LITTLE CATCH?
!
IT WAS ALWAYS MY DREAM TO PLAY CATCH WITH MY SON...
...IF WE EVER HAD ONE.
AREN'T YOU BOTH A LITTLE OLD FOR THAT?

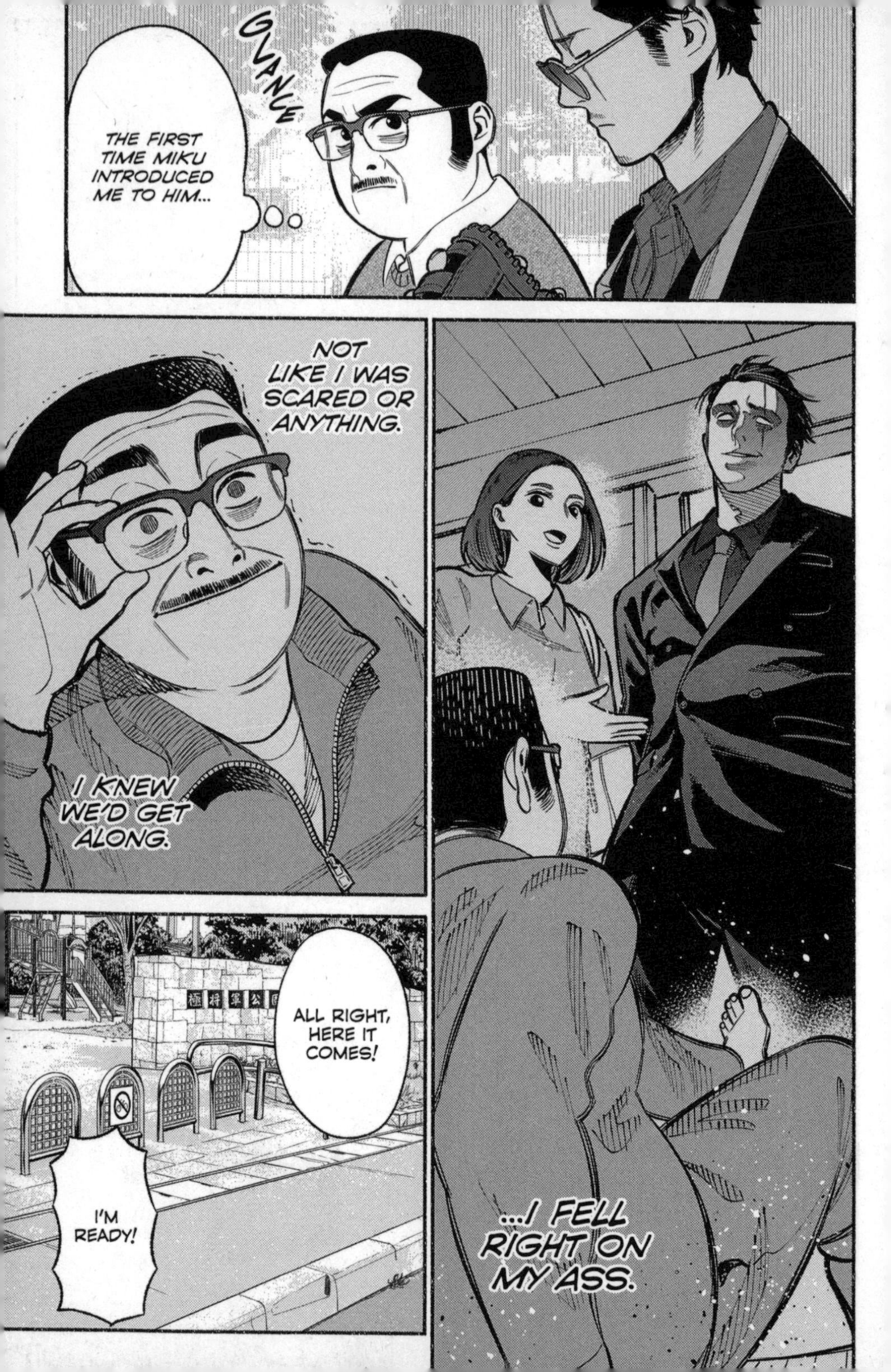
GLANCE
THE FIRST TIME MIKU INTRODUCED ME TO HIM...
...I FELL RIGHT ON MY ASS.
NOT LIKE I WAS SCARED OR ANYTHING.
I KNEW WE'D GET ALONG.
ALL RIGHT, HERE IT COMES!
I'M READY!

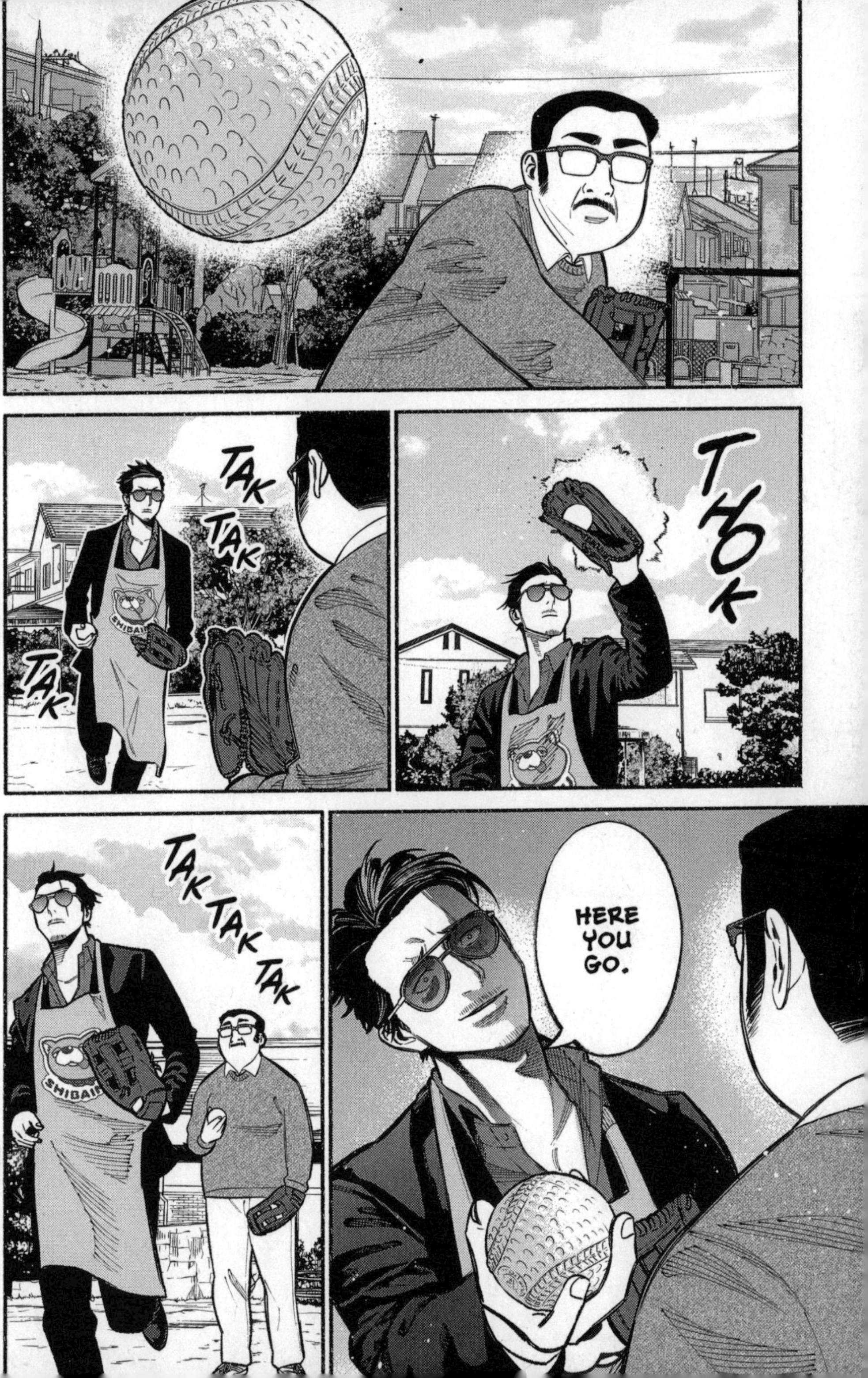
THOK
TAK TAK
TAK TAK
HERE YOU GO.
TAK TAK TAK TAK

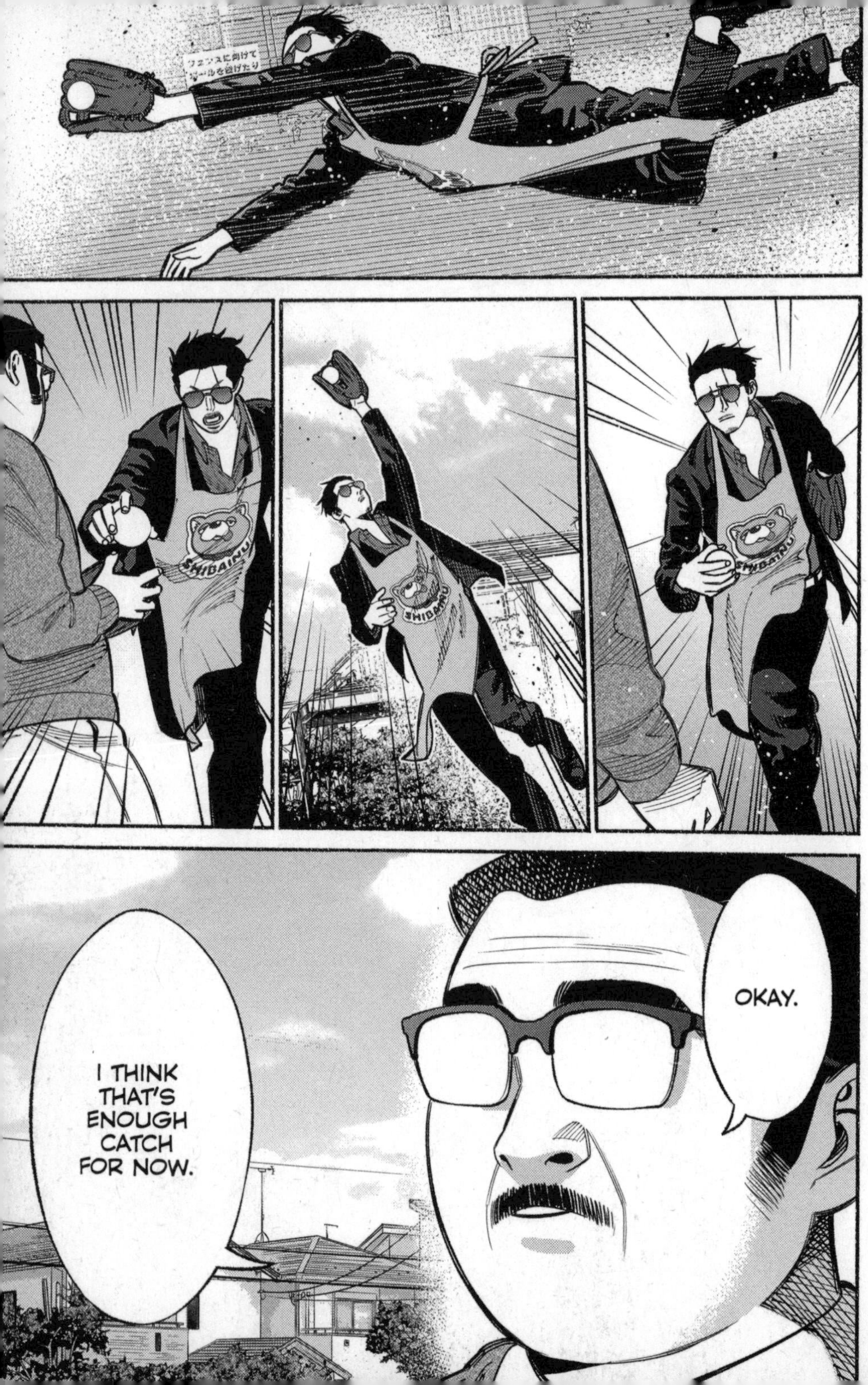
フェンスに向けて
ボールを投げたり
OKAY.
I THINK THAT'S ENOUGH CATCH FOR NOW.

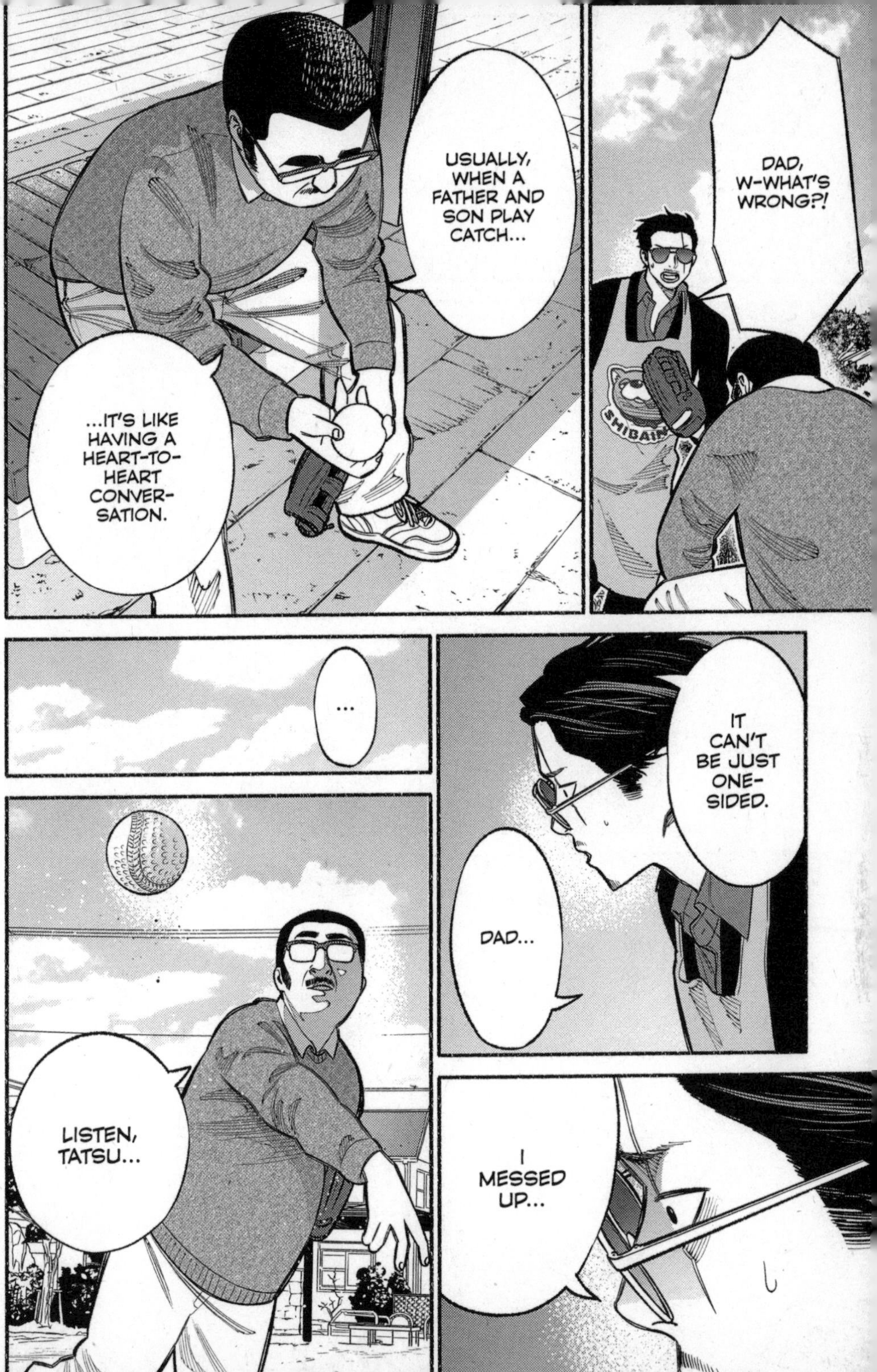
DAD, W-WHAT'S WRONG?!
USUALLY, WHEN A FATHER AND SON PLAY CATCH...
...IT'S LIKE HAVING A HEART-TO-HEART CONVERSATION.
SHIBAIN
IT CAN'T BE JUST ONE-SIDED.
DAD...
...
LISTEN, TATSU...
I MESSED UP...

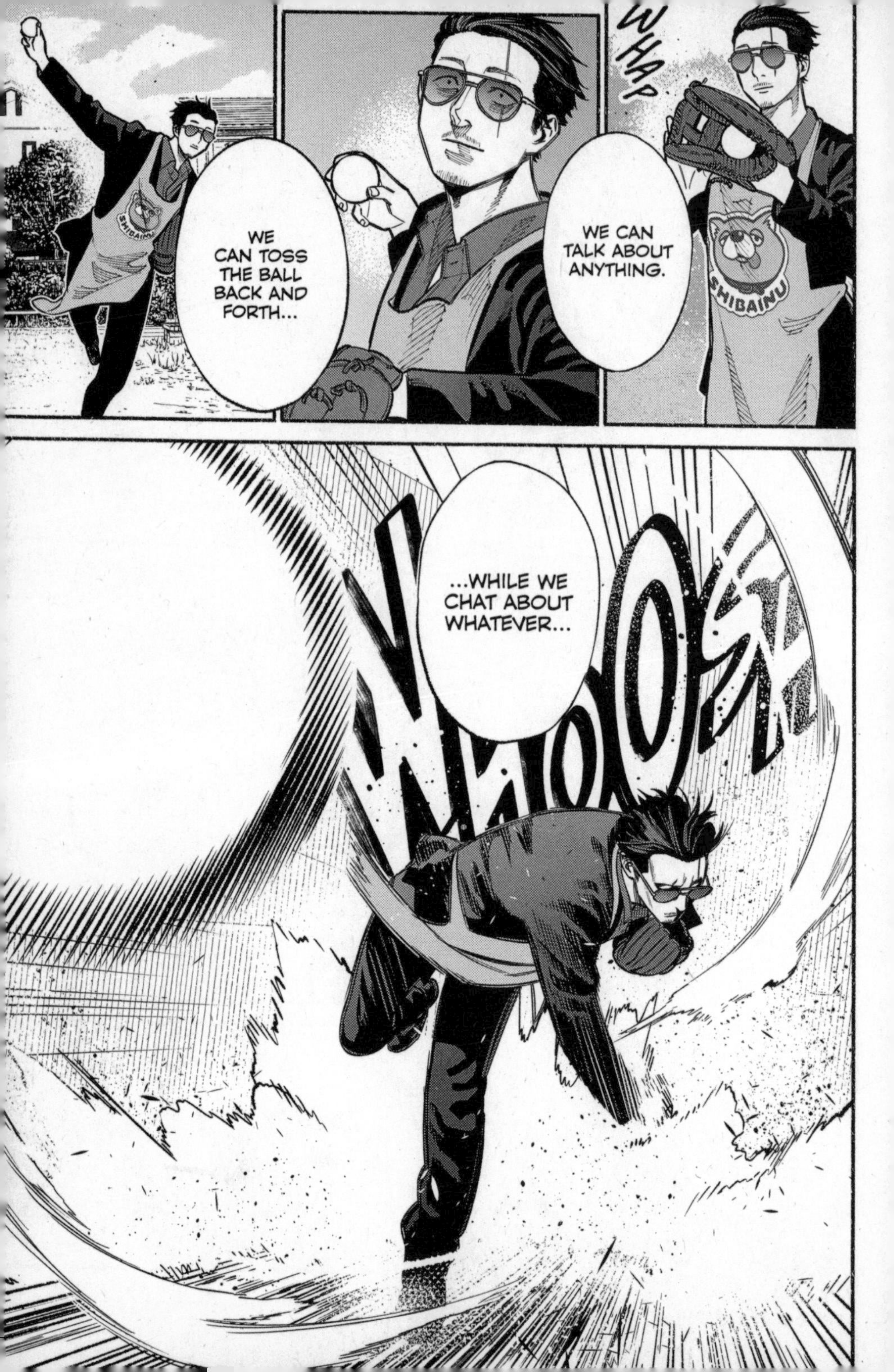
WHAP
WE CAN TALK ABOUT ANYTHING.
WE CAN TOSS THE BALL BACK AND FORTH...
...WHILE WE CHAT ABOUT WHATEVER...
WHOOOSH

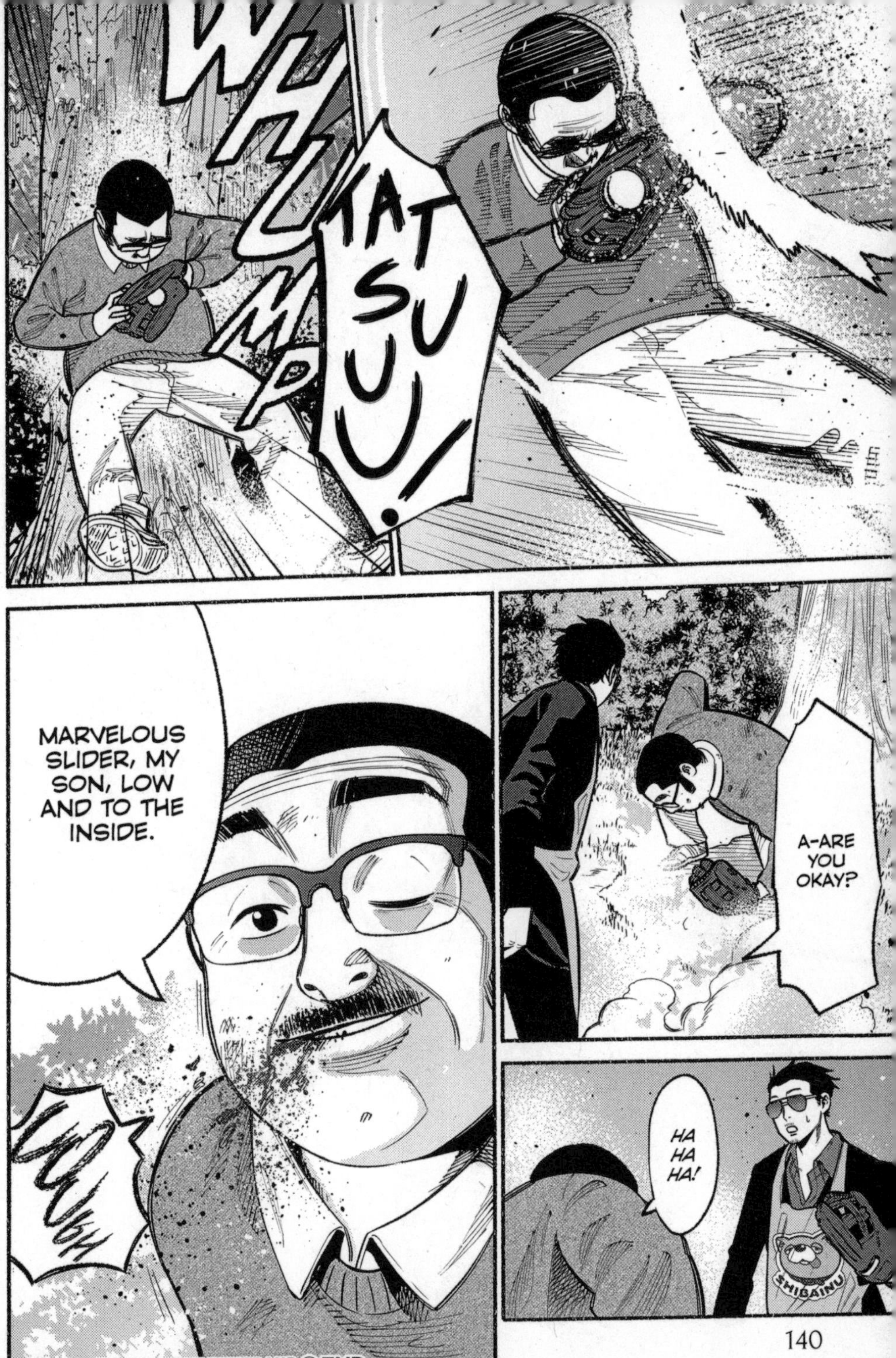
TATSUUU!
WHUMP
A-ARE YOU OKAY?
HA HA HA!
MARVELOUS SLIDER, MY SON, LOW AND TO THE INSIDE.

THE WAY OF THE HOUSEHUSBAND ② END

FELL ON HIS ASS.

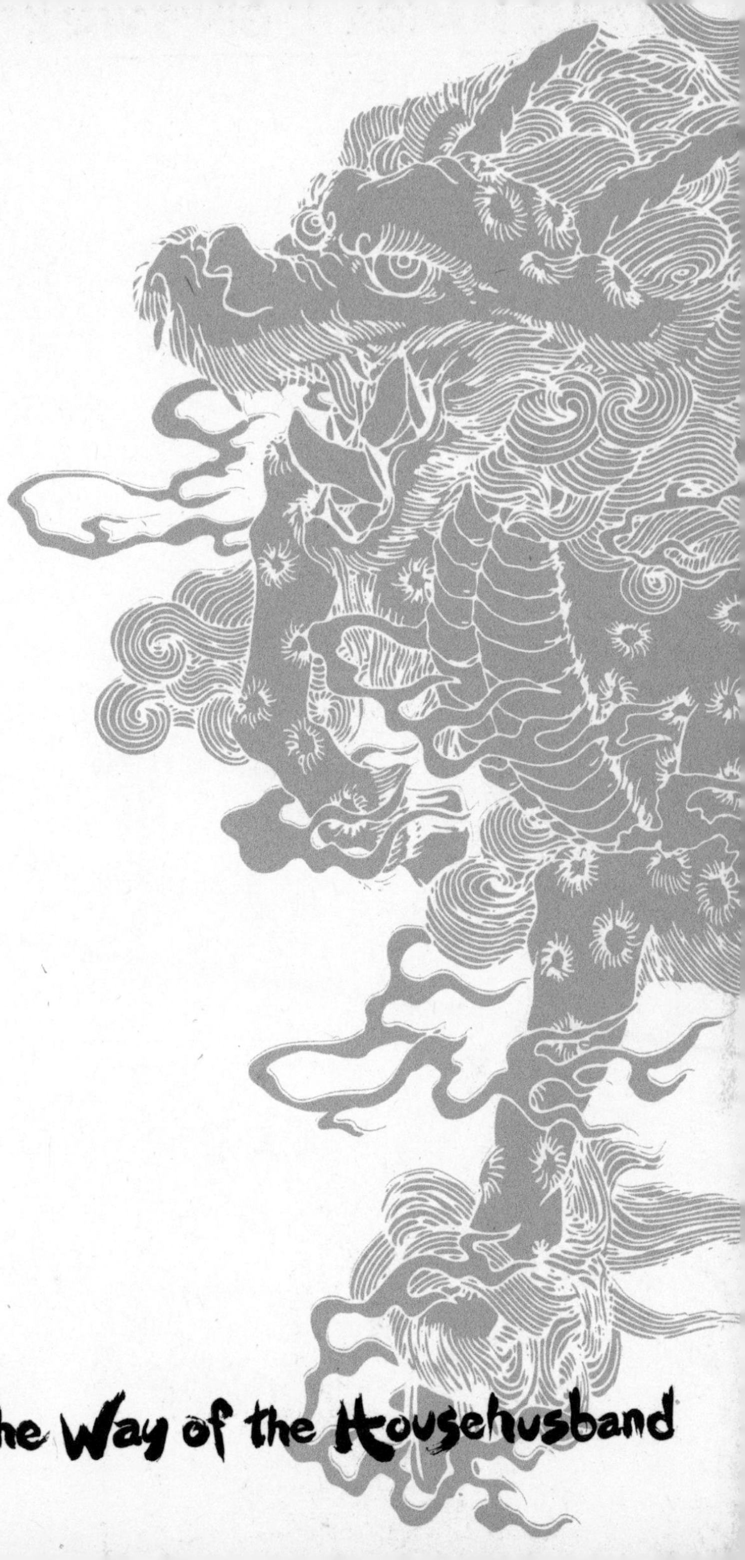

The Way of the Househusband

BONUS MANGA ① GIN'S WALK ②

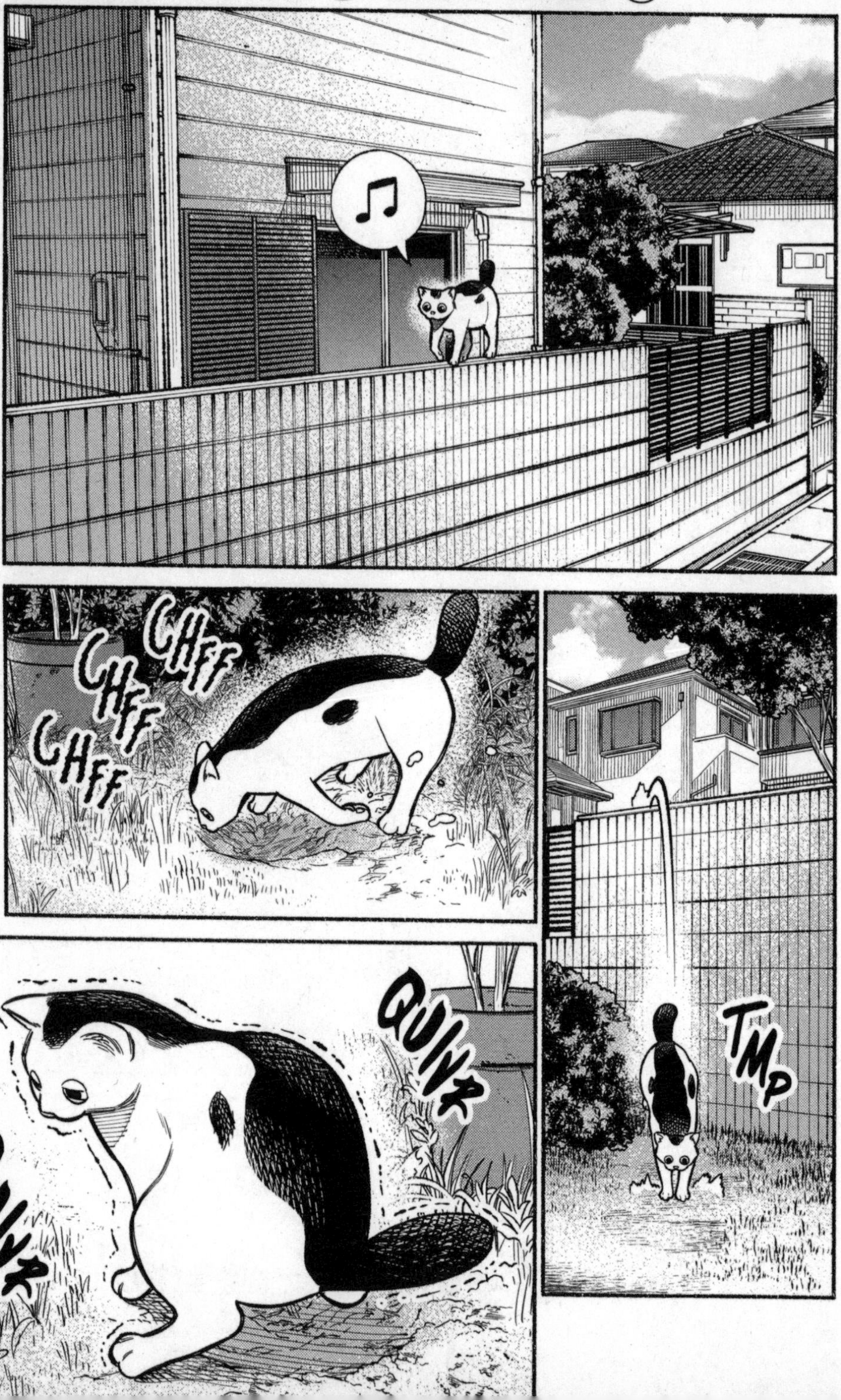
♫
TMP
CHFF CHFF CHFF
QUIVR QUIVR

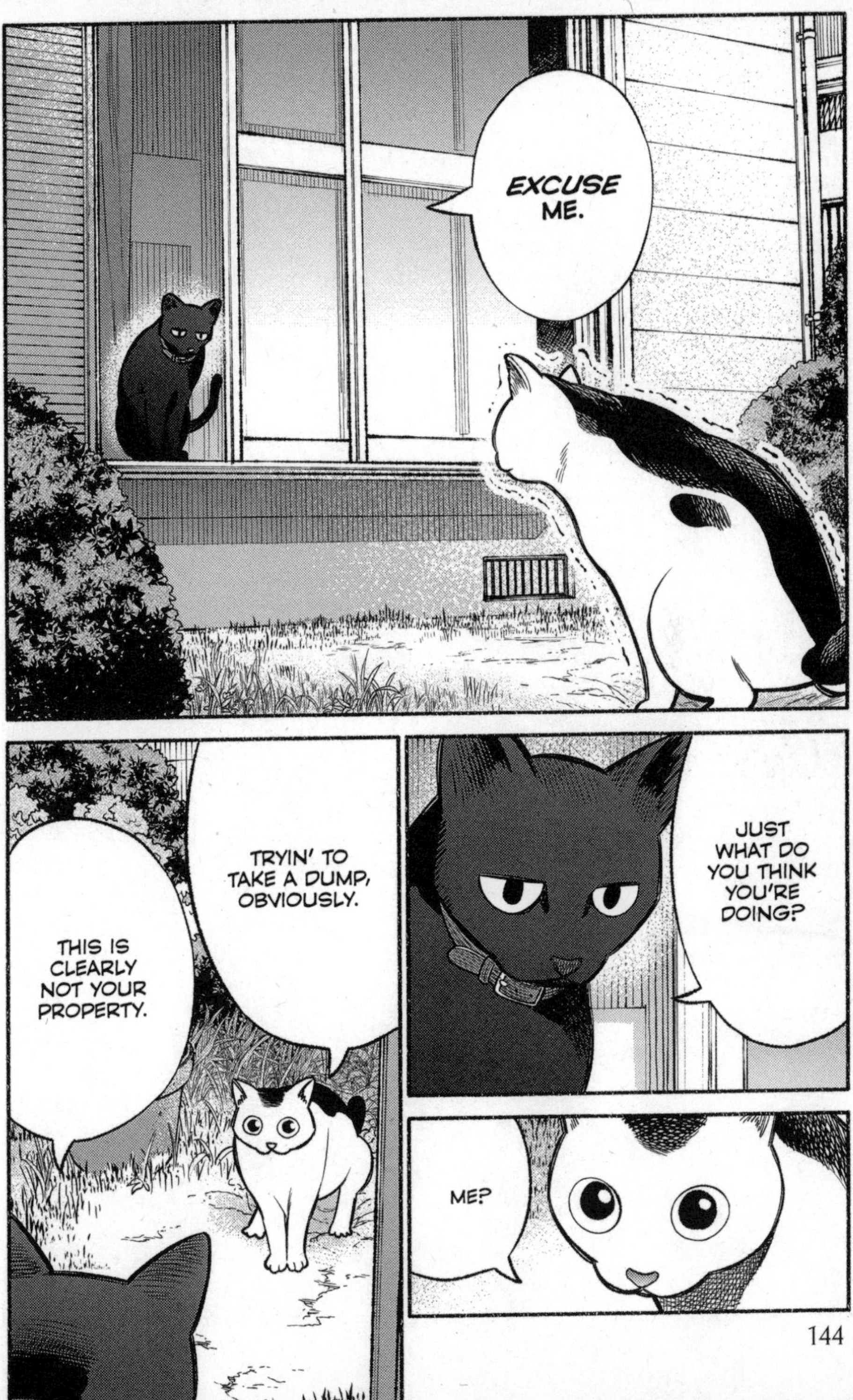
EXCUSE ME.
JUST WHAT DO YOU THINK YOU'RE DOING?
ME?
TRYIN' TO TAKE A DUMP, OBVIOUSLY.
THIS IS CLEARLY NOT YOUR PROPERTY.

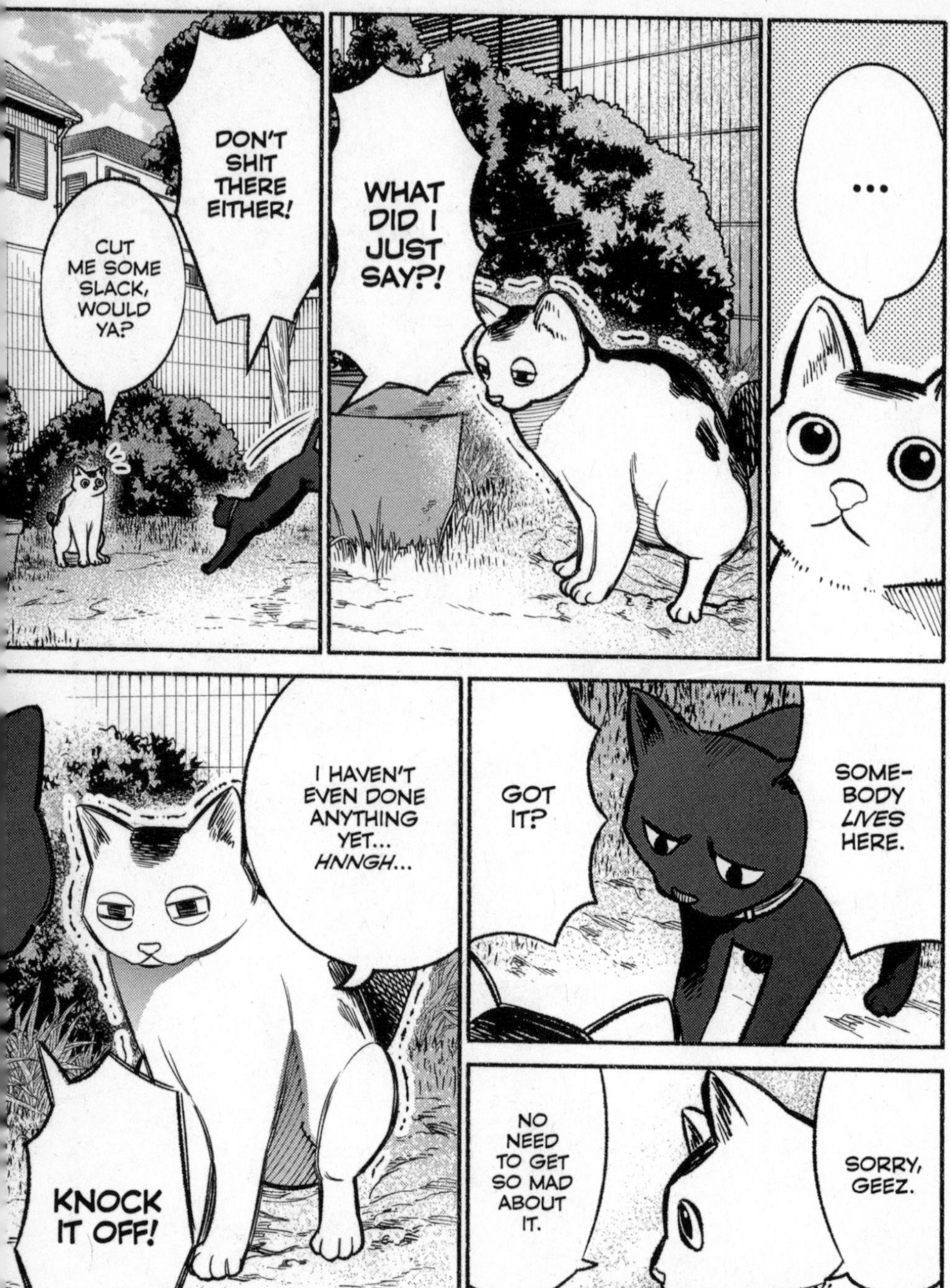
...
WHAT DID I JUST SAY?!
DON'T SHIT THERE EITHER!
CUT ME SOME SLACK, WOULD YA?
SOME-BODY *LIVES* HERE.
GOT IT?
SORRY, GEEZ.
NO NEED TO GET SO MAD ABOUT IT.
I HAVEN'T EVEN DONE ANYTHING YET... *HNNGH*...
KNOCK IT OFF!

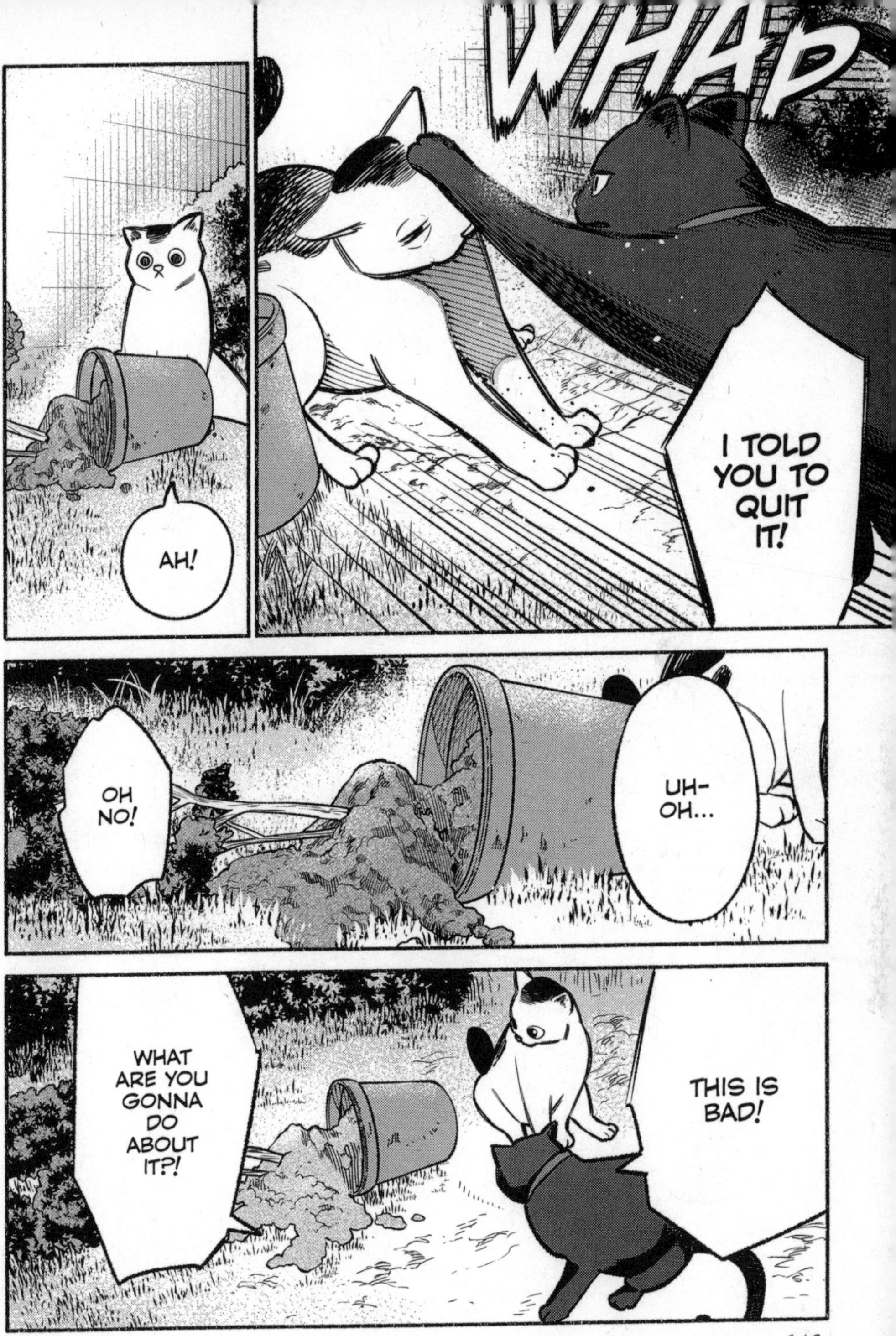
WHAP
I TOLD YOU TO QUIT IT!
AH!
UH-OH...
OH NO!
THIS IS BAD!
WHAT ARE YOU GONNA DO ABOUT IT?!

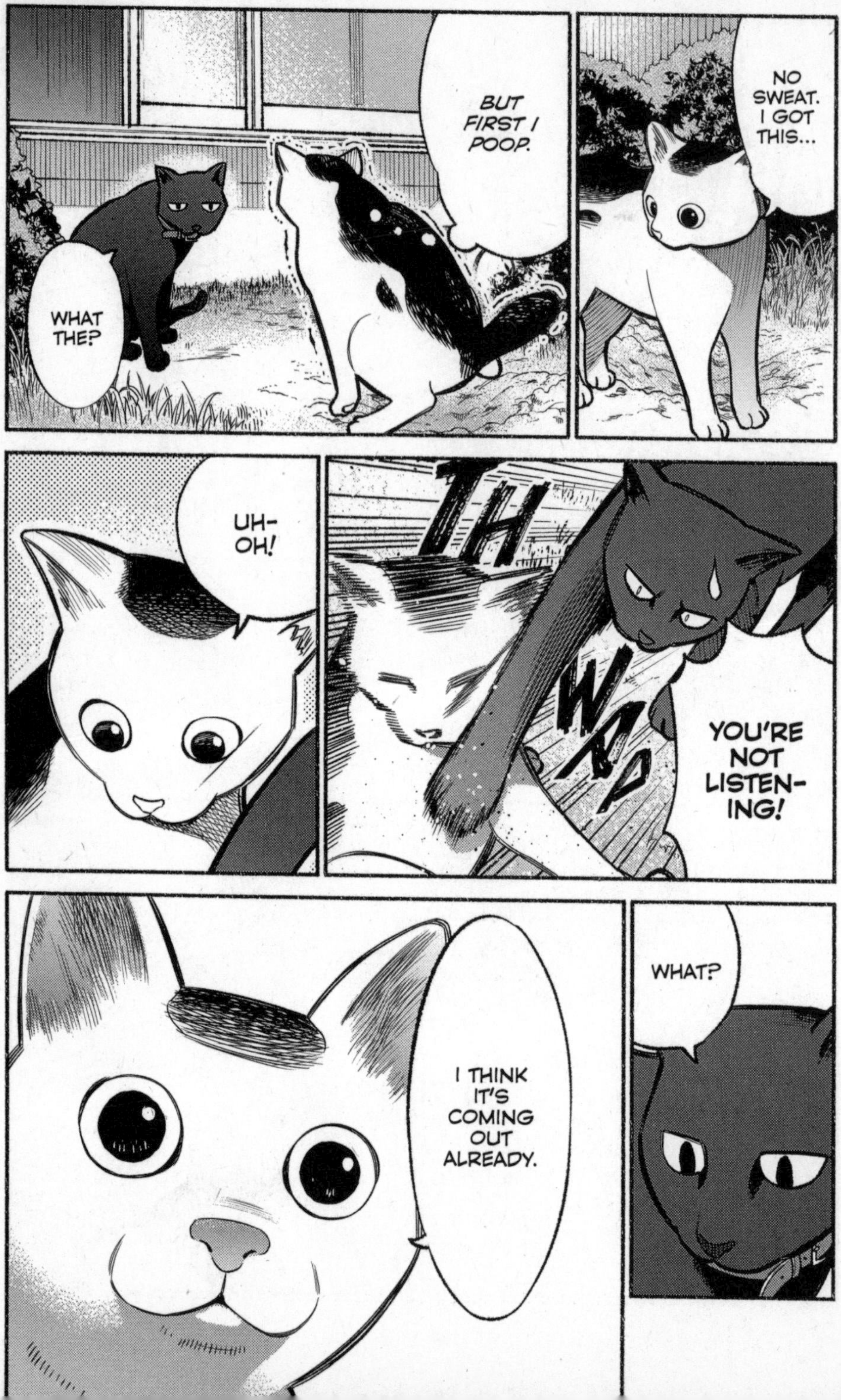
NO SWEAT. I GOT THIS...
BUT FIRST I POOP.
WHAT THE?
THWAP
YOU'RE NOT LISTEN-ING!
UH-OH!
WHAT?
I THINK IT'S COMING OUT ALREADY.

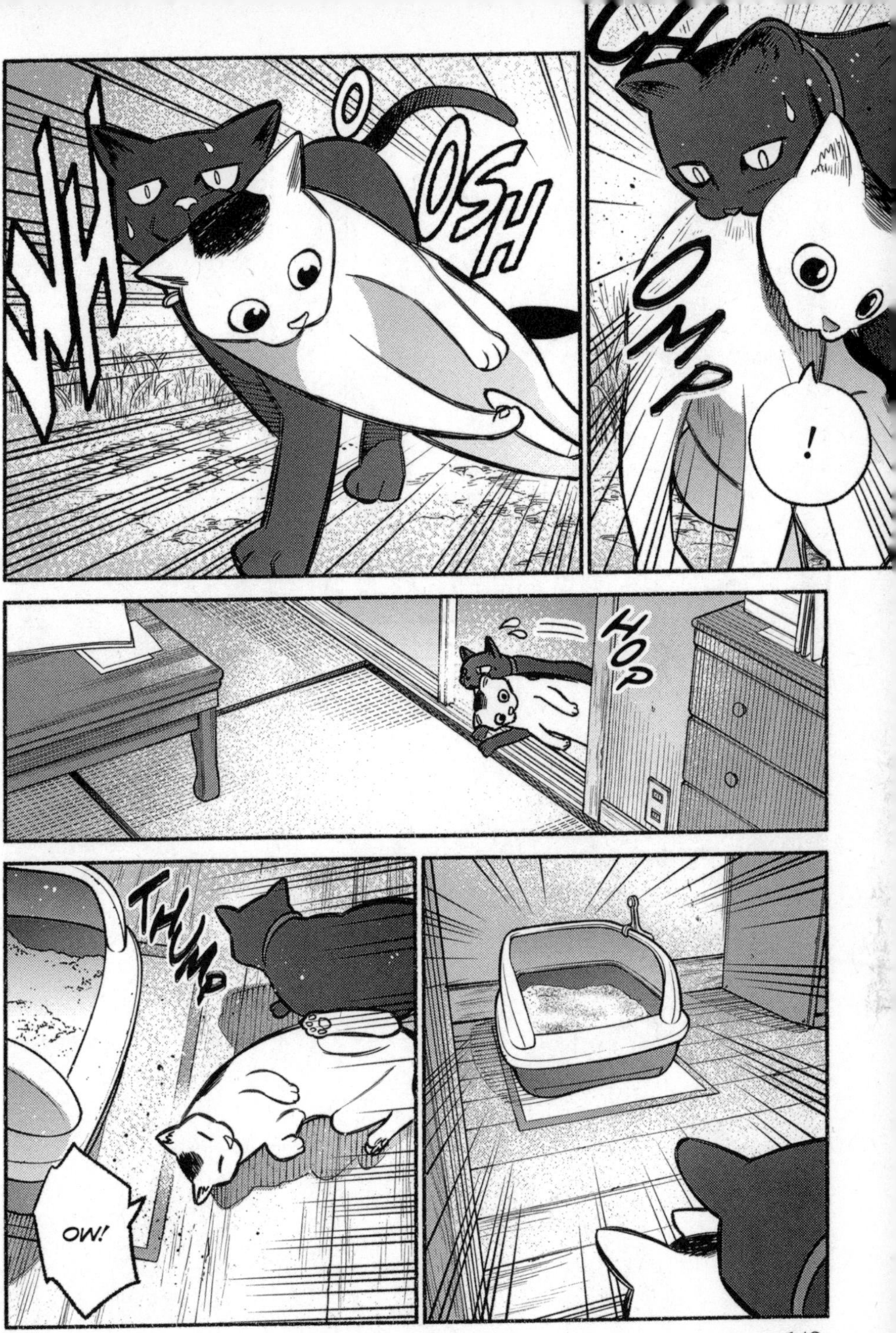
CH
OMP
!
WH
OOSH
HOP
THUMP
OW!

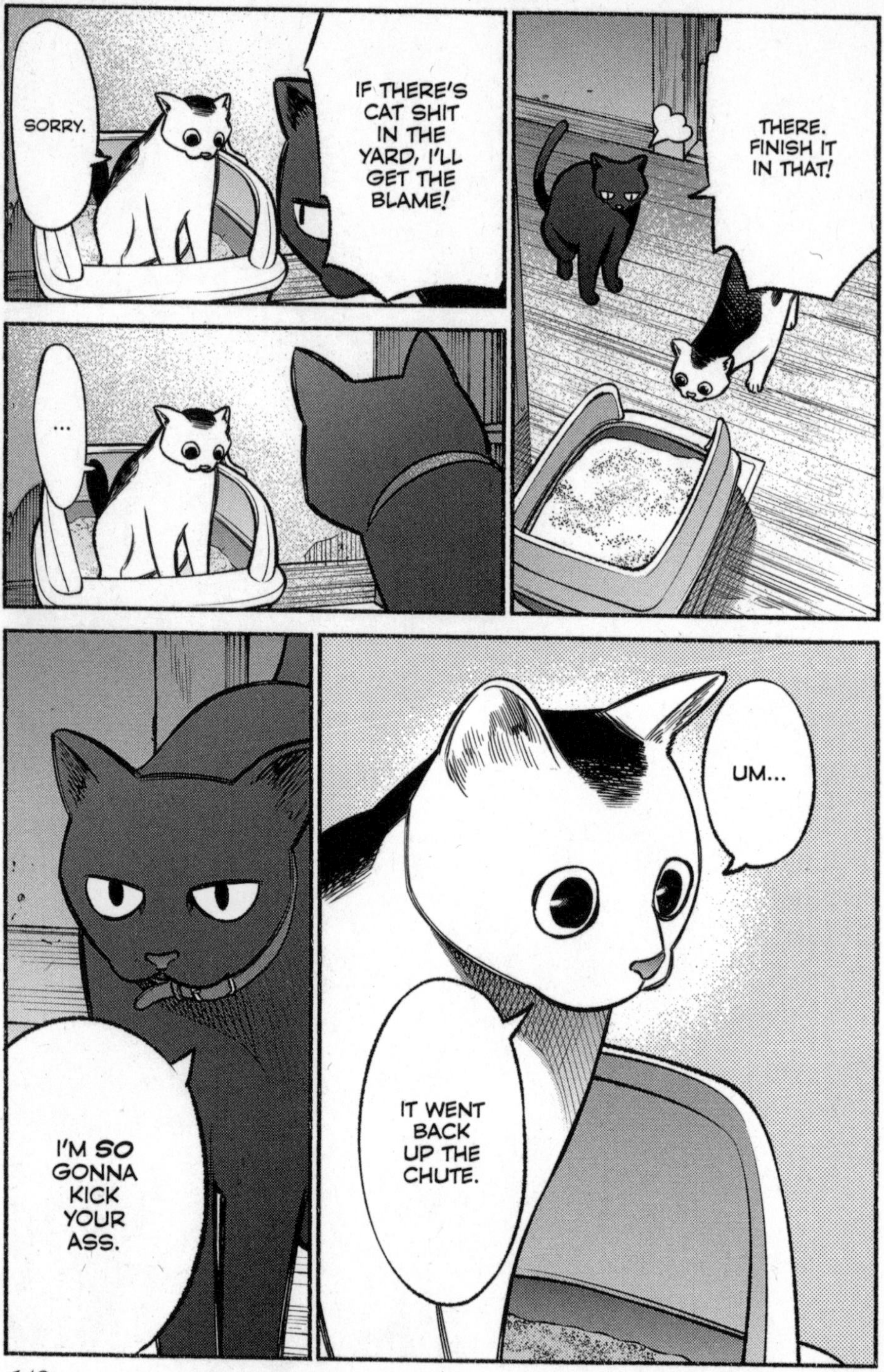
THERE. FINISH IT IN THAT!
IF THERE'S CAT SHIT IN THE YARD, I'LL GET THE BLAME!
SORRY.
...
UM...
IT WENT BACK UP THE CHUTE.
I'M SO GONNA KICK YOUR ASS.

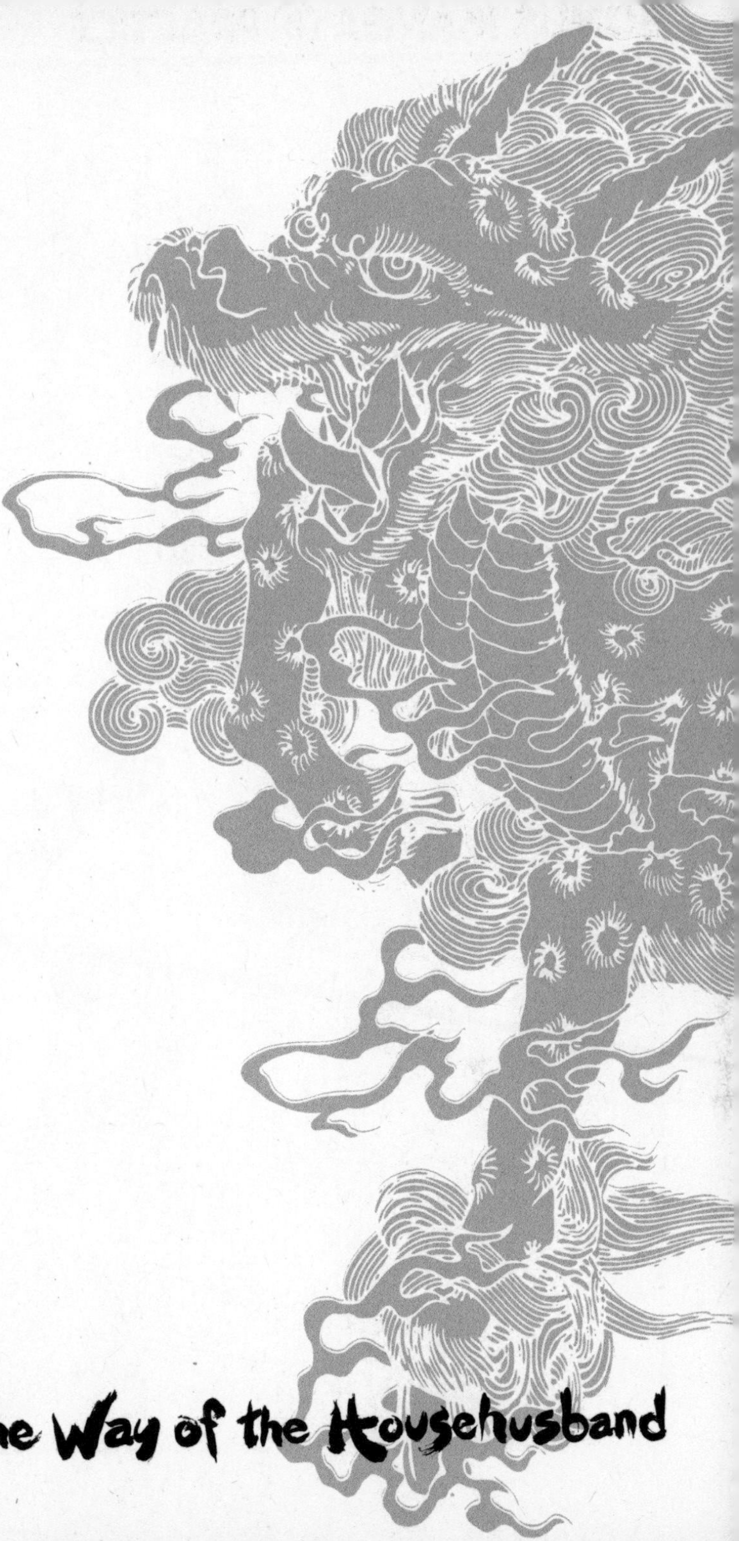

The Way of the Househusband

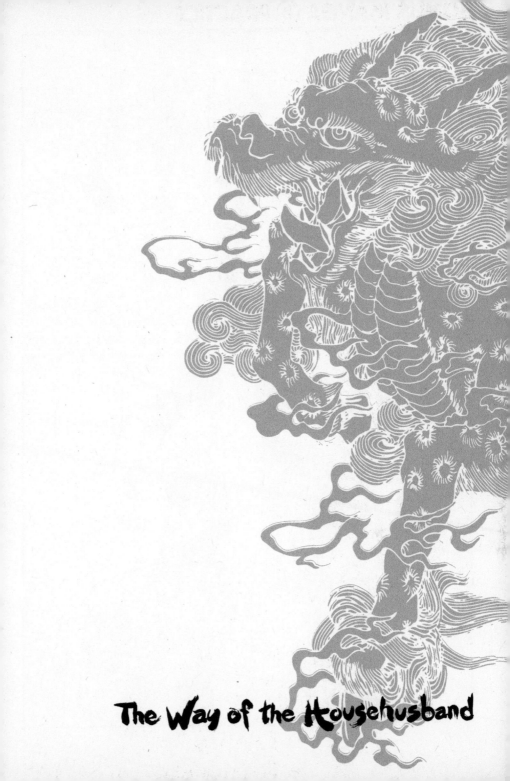

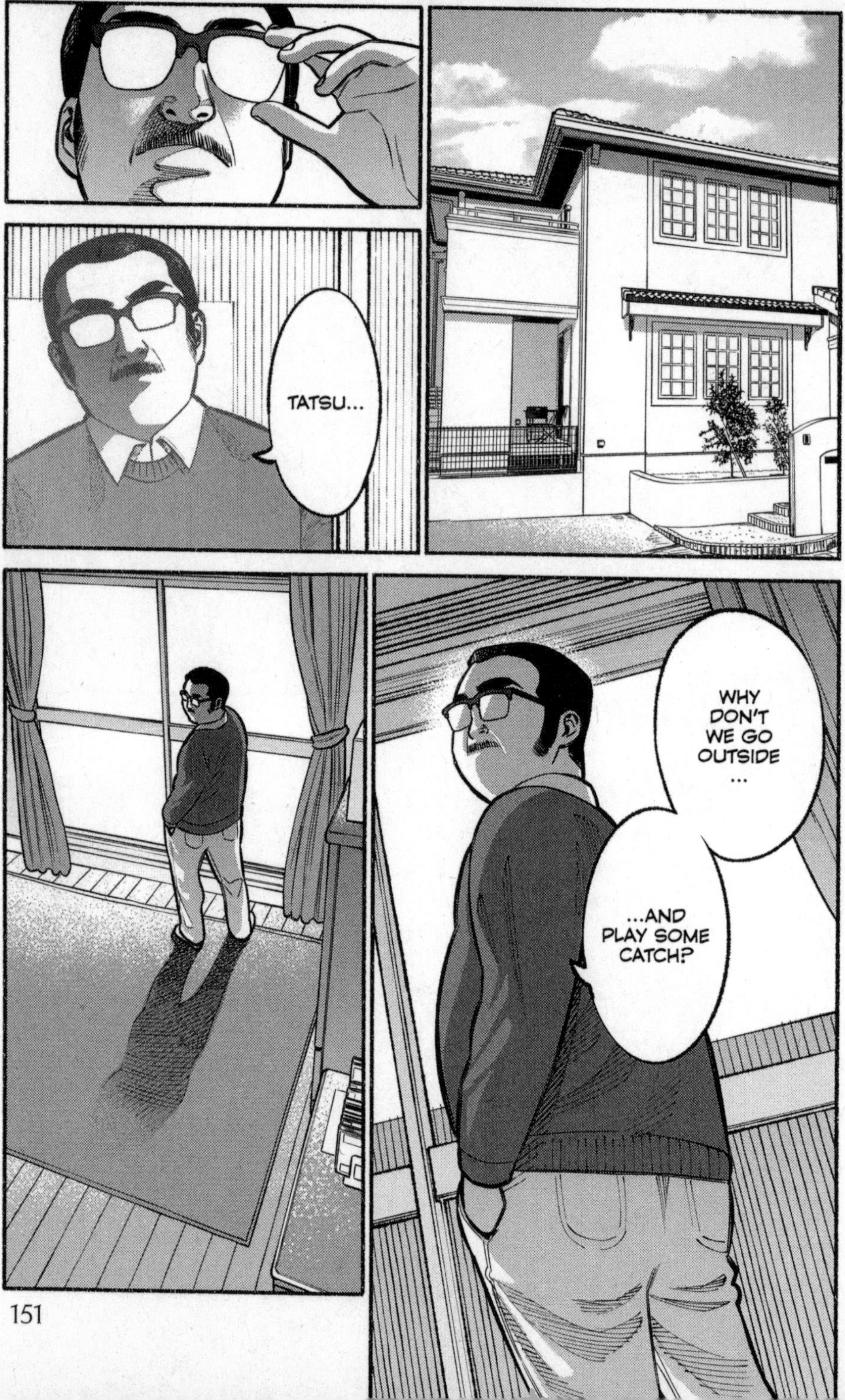
TATSU...
WHY DON'T WE GO OUTSIDE ...
...AND PLAY SOME CATCH?

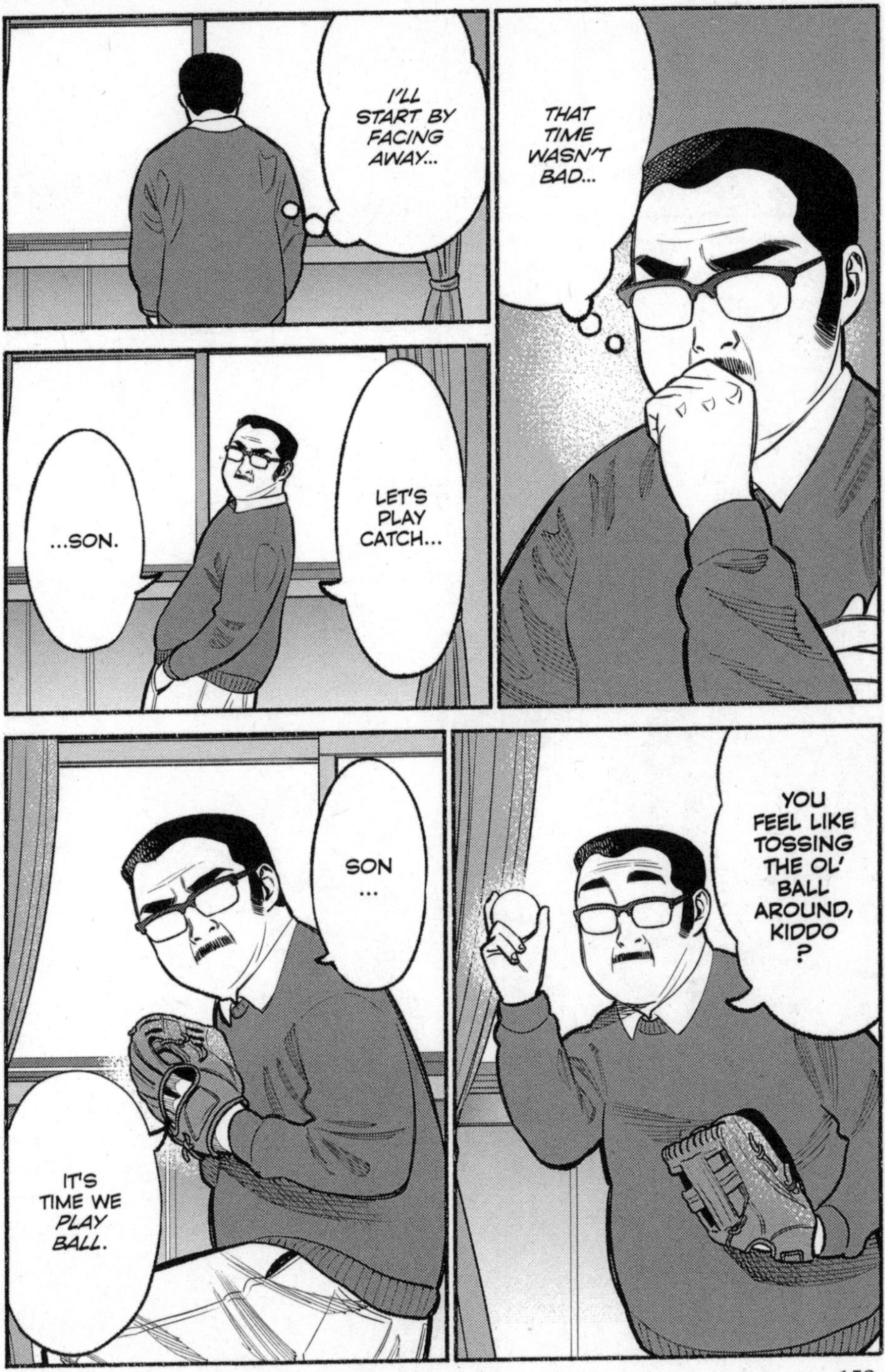
THAT TIME WASN'T BAD...
I'LL START BY FACING AWAY...
LET'S PLAY CATCH...
...SON.
YOU FEEL LIKE TOSSING THE OL' BALL AROUND, KIDDO?
SON ...
IT'S TIME WE *PLAY BALL*.

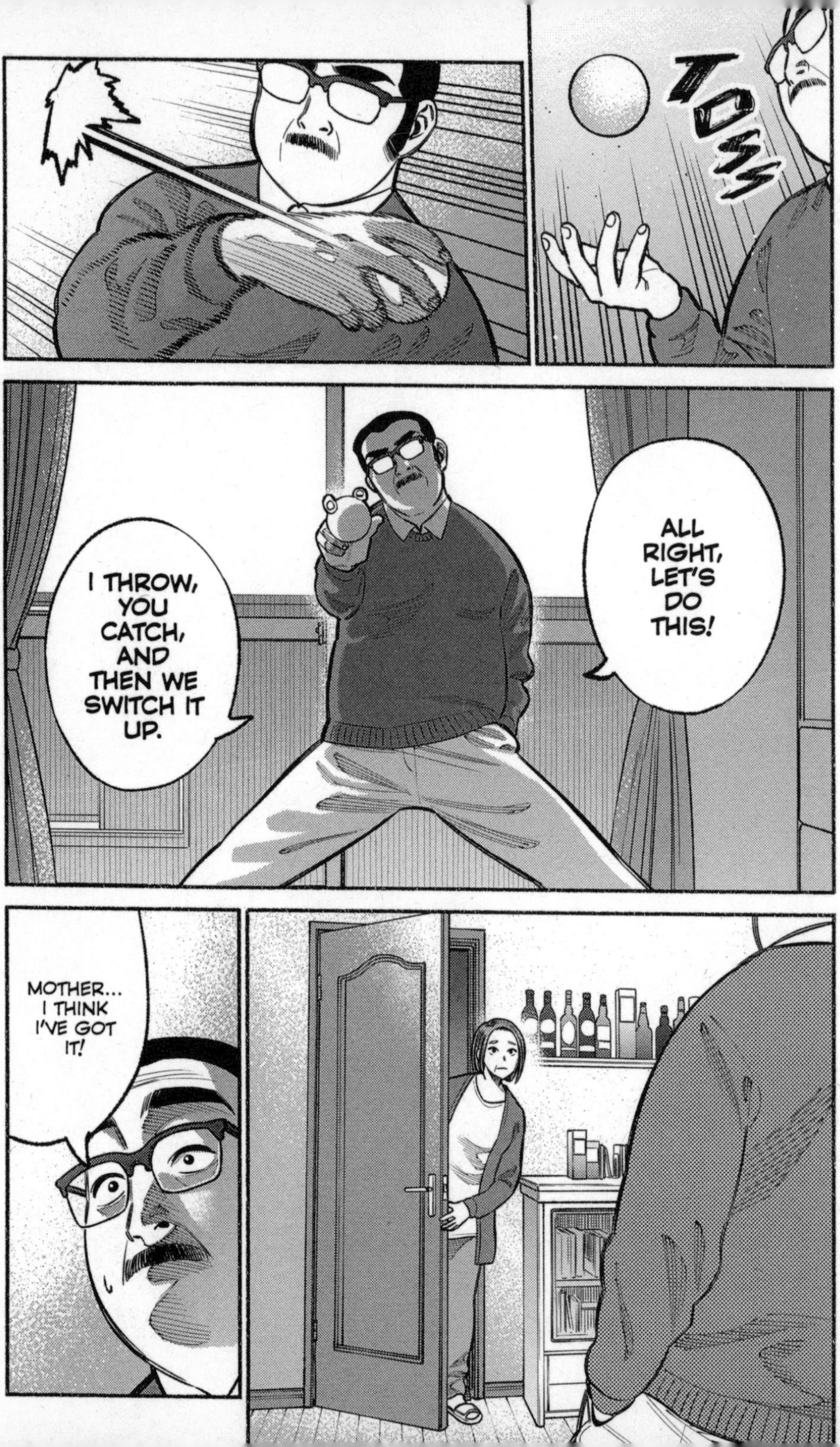
TOSS
ALL RIGHT, LET'S DO THIS!
I THROW, YOU CATCH, AND THEN WE SWITCH IT UP.
MOTHER... I THINK I'VE GOT IT!

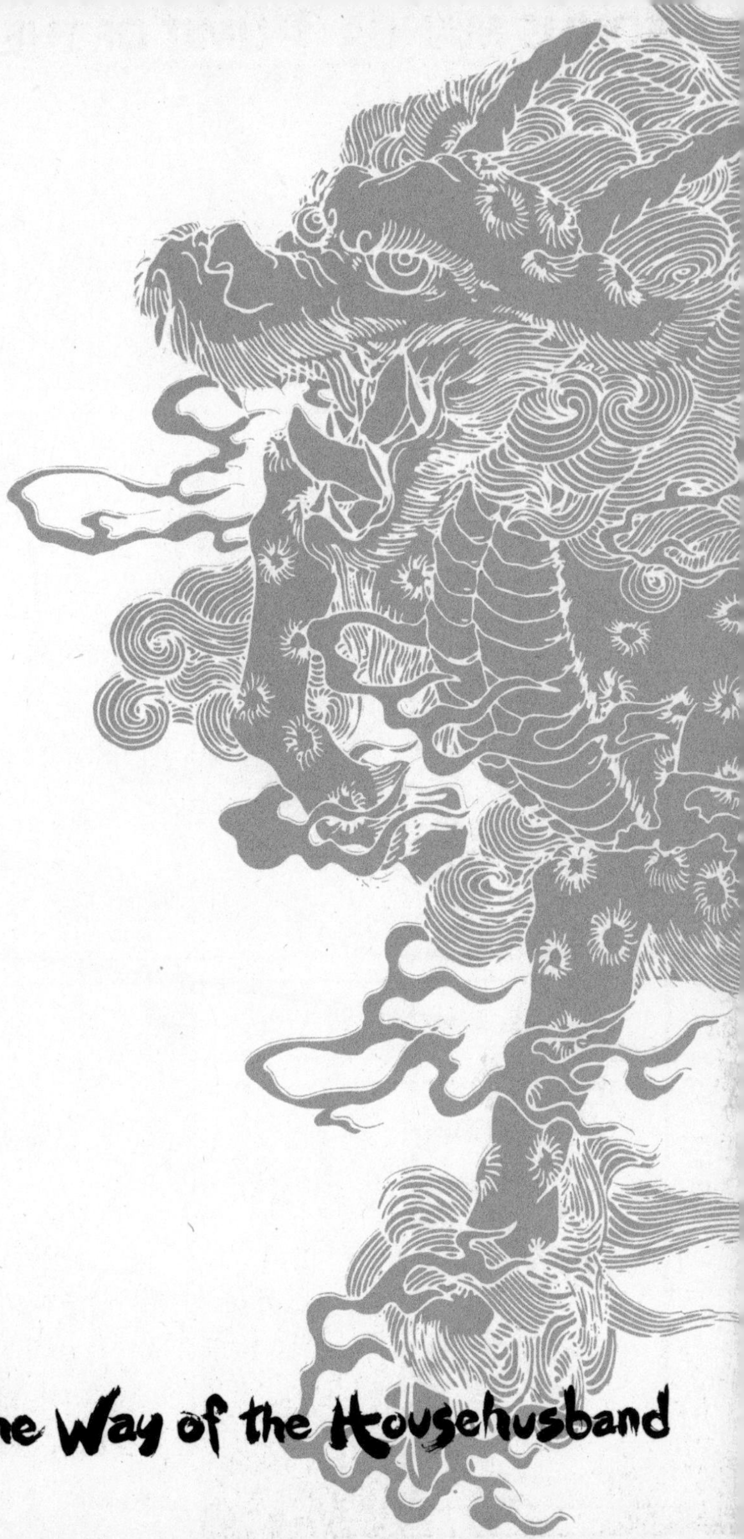

The Way of the Househusband

BONUS MANGA ③ LIMIT OF THE KNEES

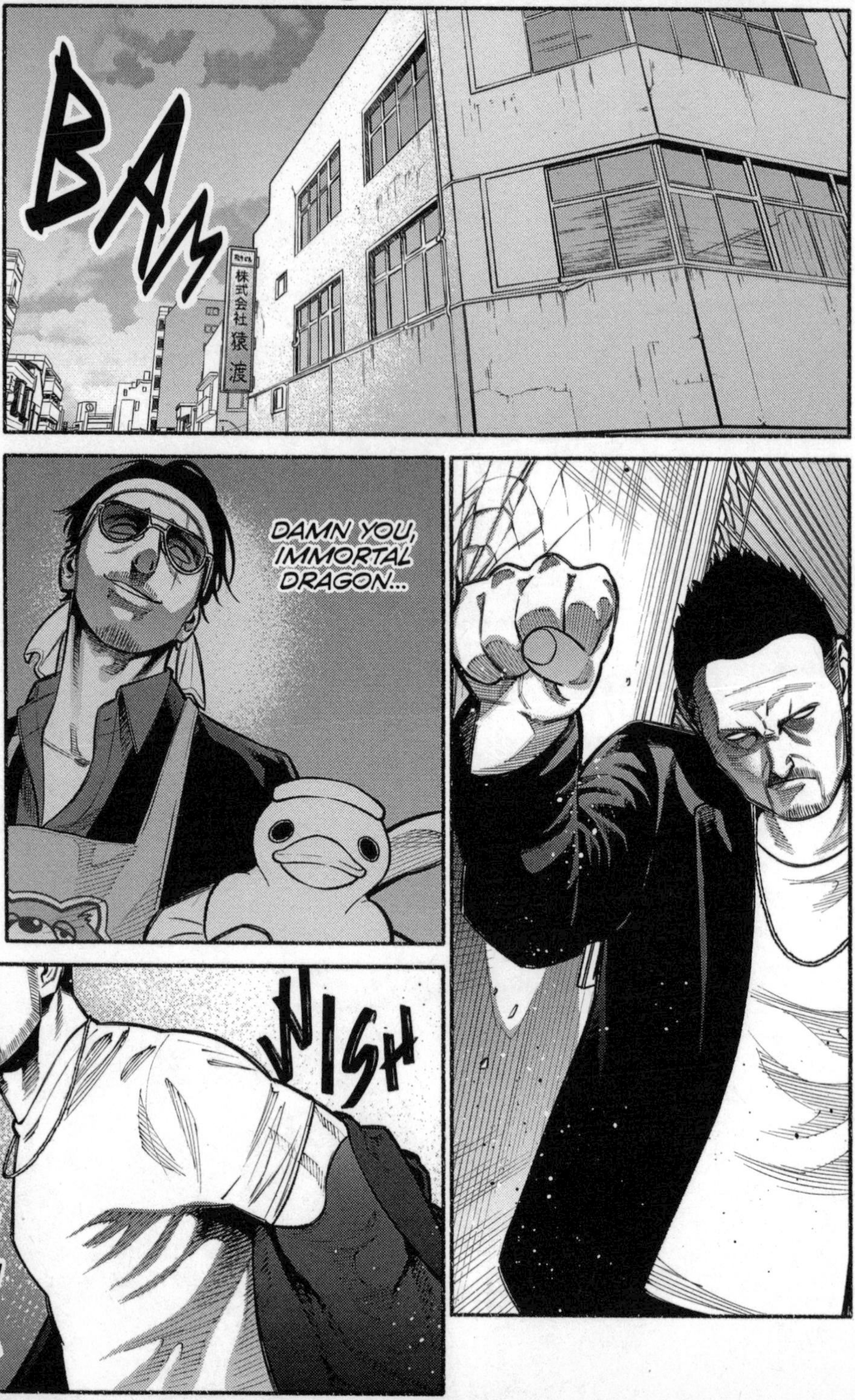
BAM
株式会社 猿渡
DAMN YOU, IMMORTAL DRAGON...
WISH

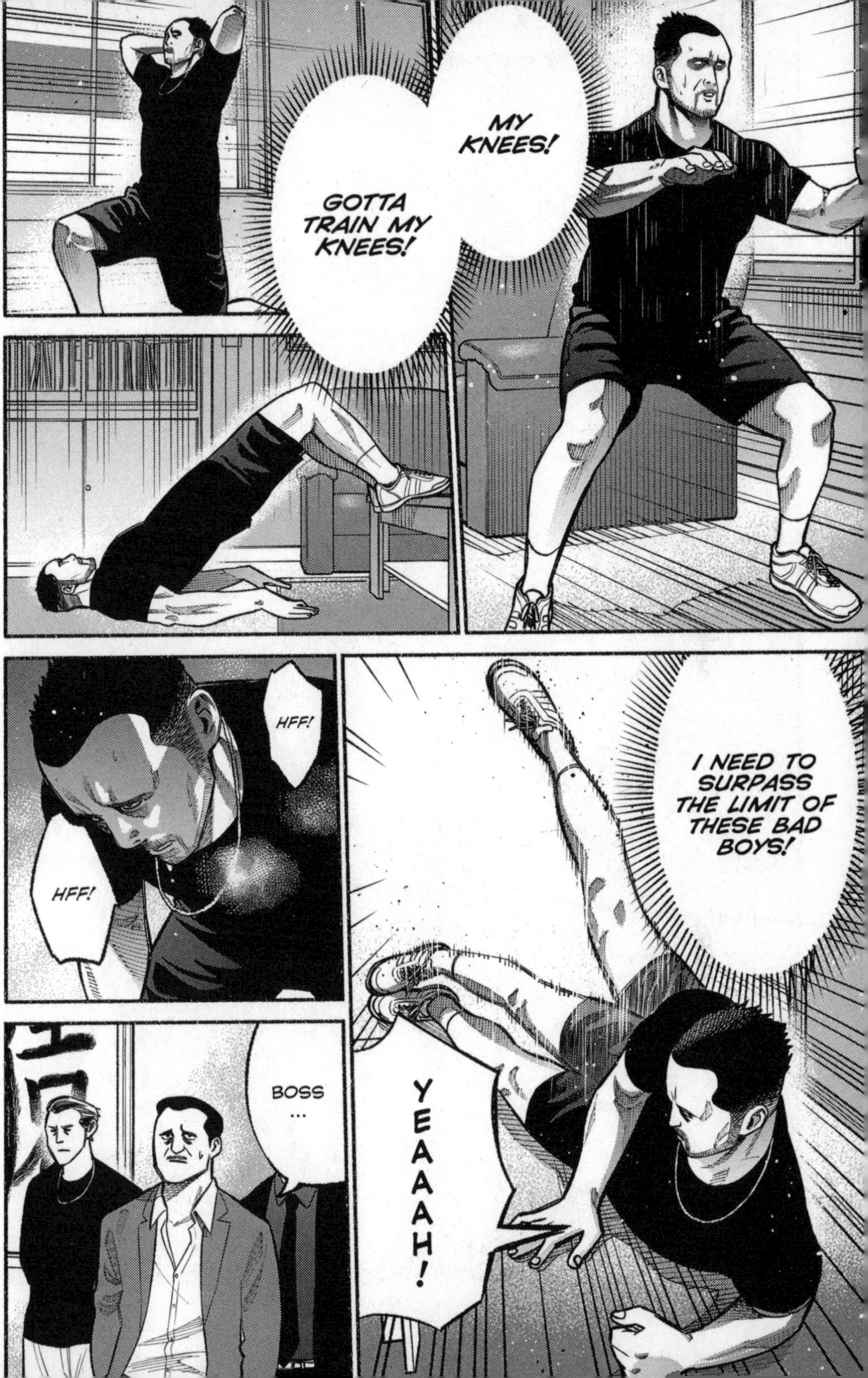
MY KNEES!
GOTTA TRAIN MY KNEES!
I NEED TO SURPASS THE LIMIT OF THESE BAD BOYS!
YEAAAH!
HFF!
HFF!
BOSS ...

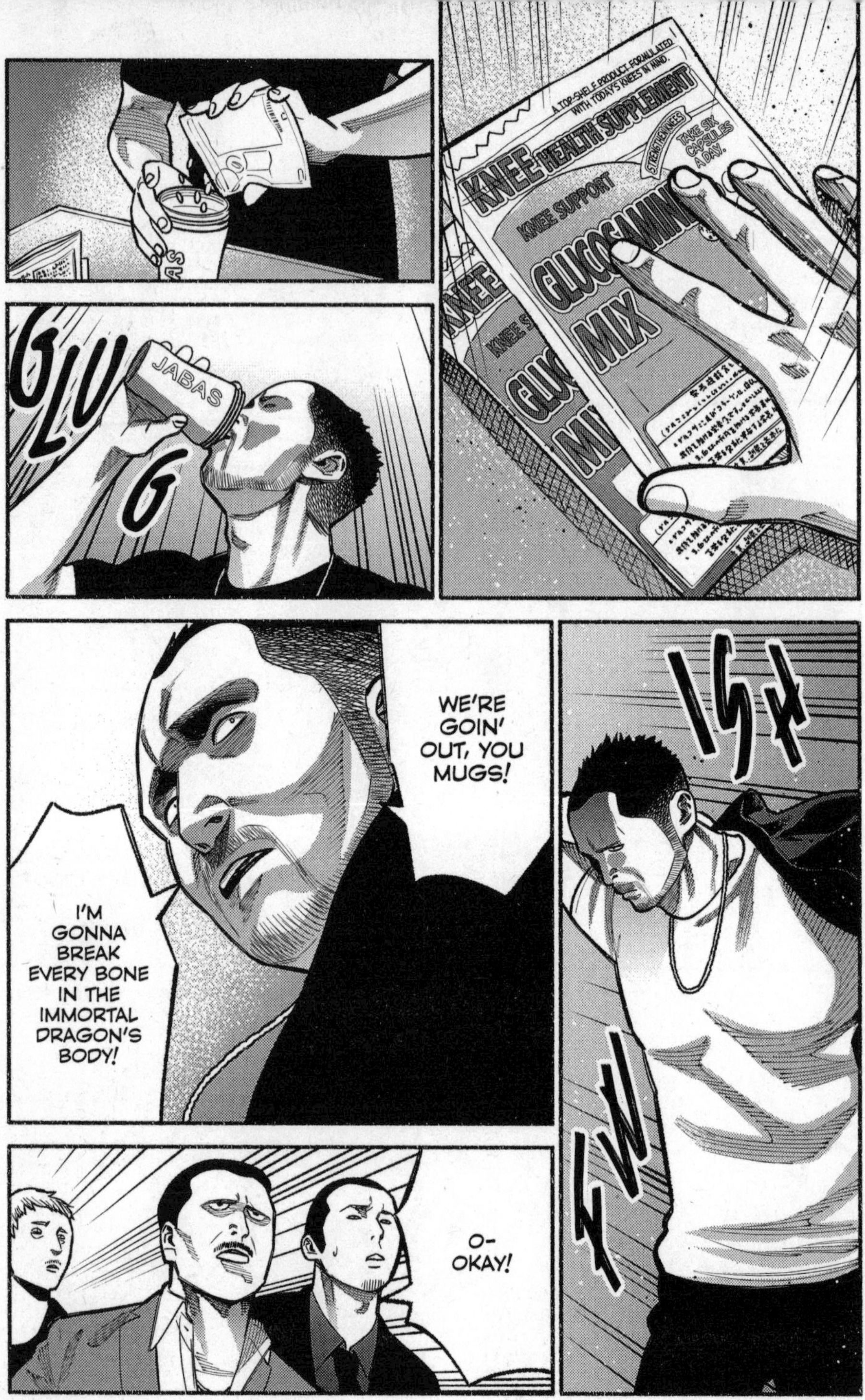
A TOP-SHELF PRODUCT FORMULATED WITH TODAY'S KNEES IN MIND.
KNEE HEALTH SUPPLEMENT
STRENGTHEN KNEES
TAKE SIX CAPSULES A DAY.
KNEE SUPPORT
MIX
JABAS
GLUG
WE'RE GOIN' OUT, YOU MUGS!
I'M GONNA BREAK EVERY BONE IN THE IMMORTAL DRAGON'S BODY!
O-OKAY!

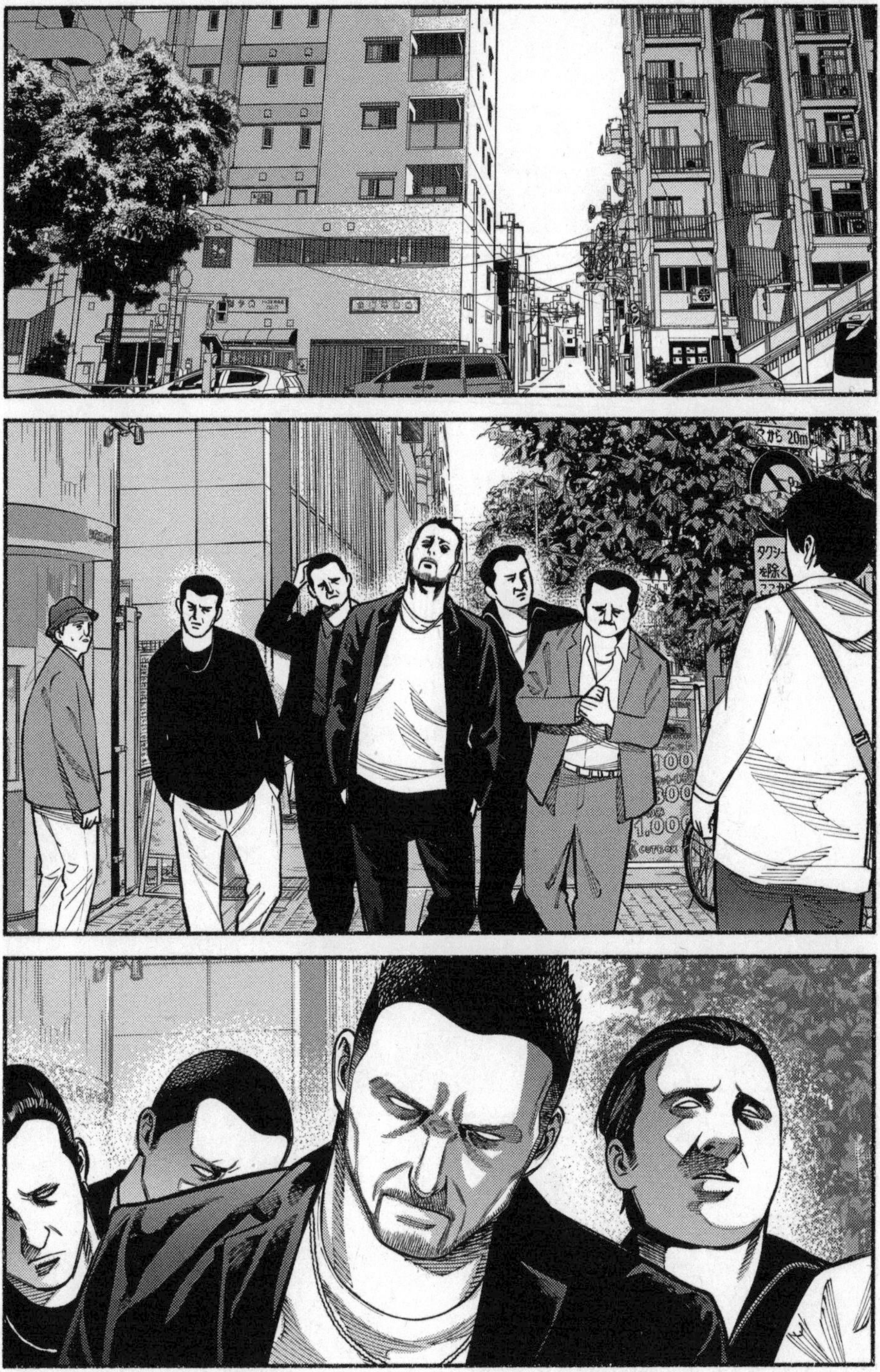
20m
タクシー
を除く

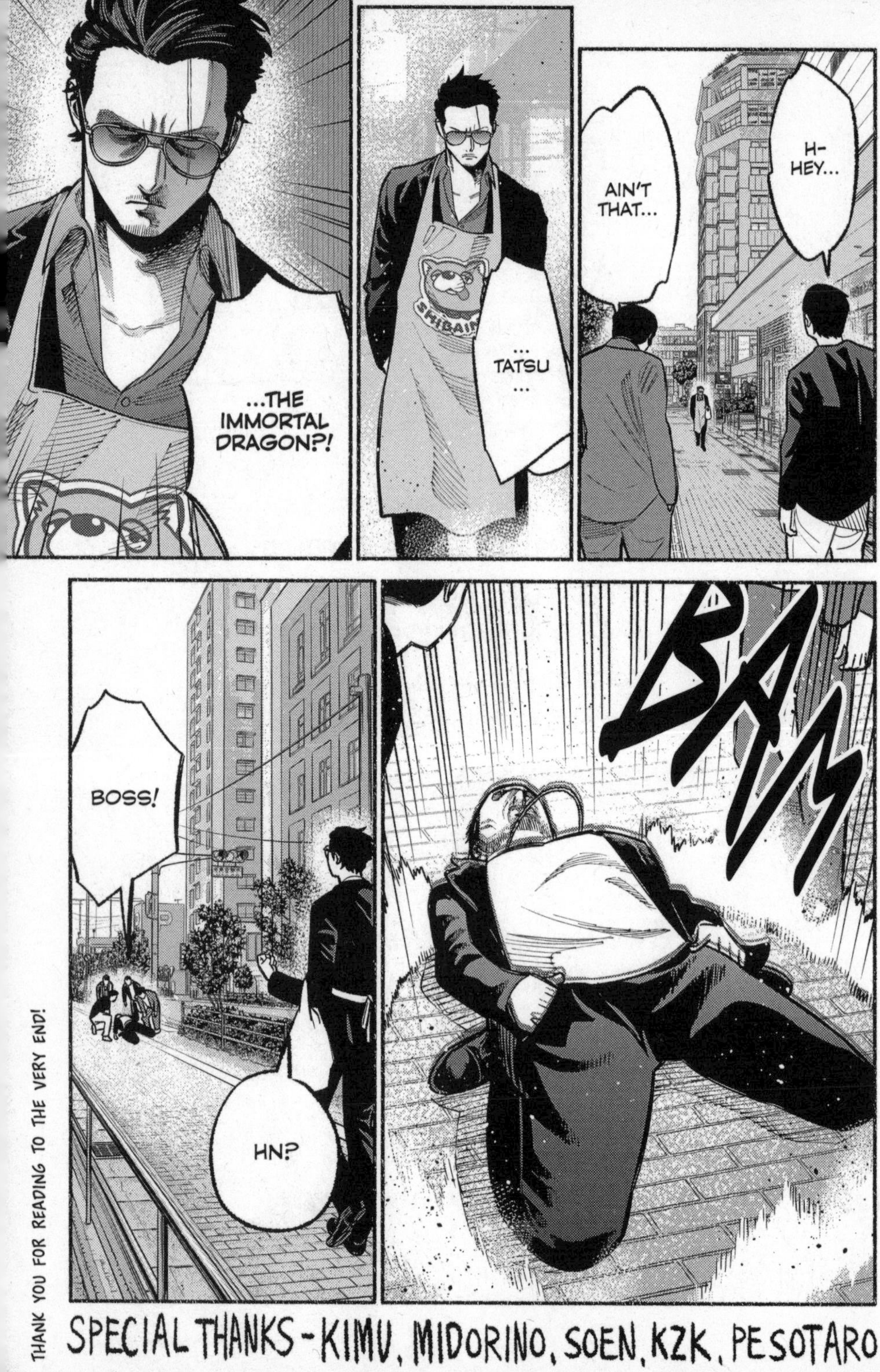
H-HEY...
AIN'T THAT...
...TATSU...
...THE IMMORTAL DRAGON?!
BAM
BOSS!
HN?

SPECIAL THANKS - KIMU, MIDORINO, SOEN, KZK, PESOTARO

THANK YOU FOR READING TO THE VERY END!

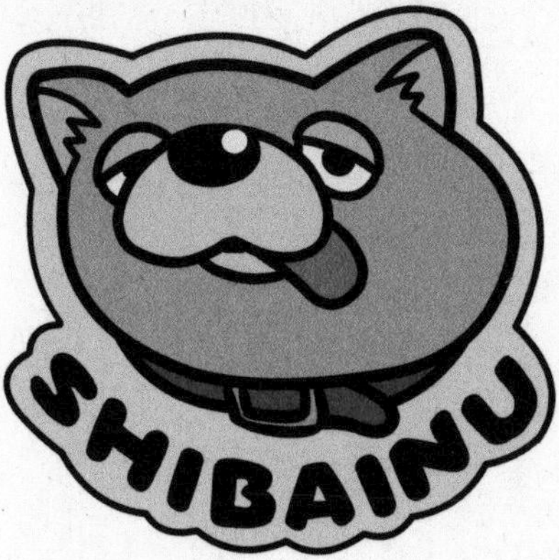
SHIBAINU

Thanks to you, we've reached volume 2. This volume is coming out in the winter, the season when my Shiba Inu engages in some tricky molting, replacing its winter coat with one for summer.

KOUSUKE OONO

Kousuke Oono began his professional manga career in 2016 in the manga magazine *Monthly Comics @ Bunch* with the one-shot "Legend of Music." Oono's follow-up series, *The Way of the Househusband*, is the creator's first serialization as well as his first English-language release.